D0953332

ALSO BY JONATHAN SACKS

Arguments for the Sake of Heaven: Emerging Trends in Traditional Judaism

Celebrating Life: Finding Happiness in Unexpected Places

Community of Faith

Crisis and Covenant: Jewish Thought After the Holocaust

The Dignity of Difference: How to Avoid the Clash of Civilizations

Exodus: The Book of Redemption

Faith in the Future: The Ecology of Hope and the Restoration
of Family, Community, and Faith

From Optimism to Hope: Thoughts for the Day

Future Tense: Jews, Judaism, and Israel in the Twenty-first Century

Genesis: The Book of Beginnings

The Great Partnership: Science, Religion, and the Search for Meaning

The Home We Build Together: Re-creating Society

A Letter in the Scroll: Understanding Our Jewish Identity and
Exploring the Legacy of the World's Oldest Religion

Leviticus: The Book of Holiness

Morals and Markets

One People?: Tradition, Modernity, and Jewish Unity

The Persistence of Faith: Religion, Morality, and Society in a Secular Age

The Politics of Hope

To Heal a Fractured World: The Ethics of Responsibility

Tradition in an Untraditional Age

Will We Have Jewish Grandchildren?: Jewish Continuity
and How to Achieve It

Not in God's Name

Not in God's Name

Confronting Religious Violence

Jonathan Sacks

SCHOCKEN BOOKS, NEW YORK

All rights reserved. Published in the United States by Schocken Books, a division of Penguin Random House LLC, New York, and distributed in Canada by Random House of Canada, a division of Penguin Random House Ltd., Toronto. Originally published in Great Britain by Hodder & Stoughton, a Hachette UK company, London, in 2015.

Schocken Books and colophon are registered trademarks of Penguin Random House LLC.

All Scripture references are taken from the author's own translation, unless otherwise indicated. (Scripture references marked KJV are taken from The Holy Bible, King James Version.)

Grateful acknowledgment is made for permission to reprint the following previously published material:
Scripture references marked NIV are taken from The Holy Bible, New International Version, copyright © 1979, 1984, 2011 by Biblica, formerly International Bible Society. Used by permission. All rights reserved.
"Written with a Pencil in a Sealed Wagon" by Dan Pagis, translated by Anthony Rudolf and Miriam Neiger-Fleishchmann. Copyright © Anthony Rudolf and Miriam Neiger-Fleishchmann. First published in *Silent Conversations: A Reader's Life* by Anthony Rudolf, Seagull Books/University of Chicago Press, in 2013.
"Faces of the Enemy" by Sam Keen, first published in *Faces of the Enemy: Reflections of the Hostile Imagination* by Sam Keen, HarperSanFrancisco, in 1992. Used by permission.

Library of Congress Cataloging-in-Publication Data
Sacks, Jonathan, [date]
Not in God's name : confronting religious violence / Jonathan Sacks.
pages cm
Includes bibliographical references.
ISBN 978-0-8052-4334-5 (hard cover : alk. paper). ISBN 978-0-8052-4335-2 (e-book).
1. Violence—Religious aspects. 2. Abrahamic religions. 3. Bible. Genesis—Criticism, interpretation, etc. I. Title.
BL65.V55S24 2015   201'.76332—dc23   2015016809

www.schocken.com

Jacket image: Total solar eclipse by Dan Suzio/Science Source/Getty Images
Jacket design by Oliver Munday

Printed in the United States of America
First American Edition

8 9

To my brother Eliot,
With love

Contents

Acknowledgements

I could not have completed this work without the help of some remarkable people who read the manuscript and made many insightful suggestions. My thanks go to Mark Berner, Dayan Ivan Binstock, Dr Megan Burridge, Revd. Canon Professor Richard Burridge, David Frei, Professor Robert P. George, Rabbi Alex Greenberg, Ed Husain, Justin Mclaren, Geoffrey Paul, Rabbi Yehudah Sarna, Professor Leslie Wagner and Professor N. T. Wright. Their comments saved me from many inaccuracies and infelicities. The errors that remain are my own. I also owe an enormous debt to Prince El Hassan bin Talal and Professor Akbar Ahmed, two figures who over the years have inspired me with their generous and deeply humane vision of Islam.

Special thanks to my office team of Joanna Benarroch, Dan Sacker and Val Sheridan for the kindness and efficiency they show daily; to my indefatigable and motivating literary agent Louise Greenberg; and to Altie Karper and her team at Schocken for their enthusiasm and professionalism. My greatest thanks as always go to my wife Elaine, my best reader and constant support.

Ultimately this book could not have been written without many encounters over the years with people of different faiths who have known, and had the courage to show, that our overarching humanity transcends our religious differences. They and what they stand for are our best hope for the future. Religious extremism flourishes when 'the best lack all conviction, while the worst are filled with passionate intensity.' That must no longer be the case. Religiously motivated violence must be fought religiously as well as militarily, and with passionate intensity, for this will be one of the defining battles of the twenty-first century.

Jonathan Sacks

March 2015 / Adar 5755

PART ONE

Bad Faith

I

Altruistic Evil

Men never do evil so completely and cheerfully as when they do it from religious conviction.

Blaise Pascal

When religion turns men into murderers, God weeps.

So the book of Genesis tells us. Having made human beings in his image, God sees the first man and woman disobey the first command, and the first human child commit the first murder. Within a short space of time 'the world was filled with violence'. God 'saw how great the wickedness of the human race had become on the earth'. We then read one of the most searing sentences in religious literature. 'God regretted that he had made man on the earth, and his heart was filled with pain' (Gen. 6:6).

Too often in the history of religion, people have killed in the name of the God of life, waged war in the name of the God of peace, hated in the name of the God of love and practised cruelty in the name of the God of compassion. When this happens, God speaks, sometimes in a still, small voice almost inaudible beneath the clamour of those claiming to speak on his behalf. What he says at such times is: *Not in My Name*.

Religion in the form of polytheism entered the world as the vindication of power. Not only was there no separation of church and state; religion was the transcendental justification of the state. Why was there hierarchy on earth? Because there was hierarchy in heaven. Just as the sun ruled the sky, so the pharaoh, king or emperor ruled the land. When some oppressed others, the few ruled the many, and whole populations were turned into slaves, this was – so it was said – to defend the sacred order written into the fabric of reality itself. Without it, there would be chaos. Polytheism was the cosmological vindication of the hierarchical society. Its monumental buildings, the ziggurats of Babylon and pyramids of Egypt, broad at the base, narrow at the top, were hierarchy's visible symbols. Religion was the robe of sanctity worn to mask the naked pursuit of power.

It was against this background that Abrahamic monotheism emerged as a sustained protest. Not all at once but ultimately it made extraordinary claims. It said that every human being, regardless of colour, culture, class or creed, was in the image and likeness of God. The supreme Power intervened in history to liberate the supremely powerless. A society is judged by the way it treats its weakest and most vulnerable members. Life is sacred. Murder is both a crime and a sin. Between people there should be a covenantal bond of righteousness and justice, mercy and compassion, forgiveness and love. Though in its early books the Hebrew Bible commanded war, within centuries its prophets, Isaiah and Micah, became the first voices to speak of peace as an ideal. A day would come, they said, when the peoples of the earth would turn their swords into ploughshares, their spears into pruning hooks, and wage war no more. According to the Hebrew Bible, Abrahamic monotheism entered the world as a rejection of imperialism and the use of force to make some men masters and others slaves.

Abraham himself, the man revered by 2.4 billion Christians, 1.6 billion Muslims and 13 million Jews, ruled no empire, commanded no army, conquered no territory, performed no miracles and delivered no prophecies. Though he lived differently from his neighbours, he fought for them and prayed for them in some of the most audacious language ever uttered by a human to God – 'Shall the Judge of all the earth not do justice?' (Gen. 18:25) He sought to be true to his faith and a blessing to others regardless of their faith.

That idea, ignored for many of the intervening centuries, remains the simplest definition of the Abrahamic faith. It is not our task to conquer or convert the world or enforce uniformity of belief. It is our task to be a blessing to the world. The use of religion for political ends is not righteousness but idolatry. It was Machiavelli, not Moses or Mohammed, who said it is better to be feared than to be loved: the creed of the terrorist and the suicide bomber. It was Nietzsche, the man who first wrote the words 'God is dead', whose ethic was the will to power.

To invoke God to justify violence against the innocent is not an act of sanctity but of sacrilege. It is a kind of blasphemy. It is to take God's name in vain.

*

Since the attack on New York's Twin Towers and the Pentagon on 11 September 2001, religiously motivated violence has not diminished. After wars in Afghanistan and Iraq, interventions in Libya and Syria, regime changes in many Middle Eastern countries and the rise of ISIS (commonly known as Islamic State), after more than a decade in which to think the problem through, the West has grown weaker while radical political Islam has grown stronger.

Al-Qaeda and the Islamist ideology from which it derived have generated dozens, perhaps hundreds, of associated or imitative groups throughout the world and neither they nor their acts of terror show any signs of diminution. In November 2014, for example, there were 664 jihadist attacks in 14 countries, killing a total of 5,042 people. A December 2014 report by the BBC World Service and the International Centre for the Study of Radicalisation at King's College London concluded that Islamist extremism is 'stronger than ever' despite al-Qaeda's declining role.[1]

We have grown used to seeing sights on television and the social media that we thought had been consigned to the Middle Ages. Hostages beheaded. Soldiers hacked to death with axes. A Jordanian pilot burned alive. Innocent populations butchered. Schoolchildren murdered in cold blood. Young girls sexually assaulted and sold as slaves. Ten-year-olds turned into suicide bombers. A February 2015 report by the United Nations Committee on the Rights of the Child spoke of mass executions of boys by ISIS, and of children being beheaded or buried alive.[2] Churches, synagogues and mosques have been destroyed, holy sites desecrated, people at prayer assassinated, and Christians abducted and crucified. Ancient communities have been driven from their homes.

Christians are being systematically persecuted in many parts of the world. Throughout the Middle East they are facing threat, imprisonment and death. In Afghanistan Christianity has almost been extinguished. In 2010 the last remaining church was burned to the ground. People converting to Christianity face the death sentence. In Syria, an estimated 450,000 Christians have fled. Members of other religions, among them Mandeans, Yazidis, Baha'i and people from Muslim minority faiths, have also suffered persecution and death.

In Egypt, 5 million Copts live in fear. In 2013, in the largest single attack on Christians since the fourteenth century, more than fifty churches were bombed or burned in an attack that has been called Egypt's Kristallnacht.[3] Young Coptic girls are abducted, converted to Islam against their will and forcibly married to Muslim men. If they attempt to return to their Christian faith, they face imprisonment and death.[4]

In 2001 there were 1.5 million Christians in Iraq: today barely 400,000. In 2014 ISIS began a programme of beheading and butchering Christians, announcing that anyone refusing to convert to Islam will be 'killed, crucified or have their hands and feet cut off'. Christians have been expelled from Iraq's second city, Mosul, where they had been a presence for more than sixteen centuries.

In Sudan, an estimated 1.5 million Christians have been killed by the Arab Muslim militia Janjaweed since 1984. In Pakistan, they live in a state of fear. In November 2010, a Christian woman from Punjab Province, Asia Noreen Bibi, was sentenced to death by hanging for violating Pakistan's blasphemy law. The accusation arose from an incident in which she had drunk water together with Muslim farm workers. They had protested that as a Christian she was unfit to touch the drinking bowl. An argument ensued. The workers accused her of blasphemy. As I write, she is still being held in solitary confinement pending an appeal for her life.

A century ago Christians made up 20 per cent of the population of the Middle East. Today the figure is 4 per cent. What is happening is the religious equivalent of ethnic cleansing. It is one of the crimes against humanity of our time.

Muslims too face persecution in Myanmar, South Thailand, Sri Lanka, China and Uzbekistan. Eight thousand were murdered in the massacre at Srebrenica in 1995, and many others raped, tortured or deported. In Cambodia in the 1970s as many as half a million were killed by the Khmer Rouge, and 132 mosques were destroyed. In Hebron in 1994 a religious Jew, Baruch Goldstein, an American-born physician, opened fire on Muslim Palestinians at prayer in Abraham's Tomb, killing 29 and injuring a further 125. On 2 July 2014 a seventeen-year-old Palestinian, Mohamed Abu Khdeir, was kidnapped and gruesomely murdered in a revenge attack after the killing of three Israeli teenagers. On 10 February 2015, three Muslims were killed in Chapel Hill, North Carolina, allegedly by a militant atheist.

Muslims form the majority of victims of Islamist violence. A report from the University of Maryland's Global Terror Database estimated that between 2004 and 2013, about half of terrorist attacks and 60 per cent of fatalities occurred in Iraq, Afghanistan and Pakistan, all of which have a mostly Muslim population.[5] One of the most tragic incidents occurred in Peshawar, Pakistan, where on 15 December 2014 Taliban gunmen stormed a military-run school and massacred 141 people, 132 of them children. Many Muslims feel deeply threatened by what they see as Western hostility, whether in the form of civilian casualties of the war in Iraq, drone strikes in Pakistan, or Israeli retaliation for Hamas rocket attacks, or as generalised antagonism in countries where they are a minority.

7

Meanwhile antisemitism has returned to the world in full force within living memory of the Holocaust. In Stockholm, on 27 January 2000, the fifty-fifth anniversary of the liberation of Auschwitz, leaders of every nation in Europe committed themselves to a continuing programme of anti-racist and Holocaust education. Since then antisemitism has risen in every European country. Jews are leaving France, Holland, Norway, Sweden, Belgium and Hungary in fear. A survey by the European Union's Agency for Fundamental Rights, published in November 2013, showed that a third of Europe's Jews were contemplating leaving.

In Copenhagen on 14 February 2015, a Jewish security volunteer was killed outside a synagogue. In Paris on 9 January 2015, four Jews were shot in a kosher supermarket. In May 2014, three people were killed by a gunman in the Jewish Museum in Brussels. In Toulouse in 2012, a Jewish teacher and three schoolchildren were murdered. In these last three cases the killers were all French-born Muslims. In the summer of 2014, a synagogue near the Bastille in central Paris was surrounded by a large and angry mob chanting 'Death to the Jews'.

That the cry of 'Jews to the gas' should be heard again on the streets of Germany, and that several European countries should now be considered by Jews as unsafe places in which to live, is extraordinary, given decades of anti-racist legislation, interfaith dialogue and Holocaust education. Jews fear that 'Never again' may become 'Ever again'.

It is not only members of the Abrahamic monotheisms who are under threat. So too are Buddhists, Hindus, Sikhs, Zoroastrians and Baha'is. In Northern Iraq, the ancient sect of the Yazidis only narrowly escaped genocide at the hands of ISIS. As well as being victims, several of the non-Abrahamic faiths, especially nationalist Buddhists and Hindus, have been among the perpetrators. Religious freedom, a right enshrined in Article 18 of the Universal Declaration of Human Rights, is under threat today in more than a quarter of the world's nations. A report entitled *Religious Freedom in the World*,[6] covering the years 2012–14,

8

notes that there has been a marked deterioration in 55 of the world's 196 countries, due either to authoritarian regimes or to Islamist groups. These are deeply troubled times.

*

Hannah Arendt, writing about the trial of Nazi war criminal Adolf Eichmann, famously used the phrase 'the banality of evil', suggesting, rightly or wrongly, that many of those who implemented the Final Solution, the planned extermination of Europe's Jews, were faceless bureaucrats implementing government orders, more out of obedience than hate. There is nothing banal about the evil currently consuming large parts of the world.

Many of the perpetrators, including suicide bombers and jihadists, come from European homes, have had a university education, and until their radicalisation were regarded by friends and neighbours as friendly, likeable people. Unlike the Nazis, who took fastidious care to hide their crimes from the world, today's terrorists take equal care to advertise them to the world using professionally produced videos and the latest social media technology. Their lack of conscience in committing what leading Islamic jurists and theologians have deemed forbidden, sinful and contrary to the Qur'an is breathtaking. In Gwoza, Nigeria, one of the survivors of a massacre by the Islamist group Boko Haram described to a reporter how the radicals calmly killed their fellow Muslims one by one. 'They told us they were doing God's work even though all the men they shot in front of me were Muslims. They seemed happy.'[7]

We need a term to describe this deadly phenomenon that can turn ordinary non-psychopathic people into cold-blooded murderers of schoolchildren, aid workers, journalists and people at prayer. It is, to give it a name, *altruistic evil*: evil committed in a sacred cause, in the name of high ideals.

By this I do not mean the kind of behaviour that people argue over: abortion, for instance, or assisted suicide. Nor do I mean issues like the highly complex question of civilian casualties in asymmetric warfare. I mean evil of the kind that we all recognise as such. Killing the weak, the innocent, the very young and old is evil. Indiscriminate murder by terrorist attack or suicide bombing is evil. Murdering people because of their religion or race or nationality is evil. It was for this reason that, during the Nuremberg trials after the Second World War, the concept of a crime against humanity was born, to give global force to the principle that there are some acts so heinous that they cannot be defended on the grounds that 'I was only obeying orders'. There are acts so alien to our concept of humanity that they cannot be justified on the grounds that they were the means to a great, noble or holy end.

There is nothing specifically religious about altruistic evil. Some of the great instances in modern history – Nazi Germany, Stalinist Russia, Mao Zedong's China, Pol Pot's Cambodia – were avowedly secular. Their mass murders were undertaken to avenge past wrongs, correct perceived injustice, restore honour to the nation, or institute a social order that would bring equality and freedom to the world. Only in fiction are the great evils committed by caricatures of malevolence: Darth Vader, Lord Voldemort, Sauron or the Joker. In real history the great evils are committed by people seeking to restore a romanticised golden age, willing to sacrifice their lives and the lives of others in what they regard as a great and even holy cause. In some cases they see themselves as 'doing God's work'. They 'seem happy'.

That is how dreams of utopia turn into nightmares of hell.

*

Much has been said and written in recent years about the connection between religion and violence. Three answers have emerged. The first: Religion *is* the major source of violence. Therefore if we seek a more peaceful world we should abolish religion. The second: Religion is not a source of violence. People are made violent, as Hobbes said, by fear, glory and the 'perpetual and restless desire for power after power that ceaseth only in death'.[8] Religion has nothing to do with it. It may be used by manipulative leaders to motivate people to wage wars precisely because it inspires people to heroic acts of self-sacrifice, but religion itself teaches us to love and forgive, not to hate and fight. The third answer is: Their religion, yes; our religion, no. We are for peace. They are for war.

None of these is true. As for the first, Charles Phillips and Alan Axelrod surveyed 1,800 conflicts in the *Encyclopedia of Wars* and found that less than 10 per cent involved religion at all.[9] A 'God and War' survey commissioned by the BBC found that religion played some part in 40 per cent of conflicts but usually a minor one.[10]

The second answer is misguided. When terrorist or military groups invoke holy war, define their battle as a struggle against Satan, condemn unbelievers to death and commit murder while declaring 'God is great', to deny that they are acting on religious motives is absurd. Religions seek peace, but on their own terms. This is not a recipe for peace but for war.

The third is a classic instance of in-group bias. Almost invariably people regard their group as superior to others. Henry Tajfel, one of the pioneers of social identity theory, showed how deeply this runs in even the most trivial of groupings. In one experiment he divided people into groups on the basis of the mere toss of a coin, yet they still rated the members of their own group as more likeable than the others, despite the fact that they had never met one another before and knew that they had been selected on a purely random basis. Groups, like individuals, have a need for self-esteem and they will interpret facts to confirm their sense of superiority.[11] Judaism, Christianity and Islam define themselves as religions of peace yet they have all given rise to violence at some points in their history.

My concern in this book is less the general connection between religion and violence than the specific challenge of politicised religious extremism in the twenty-first century. The re-emergence of religion as a global force caught the West unprotected and unprepared because it was in the grip of a narrative that told a quite different story.

It is said that 1989, the year of the collapse of the Berlin Wall and the end of the Cold War, marked the final act of an extended drama in which first religion, then political ideology, died after a prolonged period in intensive care. The age of the true believer, religious or secular, was over. In its place had come the market economy and the liberal democratic state, in which the individual and his or her right to live as they chose took priority over all creeds and codes. The hymn of the new dispensation was John Lennon's 'Imagine', with its vision of a post-ideological, post-religious world with 'Nothing to kill or die for/And no religion too.'

It was the last chapter of a story that began in the seventeenth century, the last great age of wars of religion. The West had undergone a process of secularisation that had taken four centuries.

First, in the seventeenth century, came the secularisation of *knowledge* in the form of science and philosophy. Then in the eighteenth century came the secularisation of *power* by way of the American and French Revolutions and the separation – radical in France, less doctrinaire in the United States – of church and state. In the nineteenth century came the secularisation of *culture* as art galleries and museums were seen as alternatives to churches as places in which to encounter the sublime. Finally in the 1960s came the secularisation of *morality*, by the adoption of a principle first propounded by John Stuart Mill a century earlier – namely that the only ground on which anyone, including the state, is justified in intervening in behaviour done in private is the prevention of harm to others. This was the beginning of the end of traditional codes of ethics, to be replaced by the unfettered sanctity of the individual, autonomy, rights and choice.

By the late twentieth century most secularists had come to the conclusion that religion, if not refuted, had at least been rendered redundant. We no longer need the Bible to explain the universe. Instead we have science. We do not need sacred ritual to control human destiny. In its place we have technology. When we are ill, we do not need prayer. We have doctors, medicine and surgery. If we are depressed there is an alternative to religious consolation: antidepressant drugs. When we feel overwhelmed by guilt, we can choose psychotherapy in place of the confessional. For seekers of transcendence there are rock concerts and sports matches. As for human mortality, the best thing to do, as the advice columns tell us, is not to think about it too often. People may be uncertain about the existence of God, but are reasonably sure that if we don't bother him, he won't bother us.

What the secularists forgot is that Homo sapiens is the meaning-seeking animal. If there is one thing the great institutions of the modern world do not do, it is to provide meaning. Science tells us how but not why. Technology gives us power but cannot guide us as to how to use that power. The market gives us choices but leaves us uninstructed as to how to make those choices. The liberal democratic state gives us freedom to live as we choose but on principle refuses to guide us as to how to choose.

Science, technology, the free market and the liberal democratic state have enabled us to reach unprecedented achievements in knowledge, freedom, life expectancy and affluence. They are among the greatest achievements of human civilisation and are to be defended and cherished. But they do not and cannot answer the three questions every reflective individual will ask at some time in his or her life: Who am I? Why am I here? How then shall I live? These are questions to which the answer is prescriptive not descriptive, substantive not procedural. The result is that the twenty-first century has left us with a maximum of choice and a minimum of meaning.

Religion has returned because it is hard to live without meaning. That is why no society has survived for long without either a religion or a substitute for religion. The twentieth century showed, brutally and definitively, that the great modern substitutes for religion – the nation, the race and the political ideology – are no less likely to offer human sacrifices to their surrogate deities.

The religion that has returned is not the gentle, quietist, eirenic and ecumenical form that, in the West, we had increasingly come to expect. Instead it is religion at its most adversarial and aggressive, prepared to do battle with the enemies of the Lord, bring the apocalypse, end the reign of decadence and win the final victory for God, truth and submission to the divine will.

Not all anti-modern religion is violent. To the contrary, highly religious Jews (*Haredim*) are usually quietist, as are Christian groups like the Mennonites and the Amish, and Muslim groups like the Sufis. What they seek is simply the opportunity to live apart from the world, construct communities in the light of their values, and come close to God in mind and soul. In their different ways they are testaments to grace.

Undeniably, though, the greatest threat to freedom in the post-modern world is radical, politicised religion. It is the face of altruistic evil in our time.

*

It demands a response, but from whom? Intellectuals have faced extraordinarily violent reactions to their work. The controversy over *The Satanic Verses* (1989) led to the assassination of its Japanese translator, the stabbing of its Italian translator, the shooting of its Norwegian publisher and the death by fire of thirty-five guests at a reception for the book's publication in Turkey.

In Holland in 2004, Theo van Gogh, who made the film *Submission*, was murdered in broad daylight in central Amsterdam, shot several times at close range, then knifed in an attempted beheading. The 2005 Danish cartoons led to violent demonstrations across Africa, Asia and the Middle East in which at least two hundred people died.

After a 2006 lecture at the University of Regensburg by Pope Benedict XVI, five churches were attacked in the West Bank and

Gaza, a sixty-five-year-old Italian nun was murdered in Mogadishu and a Christian priest abducted and beheaded in Mosul. In Paris the offices of *Charlie Hebdo*, the French satirical magazine, were firebombed in 2011 and attacked by terrorists in January 2015 and the editor, cartoonists and other staff killed. In a global age, speech is no longer free.

The most vociferous response has come from the 'new atheists', a group that emerged after the 9/11 attacks. Sadly they ruined their case by caricature, making the claims, palpably false, that all religion leads to violence and most violence can be traced back to religion. This is taking a pneumatic drill to perform micro-surgery. All religions have had their violent moments, as have all substitutes for religion, and they have all also achieved periods of tolerance, generosity of spirit and peace.

In general, the West has suffered from the tendency to fight the last battle, not the next. The Cold War produced, in figures like Friedrich Hayek, Karl Popper and Isaiah Berlin, great defenders of freedom. Their target, though, was the totalitarian regime of Stalinist Russia. They showed, successfully, that a Marxist utopia is in principle impossible since the great ideals, such as freedom and equality, conflict so that the more you have of one, the less you have of the other.

The trouble was that they also argued that the worst thing you can have is certainty. Conviction, they said, leads to tyranny. On this they were wrong, indeed self-contradictory. Hayek was certain that freedom was preferable to slavery, Popper that open societies were better than closed ones, and Berlin that negative liberty was better than its positive counterpart. But so insistent were they that no truth is final that the effect of their work, albeit unintention-ally, was to give strength to the principle of moral relativism.

Moral relativism is no defence whatsoever against those currently waging war against the West and its freedoms. If rela-tivism is true, then nothing can be said truly or absolutely to be wrong. As a matter of subjective belief I may regard the killing of civilians, the use of children as human shields and the enslavement of young girls as bad. However, I will then have to concede that you see things differently. You believe it is a sacred imperative undertaken for the greater glory of God. Our values are different because our worldviews are, to use Isaiah Berlin's word, incommensurable. Such discourse may have made compelling sense in the serene surroundings of Oxford during the long peace that prevailed for half a century after the Second World War. But it is utterly inadequate to the challenge today.

What then is the alternative? For this we need to travel back to the wars of religion in the sixteenth and seventeenth centuries following the Reformation. There was war in France between Catholics and Huguenots between 1562 and 1598, followed by the devastating Thirty Years War between 1618 and 1648. There are striking parallels between then and today.

*

As now, the unrest began with a revolution in information technology. The technology was printing, developed by Gutenberg in the mid-fifteenth century. Many inventions have changed the world, but when there is a change in the way we record and transmit information, the repercussions are more systemic, transforming institutions, cultures and even the way people think.

The new technology made it easier and cheaper to connect with ever wider populations. The result was a spread of literacy, a democratisation of access to knowledge, and a subsequent challenge to all existing hierarchies of power. Then as now, the primary expression of the change was religious – Luther's Reformation, begun when he nailed his ninety-five theses to the door of All Saints Church in Wittenberg on 31 October 1517.

Most of the basic doctrines set out by Luther in the early sixteenth century had already been formulated two centuries earlier by John Wycliffe in Oxford. The reason they did not spread then but did later was the impact of printing itself. The first book to be widely printed was the Bible. In England alone it has been estimated that more than a million Bibles and New Testaments were published between 1517 and 1640. Luther's own declaration was transmitted by the press. Within fifteen days it had appeared throughout Germany and within three weeks printing presses in three different towns were turning out copies. By 1546, a total of 430 separate editions of his biblical translations had appeared in print.

The result was a century of religious war, transformation of the map of Europe, the beginning of the end of the Holy Roman Empire and the birth of a new political dispensation, ushered in by the Treaty of Westphalia in 1648, based on sovereign nation states and the balance of power. It is this entire system that, according to Henry Kissinger's *World Order*, is currently at risk.

What printing was to the Reformation, the Internet is to radical political Islam, turning it into a global force capable of inciting terror and winning recruits throughout the world. The extremists have understood that in many ways religion was made for the twenty-first century. It is a more global force than nation states. Religious radicals use the new electronic media with greater sophistication than their secular counterparts. And they have developed organisational structures to fit our time.

Ori Brafman and Rod Beckstrom argued in *The Starfish and the Spider* that leaderless organisations will dominate the future. The starfish and the spider have similar shapes but different internal structures. A decapitated spider dies, but a starfish can regenerate itself from a single amputated leg. That is what has happened to the many successor movements of al-Qaeda.

So it is worth returning to the seventeenth century to see what ended the wars of religion then, giving birth to the modern world and transforming the West into the vanguard of civilisation, overtaking China on the one hand and the Ottoman Empire on the other.

Weapons win wars, but it takes ideas to win the peace. In the case of the seventeenth century the transformative ideas emerged from a series of outstanding thinkers, among them John Milton, Thomas Hobbes, Benedict Spinoza and John Locke. Their key principles were the social contract, the limits of state power, the doctrine of toleration, liberty of conscience and the concept of human rights.

Not all of these thinkers were religious. Hobbes and Spinoza were both considered atheists in their time. Milton was one of the great religious poets and Locke was a Socinian Christian. Nonetheless, all four drew their political ideas primarily from the Hebrew Bible. One of their most important principles, found also in the Qur'an (*Al-Baqara* 256), is that there should be no compulsion in religion.

Those principles remain valid today, but there is one major difference between now and then. In the seventeenth century, the primary movement was against the religious power of the Catholic Church in favour of the secularisation of the various societal domains. Today the revolution, at least in the Middle East, is against secularism of two different kinds. The first is the secular nationalism of Nasser, Sadat and Mubarak in Egypt, Assad in Syria and Saddam Hussein in Iraq, regimes widely seen to be corrupt and oppressive. The second is the secular culture of the West, judged by those for whom tradition resonates to be decadent, materialist and soul-destroying. To put it simply: *The seventeenth century was the dawn of an age of secularisation. The twenty-first century will be the start of an age of desecularisation.*

The twenty-first century will be more religious than the twentieth for several reasons. One, as we have seen above, is that in many ways religion is better adapted to a world of global instantaneous communication than are nation states and existing political institutions.

Second, as we will see in the next chapter, is the failure of Western societies after the Second World War to address the most fundamental of human needs: the search for identity. The world's great faiths provide identity. They offer meaning, direction, a code of conduct and a set of rules for the moral and spiritual life in ways that the free-market, liberal democratic West does not.

The Abrahamic monotheisms in particular offer ordinary

individuals – and we are, most of us, ordinary individuals – a sense of pride and consequence. A creed that tells us that we are no more than selfish genes, with nothing in principle to separate us from the animals, in a society whose strongest motivators are money and success, in a universe that came into existence for no reason whatsoever and for no reason will one day cease to be, will never speak as strongly to the human spirit as one that tells us we are in the image and likeness of God in a universe he created in love.

The third reason has to do with demography. Not a single member state of Europe has a replacement-level birth rate (2.1 children per female). Having dropped at one point to 1.47, the European average is now 1.6 (the increase largely being due to immigrant populations), but this means that the native populations of Europe are all in long, slow decline. The gap will be filled by immigration and the high birth rates of ethnic minority populations.

Worldwide, the most religious groups have the highest birth rates. Over the next half-century, as Eric Kaufmann has documented in *Shall the Religious Inherit the Earth?*, there will be a massive transformation in the religious make-up of much of the world, with Europe leading the way. With the sole exception of the United States, the West is failing to heed the Darwinian imperative of passing on its genes to the next generation.

All of this means that we can no longer defer the task that was essentially avoided in the seventeenth century. What then stopped Catholics and Protestants from murdering one another was *to deprive religion of power*. The theology that led to conflict in the first place was, by and large, left untouched. It lay dormant like frozen DNA. For four centuries people have known that religious doctrines might be harmful in many ways, but since power had been taken out of religious hands, there was little damage they could do.

That is no longer the case. In a world of declining superpowers, sclerotic international institutions, a swathe of failed or failing states and a Hobbesian chaos of civil and tribal wars, religious extremists are seizing power. This means that we have little choice but to re-examine the theology that leads to violent conflict in the first place. *If we do not do the theological work, we will face a continuation of the terror that has marked our century thus far, for it has no other natural end.*

It cannot be ended by military means alone. Moisés Naím, in his seminal work *The End of Power*, makes this absolutely clear. Wars, he says, are becoming increasingly asymmetric, large armies against smaller, non-traditional ones. They are also being *increasingly won by the militarily weaker side.* A Harvard study has shown that in asymmetric conflicts between 1800 and 1849, the weaker side in terms of soldiers and arms achieved its aim in 12 per cent of cases. In the wars between 1950 and 1998, the weaker side won in 55 per cent of cases. Hence Naím's conclusion that 'when nation-states go to war these days, big military power delivers less than it once did'.[12]

The work to be done now is theological. The point was made in an historic speech at Al-Azhar University at the beginning of 2015 by Egypt's President Abdel Fattah el-Sisi. Calling for a 'religious revolution', he said, 'The Islamic world is being torn, it is being destroyed, it is being lost. And it is being lost by our own hands.'

The challenge is not only to Islam, but to Judaism and Christianity also. In November 1995 a young Jewish student, Yigal Amir, assassinated Israel's prime minister, Yitzhak Rabin, whom he saw as endangering the future of the State by the peace process in which he was engaged. Like Barukh Goldstein, who killed twenty-nine Muslims at prayer, Amir was university trained, religious, and acting on religious principle. Goldstein, as far as we can surmise, believed he was fulfilling the command to 'wipe out the memory' of Amalek, the biblical symbol of evil (Deut. 25:19). Amir regarded Rabin as a *rodef*, that is, a threat to the welfare of others, or a *moser*, a traitor to his people. I believe with perfect faith that Judaism is a religion of peace. But not everyone interprets a religion the same way. None of the great religions can say, in unflinching self-knowledge, 'Our hands never shed innocent blood.'

As Jews, Christians and Muslims, we have to be prepared to ask the most uncomfortable questions. Does the God of Abraham want his disciples to kill for his sake? Does he demand human sacrifice? Does he rejoice in holy war? Does he want us to hate our enemies and terrorise unbelievers? Have we read our sacred texts correctly? What is God saying to us, here, now? We are not prophets but we are their heirs and we are not bereft of guidance on these fateful issues.

*

Why has this happened now? Because the world is changing faster than at any time in history, and since change disorients, it leads to a sense of loss and fear that can turn rapidly into hate. Our world is awash with hate. The Internet, alongside its many blessings, can make it contagious. You can spread hate globally through social media. You can have worldwide impact through YouTube videos of burnings and beheadings.

The multiplication of channels of communication means that we no longer rely for news on established newspapers and television channels. Broadcasting is being replaced by narrowcasting. The difference is that broadcasting speaks to a mixed public, exposing them to a range of views. Narrowcasting speaks to a targeted public and exposes them only to facts and opinions that support their prejudices. It fragments a public into a set of sects of the like-minded.

The Internet also globalises hate. Events that would in the past have had purely local impact now send shockwaves around the world. A provocation somewhere can create anger everywhere. Never has paranoia been easier to create and communicate. It is easy to portray an unintentional slight as a deliberate insult if you are communicating with people thousands of miles away who have no means of checking the facts.

Nor has it ever been easier to demonise whole populations so effectively. Jihadists and suicide bombers are recruited by non-stop streams of images of the humiliation of Muslims at the hands of others who then become the Greater or Lesser Satan and can be murdered without qualms since you see them as persecutors of your people. Even at an everyday level, the Internet has a *disinhibition effect*: you can be ruder to someone electronically than you would be in a face-to-face encounter, since the exchange has been depersonalised. Read any Comments section on the Web, and you will see what this means: the replacement of reason by anger, and argument by vilification. Civility is dying, and when it dies, civilisation itself is in danger.

In the West we tend to have a vague sense of what is happening without always understanding why. That is because, since the eighteenth century, the West, through market economics and liberal democracy, has produced an historically unusual way of thinking and a distinctive personality type: the *rational actor* who makes decisions on the basis of individual choice and calculation of consequences. For the rational actor there is no problem that cannot be solved, no conflict that cannot be resolved. All we need to do is sit down, brainstorm, work out alternative scenarios and opt for the outcome that is maximal for all concerned.

What rules in this universe is *interests*. Sometimes they are individual, at others collective, but interests are what are at stake. What is missing is *identity*. Identity is always a group phenomenon. It comes laden with history, memory, a sense of the past and its injustices, and a set of moral sensibilities that are inseparable from identity: loyalty, respect and reverence, the three virtues undermined by market economics, liberal democratic politics and the culture of individualism. As one who values market economics and liberal democratic politics, I fear that the West does not fully understand the power of the forces that oppose it. Passions are at play that run deeper and stronger than any calculation of interests. Reason alone will not win this particular battle. Nor will invocations of words like 'freedom' and 'democracy'. To some they sound like compelling ideals, but to others they are the problem against which they are fighting, not the solution they embrace.

*

To put the argument of this book as simply as I can: there is a connection between religion and violence, but it is oblique, not direct. Why this is so is set out in chapter 2. There is, though, a different and deeper connection between Abrahamic monotheism and the three religions to which it gave rise: Judaism, Christianity and Islam. Tracing this back to its roots is the task of chapters 3 to 5. In them I examine the social and psychological processes that lead to altruistic evil, of which violence in the name of God is a key example. There is, in these chapters, an emphasis on antisemitism, not because it is the most important instance of religiously motivated hate, but because it is the one in which we can see these processes at work most clearly. Christian and Muslim victims of violence vastly outnumber Jews, whether in the age of the Crusades or today. It is, though, by putting antisemitism under the microscope that we can trace the sequence by which fear becomes hate and then murderous violence, defeating rationality and becoming both destructive and self-destructive.

The relationship between Judaism, Christianity and Islam has been historically a poisoned one, and I seek to understand why. In these chapters I explore three phenomena: mindset, myth and sibling rivalry. First, there is a specific mindset that makes altruistic evil possible: dualism. This is incompatible with monotheism, but it has nonetheless from time to time found a home there. Second, there are myths that feed this mindset, and they are surprisingly durable and adaptable, moving from one religion to another and even to secular cultures. Third, there is the unique relationship between the three Abrahamic faiths that has set them in tension with one another.

Each initially assumed the others would disappear. Their

members would either convert or acknowledge the primacy of the new faith. Christians expected that Jews would become Christian because the founder of their faith was a Jew. Muslims expected that Jews and Christians would become Muslims because their faith incorporated Abraham, Moses, Jesus and elements of their teachings. But they did not disappear. Some converted, but most did not. Jews remained Jews. Christians remained Christians. The result is that Judaism, Christianity and Islam are each challenged, even threatened, by the existence of the others. For much of the time this hardly matters. Jews, Christians and Muslims have lived peaceably together for most of their history. But at times of intense turbulence and stress it matters very much indeed.

There is, as I show in chapter 5, a way of thinking that we can trace back to a set of narratives in the book of Genesis, shared at least loosely by all three faiths. Here is where the problem was born. To ignore these narratives is impossible. But to reinterpret them is very possible indeed. We can go further: *the very texts that lie at the root of the problem, if properly interpreted, can provide a solution.* This, though, will require a radical re-reading of those texts, through an act of deep listening to the pristine voice of monotheism itself.

Part II is that re-reading. I argue that these narratives are more profound than they have been taken to be, and that much religiously motivated violence throughout the centuries has been the result of a failure to understand these texts in their full depth and challenging complexity. Part III then looks at the other key challenges to Abrahamic monotheism in the global age. What will it take for the children of Abraham – Jews, Christians and Muslims – to live together in peace, and what is at stake if we fail?

*

What made this book possible is knowledge of the transformation that has taken place when Jews, Christians and Muslims face one another in their full humanity.

In the case of Judaism and Christianity it took the Holocaust for this to happen. The result has been dramatic. Today, after an estrangement that lasted almost two millennia, Jews and Christians meet much more often as friends – even (in the word selected by recent popes) 'brothers' – than as enemies.

Likewise with Islam. As I was writing this book an event happened that moved me greatly. On Friday 9 January 2015, an Islamist terrorist entered a kosher supermarket in Paris and killed four Jews buying food for the Sabbath. A Muslim employee, Lassana Bathily, saw what was happening and, out of sight of the gunmen, hid twenty Jewish customers in a cold storage room, saving their lives. Commended for his courage, he replied, 'We are all brothers. It's not a question of Jews, Christians or Muslims. We were all in the same boat, we had to help each other to get out of the crisis.'

Like Malala Yousafzai, the Pakistani-Muslim girl who fought for women's rights against the Taliban, surviving an attempted assassination and becoming in 2014 the youngest person ever to win the Nobel Prize, Lassana is one of the heroes of our time. What they and millions like them represent is the ability to let faith strengthen, not damage, our shared humanity. It sounds simple, but history tells us that it is not. Religious people in the grip of strong emotions – fear, pain, anxiety, confusion, a sense of loss and humiliation – often dehumanise their opponents with devastating results. Faith is God's call to see his trace in the face of the Other. But that needs a theology of the Other, which is what I offer in this book.

There is nothing accidental about the spread of radical politicised religion in our time. It came about because of a series of decisions a half-century ago that led to the creation of an entire educational network of schools and seminaries dedicated to the proposition that loving God means hating the enemies of God. The end result has been a flood of chaos, violence and destruction that is drowning the innocent and guilty alike. We now have, with equal seriousness, to educate for peace, forgiveness and love.

Until our global institutions take a stand against the teaching and preaching of hate, all their efforts of diplomacy and military intervention will fail. Ultimately the responsibility is ours. Tomorrow's world is born in what we teach our children today. That is what this book is about.

It begins with the simplest of questions: What makes people violent in the first place?

2

Violence and Identity

What a chimera, then, is man! What a novelty, what a monster, what a chaos, what a contradiction, what a prodigy! Judge of all things, feeble earthworm, repository of truth, sewer of uncertainty and error, the glory and the scum of the universe.

Blaise Pascal

Two friends are walking in the jungle when they hear the roar of a lion. The first starts thinking of places they can hide. The second puts on his running shoes. The first says, 'What are you thinking of? You can't possibly run faster than a lion.' The second replies, 'I don't need to run faster than the lion. I just need to run faster than you.'

That is the joke told in the film *The Imitation Game* by Alan Turing, the mathematical genius who conceptualised the computer and helped break the German Enigma code during the Second World War. But it took an earlier figure, Charles Darwin, to see that this was more than a joke. It expresses one of the fundamental tensions in the human condition. It was the single biggest challenge to his theory of natural selection.

The first man seeks a collective solution. He tries to think of a way of saving both him and his friend. The second opts for natural selection. He thinks of a solution that will save him at the cost of his friend. He knows that, come what may, one of them will die and he prefers it not to be him.

This is, in essence, the human dilemma. Which comes first? Altruism or survival? The common good or individual self-interest? Are we, under the skin, saints or sinners, angels or demons, moralists or Machiavellians? The joke trades on the fact that we are both. It is the central ambiguity of the human situation.

27

Darwin's problem was this: if natural selection is correct, if evolution is a competition for scarce resources such that only the best adapted survive and pass on their characteristics to the next generation, then we should expect to see the selfish survive. The altruists, those who take a risk for the safety of all, would on average die earlier and fail to pass their genes on. They are the ones who get eaten by the lion.

As Darwin put it, the bravest, most self-sacrificial individuals 'would on average perish in larger numbers than other men', and the noblest 'would often leave no offspring to inherit his noble nature'.[1] So altruism should become extinct over time. It is a bad survival strategy. Let others take the risks. Make sure you, at least, are safe.

Yet Darwin knew that altruism was admired in every human society of which he was aware. Even animals take risks for the sake of the group. The one that emits a cry to warn of the presence of a predator helps the group escape while making its own detection more likely. In the language of today: how could selfish genes come together and produce selfless people?

We can arrive at the same problem from the opposite direction. Since Socrates, philosophers have asked: Why be moral? Plato thought it was knowledge. People do wrong only through ignorance. Aristotle thought this implausible. We often suffer from *akrasia*, weakness of will. So we become good people the way we become good tennis players or violinists, through practice until the behaviour we aspire to becomes natural and instinctive. Being moral means acquiring the habits of the heart we call virtue.

In the modern age Kant thought that what makes us moral is reason (understood in a particular way). An act is right if we can prescribe it as a universal rule. We should not tell lies because if everyone else did, no one would trust us and the practice of communication on which lying depends would be undermined. Immorality is a kind of self-contradiction. Reason allows us to think our way through to virtue.

David Hume and Adam Smith thought that reason alone

cannot provide our fundamental motives for action. Feelings or emotions (what Hume called 'the passions') do that. What make us moral are the feelings we have with and for others. As Adam Smith put it in the opening sentence of *The Theory of Moral Sentiments*, 'How selfish soever man may be supposed, there are evidently some principles in his nature, which interest him in the fortune of others, and render their happiness necessary to him, though he derives nothing from it except the pleasure of seeing it.' Whether through neuroscience or biochemistry, mirror neurons or oxytocin, we have a moral sense.

The obvious question, though, on all these theories is this: if being moral is so straightforward – if knowledge, habit, character, reason and emotion all point the way to the right and the good – how is it that people have, throughout the ages, lied, cheated, robbed, stolen, insulted, offended, oppressed, exploited and killed? This is Darwin's question from the opposite direction. If we are so good, why are we so bad?

The third starting point, a religious one, is the one with which this book began. How is it that people kill in the name of the God of life, wage war in the name of the God of peace, hate in the name of the God of love and practise cruelty in the name of the God of compassion? How, if we are the image of God, do we so often harm the work of God, especially our fellow humans?

*

The answer in its essentials was given by Darwin himself. In *The Descent of Man* he wrote, 'There can be no doubt that a tribe including many members who, from possessing in high degree the spirit of patriotism, fidelity, obedience, courage, and sympathy, were always ready to aid one another, and to sacrifice themselves for the common good would be victorious over most other tribes; and this would be natural selection.'

We are social animals. We hand on our genes as individuals, but we survive only in groups. Nor is this unique to humans. Ants, bees and most mammals scout, feed and live in groups. In the wild the individual separated from the group is essentially dead. The lone individual is the one that gets eaten by the lion.

Supremely, this is the evolutionary advantage of Homo sapiens. We are the most effective of all life forms in creating and sustaining groups. We are the most social of animals. Indeed, according to many biologists it was for the sake of enhancing this ability that we developed language. It is also the reason for our prodigious brain size, a full 300 per cent larger than our evolutionary ancestors.

We co-operate and we compete. We co-operate in order to compete. One man will not survive against a lion. But ten or a hundred might, if they formed an effective team. Their greatest danger would then be posed not by a predator but by another human group in pursuit of the same scarce resources: food, shelter and territory. The stronger the group, the more chance it has against rivals. In the Darwinian struggle to survive, the most cohesive team, adept at co-ordinating its various talents and tasks, will live to fight another day.

It follows that we have two sets of instincts, honed and refined by many centuries of evolutionary history. One set – Darwin's 'patriotism, fidelity, obedience, courage and sympathy' – inclines us in the direction of altruism. We work for the good of the group because our very viability depends on it. The stronger the group, the greater our chances of surviving to beget further generations. As Darwin said, this would be natural selection.

The other set – our most basic reactions of aggression, fear, anger and combativeness, our willingness to fight and inflict injuries on others – shapes our relationship with rival groups competing with us for scarce resources. The speed and force of these reactions are vital to our success in the competitive arena of natural selection.

So we are angels *and* demons, angels to those on our side, demons to those on the other side. This follows from the human – and wider than human – instinct to form groups. Groups unite and divide. They divide as they unite. Every group involves the coming together of multiple individuals to form a collective Us. But every Us is defined against a Them, the ones not like us. The one without the other is impossible. Inclusion and exclusion go hand in hand.

Here then is the source of both violence and altruism. Darwin's question is answered. Altruism plays a major role in survival of the group. Whether natural selection operates at the level of the individual or whether there is such a thing as group selection has been and remains a hotly debated topic within biology. But there is no doubt that the survival of individuals depends on the willingness of members of the group to take risks and make sacrifices for the good of the group as a whole. That is the biological function of the better angels of our nature.

The same applies in the reverse direction, explaining why, when reason or emotion inclines us to morality, human evil exists. Our inclination to act well towards others, whatever its source, tends to be confined to those with whom we share a common identity. The Greeks, the world's first philosophers and scientists, regarded anyone who was not Greek as a barbarian – a word derived from the sound of a sheep bleating. Our radius of moral concern has limits. The group may be small or large, but in practice as opposed to theory, we tend to see those not like us as less than fully human.

The same is true of religion. The world's great faiths have said sublime things about love, compassion, sacrifice and charity. But these noble sentiments have often been confined to fellow believers, or at least potential fellow believers. Against non-believers – members of another faith or of none, and those of our own faith we deem to be heretics – religions can be brutal and pitiless.

*

We are potentially violent because, as social animals, we form groups to compete for resources and survive against other groups. Unlike non-human social animals, we can choose non-violent ways of interacting with other groups, but sadly all too often we do not. There is such a thing as in-group violence, but for the most part it is contained (what counts as in-group and out-group depends on context: groups may fracture into schisms, sects, denominations, parties and factions that sometimes come together and at other times see each other as completely separate groups). The violence that leads to war and terror is between groups, and it is precisely this that leads to in-group solidarity and cohesion, and fear, suspicion and aggression towards out-groups. It is neither secularism nor religious belief that makes us what we are, the curious mixture of good and bad that can lead us to the moral heights or the savage depths. It is our groupishness.

What, though, allows us to form groups in the first place if we are genetically conditioned to seek our own survival before that of others? How could altruism emerge? The answer comes at three levels, very different from one another.

The first was indicated graphically by J.B.S. Haldane when he was asked whether he would jump into a river to save his brother. He replied, 'No, but I would do so to save two brothers or eight cousins.' On the face of it, it would never make sense to risk our own life to save someone in danger of drowning. Why endanger your posterity for the sake of others? Haldane's point, elaborated in the 1960s by William Hamilton and others, is that it would make sense if the people you are trying to save are closely related to you. We share 50 per cent of our genes with our siblings, an eighth with our cousins, and so on. So by saving the lives of close relatives we would still be handing on our genes to the future. This is the logic of *kin selection* and it is determined by genetic similarity.

This makes intuitive sense. We know that the matrix of altruism is within the family. It is there that we hand on our genes to the next generation, there that we have our greatest chance of defeating mortality this side of heaven. It was Edmund Burke who said that 'we begin our public affections in our families', and Alexis de Tocqueville who wrote that 'as long as family feeling was kept alive, the antagonist of oppression was never alone'. Biology, morality and society coincide. Morality begins with kin.

How groups became wider – from kin to kith, from relatives to friends – was a major problem in evolutionary biology until the late 1970s. How would any animal, let alone a human being, come to form an association with non-related others if self-interest always defeats the common good? This was the starting point of Hobbes's famous account of life in a state of nature, in which there was 'continual fear and danger of violent death, and the life of man, solitary, poor, nasty, brutish, and short'. What stops people fighting one another for long enough to create an association?

Some brilliant work in the late 1970s and 1980s provided the answer. It used a scenario drawn from Game Theory called the Prisoner's Dilemma. This exercise imagines two criminals, suspected of a crime for which the police lack adequate evidence to secure a conviction. Their best chance of doing so is to interrogate the two men separately, giving each an incentive to inform on the other. This they both do, with the result that they end up in prison with a longer sentence than they would have received had they both stayed silent. This sounds like a minor curiosity, but it upset the major assumption on which economics had been based since Adam Smith's *Wealth of Nations*, namely that division of labour combined with individual self-interest would result in collective gain. The Prisoner's Dilemma shows that this is so only if we add one other ingredient: trust. What stops the two accused men from staying silent is that neither can trust the other to do likewise.

What mathematicians discovered was that the Prisoner's Dilemma yields a negative outcome if played only once. If played many times, the two men eventually learn to trust each other because they learn that they gain if they do and lose if they don't. A competition to find the most effective computer programme for survival in multiple encounters with strangers was won in 1979 by a simple programme, designed by Anatol Rapoport, a political scientist with an interest in nuclear confrontation who had once been a concert pianist. He called it Tit-for-Tat. It said: on the first encounter be nice, and on subsequent encounters repeat the other person's last move. If he is nice, so should you be, and if not, then respond in kind. This was the first moral principle whose survival value was shown by computer simulation. What it did was to show the gold in the Golden Rule. It said, in a world where people will probably do to you what you did to them, it pays to act to others as you would wish them to act to you – a basic principle of most cultures.

This solves the Darwinian dilemma of how non-genetically related individuals can co-operate to form groups. If you do to others what you expect them to do for you – share food, give warning of impending danger and the like – then the group will function effectively and survive. If not, you will be punished by reprisals and possible exclusion from the group. Biologists call this *reciprocal altruism*. Some deny that this is altruism at all. It is 'self-interest rightly understood', or what Bishop Butler called 'cool self-love'. But the terminology is neither here nor there. This is the simplest basis of the moral life. If you start with benevolence, then apply the rules of reciprocity, you create a basis of trust on which groups can form. For this you do not need religion. All social animals work this out, because those who do not, do not survive.

It depends, though, on repeated face-to-face encounters. I have to be able to remember what you did to me last time if I am to trust you now. This requires a fair amount of memory, which explains why animal groups like chimpanzees and bonobos are small. Some biologists think that humans developed language so that they could better co-ordinate their activities. It also allowed them to gossip, sharing information about which individuals were trustworthy and which were not. It even allowed them to 'stroke' one another verbally rather than physically, thus strengthening the emotional bonding between them.

One ingenious biologist, Robin Dunbar, worked out that there is a correlation among species between brain size and the average size of groups. On this basis he calculated that for humans, the optimal size is 150. That is why the first human groups, even after the domestication of animals and the invention of agriculture, were quite small: the tribe, the village, the clan. Associations larger than this were federations of smaller groups.

How then did humans develop much larger concentrations of population? How did they create cities and civilisation? Reciprocal altruism creates trust between neighbours, people who meet repeatedly and know about one another's character. The birth of the city posed a different and much greater problem: *how do you establish trust between strangers?*

*

This was the point at which culture took over from nature, and religion was born – that is, religion in the sense of an organised social structure with myths, rituals, sacred times and places, temples and a priesthood. Recall that we are speaking in evolutionary not theological terms. Regardless of whether we regard religion as true or false, it clearly has adaptive value because it appeared at the dawn of civilisation and has been a central feature of almost every society since.

The early religions created moral communities, thus solving the problem of trust between strangers. They sanctified the social order. They taught people that society is as it is because this is the will of the gods and the basic structure of the universe. The fundamental theme of the early religions in Mesopotamia and Egypt was the tension between cosmos and chaos, order and anarchy, structure and disarray. The universe began in chaos, a formless ocean or unformed matter, and if the rules are not followed, it will become chaos again. As Shakespeare put it in Ulysses' speech in Act 1, scene 3 of *Troilus and Cressida*, the finest-ever account of the cosmological mind:

> The heavens themselves, the planets and this centre
> Observe degree, priority and place,
> Insisture, course, proportion, season, form,
> Office and custom, in all line of order.

There is an order in heaven and earth, and if its rules are broken, 'hark, what discord follows!' The sea will flood the earth. Social distinctions will dissolve. Law will be replaced by anarchy. Children will no longer obey their parents. All that will be left is violence:

> Then every thing includes itself in power,
> Power into will, will into appetite;
> And appetite, an universal wolf,
> So doubly seconded with will and power,
> Must make perforce an universal prey,
> And last eat up himself.

There is no biological mechanism capable of yielding order on such a scale. Ants manage it because, within groups and roles, they are clones of one another. They operate by kin selection. Humans are different from one another. That is what makes co-operation between them so difficult, and so powerful when it happens. This is when something new and distinctively human emerges. Learned habits of behaviour take over from evolved instinctual drives. Rituals make their appearance. Socialisation becomes a fundamental part of the education of the young. There are roles, rules, codes of conduct. The habits necessary to the maintenance of the group become internalised. We are the culture-creating, meaning-seeking animal. Homo sapiens became Homo religiosus.

Such, at any rate, is the argument put forward by a group of evolutionary scholars, among them David Sloan Wilson, Scott Atran and Ara Norenzayan. They point, among other things, to the research of Richard Sosis into 200 communes founded in the nineteenth century. Communes are good examples of co-operation without kinship. Sosis found that 6 per cent of secular communes were still in existence twenty years after their founding, as compared with 39 per cent of religious ones. In a follow-up study he found the more demanding the religious group, the longer its lifespan.[2] Religion creates and sustains communities.

It also creates trust. Nicholas Rauh studied social life in Delos, the centre of Roman maritime trade in pre-Christian times. What allowed merchants to develop the mutual trust that made long-distance trade possible? They created religious fraternities and invoked the watchful gods as witnesses to their agreements. 'This divine function more than anything else provides the common denominator for the features encountered in both Greek and Roman marketplaces.'[3]

In the run-up to the 2008 American presidential election, a Gallup poll in 2007 showed that over 90 per cent would vote for a candidate who was Catholic or Jewish as opposed to 45 per cent who would vote for an atheist.[4] Nor was this unique to America. In a worldwide survey of 81 countries conducted between 1999 and 2002, two-thirds of participants said they trusted religion, a half trusted their government and a third trusted political parties.[5]

Recall that even the liberal-minded John Locke in the seventeenth century argued against granting civil rights to atheists: 'Those are not at all to be tolerated who deny the being of a God. Promises, covenants, and oaths, which are the bonds of human society, can have no hold on an atheist. The taking away of God, though but even in thought, dissolves all.'[6] This is not to endorse these sentiments, merely to note that they exist.

Others like Richard Schweder and Jonathan Haidt have shown how the rich repertoire of religious ethics, with its dimensions of respect for authority, loyalty and a sense of the sacred, furnish a more comprehensive or 'thick' morality than the relatively pared-down features of secular ethics, based on fairness and the avoidance of harm. It is not that religious people are more moral than their secular counterparts, but rather that their moralities tend to have a thicker and richer texture, binding groups together, not merely regulating the encounters of randomly interacting individuals. As Haidt puts it: 'Whatever its origins, the psychology of sacredness helps bind individuals into moral communities.'[7] Many believe that the word 'religion' comes from the Latin *religare*, meaning 'to bind'.

Indeed, as the research of Harvard political scientist Robert Putnam has shown, in his and David Campbell's book *American Grace*, it is specifically in religious communities in the United States that you find the strongest reservoirs of social capital, willingness to help strangers, to give to charity for both religious and secular causes, and to be active in voluntary associations, neighbourhood groups and so on. His view is that this has to do not with religious belief as such, but rather with membership in a religious community.

Add to this the demographic research of Eric Kaufmann, already referred to in the previous chapter, that throughout the contemporary world, the more religious the group the higher its birth rate, and we see the power of religion to sustain community over time. The converse is also true. Michael Blume notes:

> Although we looked hard at all the available data and case studies back to early Greece and India, we still have not been able to identify a single case of any non-religious population retaining more than two births per woman for just a century. Wherever religious communities dissolved, demographic decline followed suit.[8]

So religion performed, and continues to perform, a task fundamental to large groups. It links people, emotionally, behaviourally, intellectually and spiritually, into communion and thus community. It follows, incidentally, that the first fully articulated religions were integrally linked with politics, a word that itself derives from *polis*, meaning 'city'. Religion was the metaphysical grounding of the social structure, and thus the basis of political order. The head of state *was* the head of the religion. The king, ruler or pharaoh was either a god or a son of the gods or the chief intermediary with the gods. Civilisation had to undergo a revolution before it learned to separate the two. That was where Abrahamic monotheism came in, but that is a story for a later chapter.

*

We can now answer the question of the relationship between religion and violence, as well as that of the dual nature of human beings, capable of great good but also of great evil. We are good and bad because we are human, we are social animals and we live, survive and thrive in groups. Within groups we practise altruism. Between them we practise aggression. Religion enters the equation only because it is the most powerful force ever devised for the creation and maintenance of large-scale groups by solving the problem of trust between strangers.

Violence has nothing to do with religion as such. It has to do with identity and life in groups. Religion sustains groups more effectively than any other force. It suppresses violence within. It rises to the threat of violence from without. Most conflicts and wars have nothing to do with religion whatsoever. They are about power, territory and glory, things that are secular, even profane. But if religion can be enlisted, it will be.

If, then, violence has to do with identity, why not abolish identity? Why divide humanity into a Them and Us? Why not have just a common humanity? This, after all, was the utopian hope of prophets like Zechariah who imagined a time when 'The Lord will become king over all the world. On that day the Lord will be one, and his name will be one' (Zech. 14:9). A world without identities would be a world without war.

There have been three major attempts in history to realise this dream, and it is immensely important to understand why they failed. The first was Pauline Christianity. Paul famously said, 'There is neither Jew nor Gentile, neither slave nor free, nor is there male and female' (NIV, Gal. 3:28). Historically, Christianity has been the most successful attempt in history to convert the

39

world to a single faith. Today a third of the population of the world is Christian. But nations continued to exist. So did non-monotheistic faiths. Another monotheism arose, Islam, with a similar aspiration to win the world to its understanding of the will of God. Within Christianity itself there was schism, first between West and East, then between Catholic and Protestant. Within Islam there were Sunni and Shia. The result was that war did not end. There were crusades, jihads, holy wars and civil strife. These led some people to believe that religion is not a way of curing violence but of intensifying it.

The second attempt was the European Enlightenment in the eighteenth century. After a devastating series of religious wars there was a genuine belief among European intellectuals that the divisions brought about by faith and dogma could be transcended by the universal truths of reason, philosophy and science. Kant produced a secular equivalent of the idea that we are all in the image of God. He said: treat others as ends, not only means. He also revived the prophetic dream of Isaiah, turning it into a secular programme for 'perpetual peace' (1795). Its most famous expression was Beethoven's setting in the last movement of his Ninth Symphony of Schiller's 'Ode to Joy', with its vision of a time when *Alle Menschen werden Brüder* – 'All men become brothers.'

This too did not last. The age of reason was succeeded by Romanticism and the return of the old gods of nation and race. In the course of the nineteenth and twentieth centuries three substitutes for religion emerged as the basis for new identities. One was the nation state. A second was the ideological system. The third was race. The first led to two world wars, the second to Stalin's Russia, the Gulag and the KGB, and the third to the Holocaust. The cost of these three substitutes for religion was in excess of a hundred million lives. After that, no one who argues that abolishing religion will lead to peace can be taken seriously.

The first two attempts were universalist: a universal religion or a universal culture. The third attempt, the one we have been living through for the past half-century, is the opposite. It is the effort to eliminate identity by abolishing groups altogether and instead enthroning the individual. The contemporary West is the most individualistic era of all time. Its central values are in ethics, autonomy; in politics, individual rights; in culture, post-modernism; and in religion, 'spirituality'. Its idol is the self, its icon the 'selfie', and its operating systems the free market and the post-ideological, managerial liberal democratic state. In place of national identities we have global cosmopolitanism. In place of communities we have flash-mobs. We are no longer pilgrims but tourists. We no longer know who we are or why.

No civilisational order like this has ever appeared before, and we can only understand it in the light of the traumatic failure of the three substitutes for religion: nationalism, communism and race. We are now living through the discontents of individualism and have been since the 1970s. Identity has returned. The tribes are back and fighting more fiercely than ever. The old sources of conflict, religion and ethnicity, are claiming new victims. The anti-modern radicals have learned that you can use the products of modernity without going through the process that produced them, namely Westernisation. Meanwhile the energy of the West has been sapped by the decay of the very things religion once energised: marriage, families, communities, a shared moral code, the ability to defer the gratification of instinct, the covenant that linked rich and poor in a bond of mutual responsibility, and a vision of the universe that gave rise to the social virtue of hope.

The tendency of humans to form groups, of which religion is the most effective agent, is a source of violence and war. But the alternative – humanity without groups or identities – is impossible because unbearable. The thinker who saw this most clearly was French sociologist Émile Durkheim. In 1897 he published a remarkable book entitled *Suicide*. Intuitively we think that the choice of 'to be or not to be' is the most intensely personal decision of all. It has everything to do with mind and mood, and little to do with the world outside.

Durkheim argued otherwise. He said that in a society undergoing *anomie* – the loss of a shared moral code – more people will commit suicide. We cannot bear the absence of public meanings and collective moral identity. Faced with the prospect, vulnerable individuals will choose death rather than life. Though Durkheim could not have foreseen it, a variant of this is happening in our time. It is the reason why seemingly normal, well-educated and adjusted people with careers and families ahead of them become jihadists and suicide bombers, choosing death rather than life.

Vast research since the events of 11 September 2001 has shown that jihadists and suicide bombers are not for the most part people driven by poverty or social exclusion. They have no recognisable psychological profile. They are not psychopathic, nor are they driven by religious extremism as such. Many of them did not have a religious education. As children, they did not attend madrassahs. Some of them know very little about Islam.

If they are suffering from anything, it is from what they see as the emptiness, meaninglessness, materialism and narcissism of the contemporary West and the corruption of secular regimes in the Islamic world. As Eric Hoffer noted in *The True Believer* (1951) and as Scott Atran has shown in his study of suicide bombers, *Talking to the Enemy*, individuals join radical movements to alleviate the isolation of the lonely crowd and become, however briefly, part of an intense community engaged in the pursuit of something larger than the self.[9] They are motivated by genuine ideals. They feel the suffering, the pain and the humiliation of their fellow believers. They seek to dedicate and if need be sacrifice their lives to end what they see as the injustice of the world and to honour the memory of those they see as its victims. As Michael Ignatieff wrote in *The Warrior's Honor*, the book he wrote in response to the Balkan wars, 'Political terror is tenacious because it is an ethical practice. It is a cult of the dead, a dire and absolute expression of respect.'[10] Holy warriors are altruists, and what they commit is altruistic evil.

We have seen in this chapter how altruism leads us to make sacrifices for the sake of the group, while at the same time leading us to commit acts of violence against perceived threats to the group. Good and bad, altruism and aggression, peace and violence, love and hate, are born together as the twin consequences of our need to define ourselves as an Us in opposition to a Them. But we have a way further to go. Something more than simple identity is needed for good people to commit truly evil deeds.

3

Dualism

Exaggerate each feature until man is
Metamorphosized into beast, vermin, insect.
Fill in the background with malignant
Figures from ancient nightmares – devils,
Demons, myrmidons of evil.
When your icon of the enemy is complete
You will be able to kill without guilt,
Slaughter without shame.

Sam Keen, Faces of the Enemy *(1986)*[1]

One day between November 1946 and February 1947, a young Bedouin shepherd, Muhammed edh-Dhib, in the company of a cousin and a friend, discovered a number of ancient decaying leather scrolls in a cave in Qumran, amid the mountains that border the Dead Sea. The story Muhammed told was that he was tending his animals when he noticed that one had strayed from the flock. He idly tossed a stone into the small opening of a cave and became frightened when it made an unusual noise, as if it had hit not the bottom of the cave but a jar inside. Unnerved, he fled, but later returned with his two companions, climbed into the cave, retrieved the scrolls and brought them back to his family. After drying them, his father took them to some local dealers. One declared them worthless. A second bought three for low prices. A further scroll came into the possession of the Syrian archbishop of Jerusalem, who showed them to a scholar who realised their value and significance.

This prompted a dramatic search for other caves and scrolls against the background of Israel's War of Independence. It continued under Jordanian auspices until 1956. Eventually eleven caves were found to contain documents, yielding a vast library of 981 different texts. Among them were by far the oldest manuscripts of biblical texts then known, dating from the third or second century BCE (subsequently even older fragments dating to the sixth century BCE were discovered at Ketef Hinom), together with other previously unknown ancient documents.

The Dead Sea Scrolls are one of the great discoveries of modern times. Most believe that they were the work of a small community of separatists who had taken the decision, sometime in the second pre-Christian century, to leave Jerusalem and live in seclusion until the day when Israel's enemies and its own corrupt religious establishment would be overthrown and the reign of righteousness restored. Some believe they were a branch of the Essenes, others that they were a dissident group of Sadducees, yet others that they were a group in their own right, one of many in those turbulent, fissiparous times.

Less well known is another major manuscript discovery some two years earlier near Nag Hammadi, a settlement in upper Egypt. It was there in December 1945 that Muhammad Ali al-Samman and his brothers had gone to dig in Jabal al-Tarif, a mountain honeycombed with caves, for the soft soil they used to fertilise their crops. As they were digging, their spades hit a red earthenware jar containing thirteen papyrus books bound in leather. From there on the story becomes obscure. The brothers had been involved in a blood feud and were afraid that the police, investigating murder, would find the manuscripts and confiscate them. Eventually the manuscripts found their way onto the black market, but as news of their existence leaked out, the Egyptian government eventually tracked most of them down and deposited them in the Coptic Museum in Cairo.

Part of one of the codices was smuggled out of Egypt and placed for sale, attracting the attention of a Dutch scholar, Gilles Quispel, who pieced the fragments together, deciphered one of the texts and realised that it was an edition of a text hidden for many centuries, the *Gospel of Thomas*. Altogether the Nag Hammadi manuscripts represent Coptic versions of fifty-two early Christian texts, many of them hitherto unknown, including the *Gospel of Truth*, the *Gospel to the Egyptians*, the *Secret Book of James*, the *Apocalypse of Paul* and the *Apocalypse of Peter*.

Written in Coptic, they were translations, dated between 350 and 400 CE, of originals written in Greek and dating back to the second century. The reason they had been hidden soon became clear. They embody a theology radically at odds with the beliefs that became mainstream Christianity. Indeed, many of the newly discovered texts had been denounced as heretical by Irenaeus, bishop of Lyons, around the year 180.

These two libraries, hidden for centuries, belong to two quite different religious traditions, one Jewish, the other Christian. But they have one very unusual feature in common – one of the reasons that they were hidden in the first place. Judaism and Christianity are both monotheisms, but the Qumran sectarians and those of Nag Hammadi were *dualists*. They believed not in one power governing the universe, but in two.

Among the Qumran scrolls is one describing a war between the Children of Light (the Israelites or such of them as remained after their various defeats and exiles) and the Children of Darkness, the Ammonites, Moabites, Amalekites, Philistines and their allies. The Children of Light would be victorious, darkness would be vanquished, and peace would reign for ever.

The Nag Hammadi gospels are more radical, turning the conventional world of the Bible upside down. In them, the creator of the physical universe was not God but a demiurge, a second-ary power, a fallen angel who had got out of hand. It was he who made the material world with its disease and death, violence and pain. The true God had nothing to do with the physical universe but lived in heaven in a realm beyond time, death and change. For the Nag Hammadi sectarians the Hebrew Bible and the New Testament Gospels are, in significant ways, completely false. The real hero of the Garden of Eden was the serpent. It was he

46

who opened Adam's and Eve's eyes to the truth. As for the New Testament, the *Gospel of Thomas* offers the startling revelation that the only disciple who truly understood Jesus was Judas, seen in the canonical Gospels as the traitor who betrayed him.

Where did these strange ideas come from? They are clearly not indigenous to Judaism or Christianity, because dualism is not monotheism. Jews first encountered them during the period of Persian rule in the form of Zoroastrianism. This ancient faith divided the supernatural powers into two, Ahura Mazda, the god of light, and Ahriman, the god of darkness, 'the accursed destructive Spirit who is all wickedness and full of death'.[2] Aided by an army of demons and seven archfiends, Ahriman wages war against the light, changing his form into anything he chooses, from lion to lizard to handsome youth. As time proceeds and Ahriman senses his inevitable defeat, he gathers his strength for a final confrontation, during which the sun and moon will pale in the heavens and the stars will be shaken from the sky. Eventually, exhausted, he is vanquished, never to return.

The other source of dualism, more evident in Nag Hammadi than Qumran, is ancient Greece, especially Orphism. Here the division is not between good and evil but between the soul and the body, the spiritual and the physical. Orphic myth tells the story of the Titans' clash with Dionysus, son of Zeus, whom they murder and eat. Zeus burns them in his anger, and from the ash, humans are born, containing elements of both: Dionysus in the form of the soul, the Titans in the form of the body. The soul is imprisoned within the body but lives on after it and is reincarnated. Elements of this doctrine persist in the philosophy of Plato, who distinguished between the world as we encounter it through the physical senses and as we truly know it through the soul.

The sects that produced the manuscripts at Qumran and Nag Hammadi disappeared, but dualism lived on. In Persia it became known as Manichaeism (after the Iranian thinker Mani, c. 216–76 CE). In Greece it was called Gnosticism. The Nag Hammadi texts are known as the Gnostic Gospels.

It might seem strange to turn to two ancient and marginal sects to understand the connection between religion and violence, but they contain a clue that is an essential piece of the puzzle. The last chapter argued that violence is born of the need for identity and the formation of groups. These lead to conflict and war. But war is normal. Altruistic evil is not normal. Suicide bombings, the targeting of civilians and the murder of schoolchildren are not normal. Violence may be possible wherever there is an Us and a Them. But radical violence emerges only when we see the Us as all-good and the Them as all-evil, heralding a war between the children of light and the forces of darkness. That is when altruistic evil is born.

*

Why would even sectarian members of Judaism and Christianity be tempted by an idea that is clearly incompatible with their faith in a single God? *Dualism is what happens when cognitive dissonance becomes unbearable, when the world as it is, is simply too unlike the world as we believed it ought to be.* In the words of historian Jeffrey Russell, dualism 'denied the unity and omnipotence of God in order to preserve his perfect goodness'.[3]

The God of Abraham is, among other things, the Lord of history who redeemed his people from slavery in Egypt. Yet for the Jews of the second century BCE, the great prophetic visions had not come true. Israel had been defeated by Nebuchadnezzar. The Temple had been destroyed. The people had gone into exile in Babylon. Some had returned, but not all. The lost ten tribes for the most part stayed lost. The Second Temple was a pale shadow of Solomon's. The nation was not truly independent. Persian rule was succeeded by the Alexandrian Empire, eventually to be followed by Rome. Many Jews had become Hellenised, including the Hasmonean kings and high priests. It was at this point, probably around 125 BCE, that a priestly group decided to leave Jerusalem, live in purity in the lonely wastes of the Dead Sea, and wait for the end of history, when God would fight a cosmic battle and defeat the forces of evil.

Among the early Christians, the cognitive dissonance was even greater. The first Christians were Jews who believed that the Messiah had come. But the Messiah in mainstream Judaism is not a supernatural being with the power to transform the human condition. He is simply an anointed king (the word *messiah* means 'anointed') in the line of David who will fight Israel's battles, restore its independence, unite the people and usher in a reign of peace.

Manifestly that had not happened. After the death of Jesus the fate of the faithful became worse, not better. The Romans were ruthless. Religious liberty was curtailed. Jews rose in revolt but suffered devastating defeat. It became easier, particularly for some Gentile Christians, to think in dualistic terms borrowed from Greece. The physical arena with its wars and destruction was neither real nor the work of God. It was, as Plato said, a play of shadows cast on the wall of our senses by an artificial light. The real world is that of the forms, of eternity and the soul. This is where God lives. What the Messiah had done was not to change history. Rather, he had brought his disciples the truth about the other world, the realm of the spirit that lies within us if we only have the knowledge, the *gnosis*, the secret key that unlocks the door.

Dualism entered Judaism and Christianity when it became easier to attribute the sufferings of the world to an evil force rather than to the work of God.

The Qumran and Nag Hammadi sects disappeared. The mainstream in both Judaism and Christianity rejected dualism. Within Judaism, the group that survived were the rabbis. In some respects their teachings were close to those of the first Christians. They believed in the primacy of love and forgiveness. They subscribed to the morality taught in the Sermon on the Mount. They called it *lifnim mi-shurat ha-din*, going beyond the letter of the law. They saw themselves as heirs to the prophets, and believed, as did the early Christians, in the goodness of ordinary people.

They also discovered a powerful way of excluding heretical beliefs. They did not codify doctrine as the Church eventually did at the Council of Nicea in 325. Instead they fought the battle of ideas through the prayer book. The way they defeated dualism – they called it *shtei reshuyot*, 'two domains' – was elegant and effective. They chose the single most emphatic rejection of dualism in the Bible, Isaiah's statement, 'I form the light, and create darkness: I make peace, and create evil' (Isa. 45:7). Out of delicacy they substituted 'all things' for 'evil'. They then set these words as the opening line of the communal daily Morning Prayer, where they stand to this day. So whoever prayed in the synagogue denied dualism. It soon disappeared from the Jewish mainstream, surfacing from time to time only in esoteric mystical texts.

Christianity likewise rejected the Gnostic Gospels. The most significant dualistic challenge came from Marcion of Sinope in the mid-second century. He believed that the God of the Old Testament and the God of the New were two quite different deities. Like the Gnostics he believed that the Jewish God, Creator of the physical universe, was a different and lower being than the God of Christianity, who was spiritual, not physical, practising love and forgiveness rather than justice and retribution. The two religions had nothing to do with one another, so the Hebrew Bible, the 'Old Testament', had no place within the Christian canon. Marcion's views were rejected as heresy. Dualism reappeared in the eleventh century in the form of the Cathars, against whom Pope Innocent III launched the Albigensian Crusade (1209–29). Some say that suspicion of lingering dualism was one of the reasons the Inquisition was started in 1234.

Unfortunately, a mild form of dualism has a habit of reappearing. Hardly a week goes by without someone in an article or book drawing a contrast between the Old Testament God of revenge and the New Testament God of forgiveness. The well-known atheist Richard Dawkins began the second chapter of *The God Delusion* with the words, 'The God of the Old Testament

is arguably the most unpleasant character in all fiction.'⁴ He was
surprised and angry when, in conversation, I told him that those
words showed that he was a Christian atheist, not a Jewish atheist. He could not understand this, but it is quite simple. The words
'the God of the Old Testament' are only spoken by Christians.
Outside Christianity, there is no Old Testament. There is the
Hebrew Bible.

It has become one of the taken-for-granted clichés of Western
culture that the God of the Old Testament is the God of law,
letter, justice, retribution, vengeance, anger, flesh and death. The
God of the New Testament is the God of faith, spirit, forgiveness,
grace, forbearance, love and life. But this is pure Marcionism
and, in Christian terms, heresy. The essence of Christianity as
articulated by Paul and the Gospels is that the God of the Old
Testament and the God of the New are the same God. His love
is the same love. His justice is the same justice. His forgiveness is
the same forgiveness. That is why the Old Testament is part of the
Christian canon.

*

Dualism comes in many forms, not all of them dangerous. There
is the Platonic dualism that differentiates sharply between mind
and body, the spiritual and the physical. There is the theological dualism that sees two different supernatural forces at work in
the universe. There is the moral dualism that sees good and evil
as instincts within us between which we must choose. But there
is also what I will call *pathological dualism* that sees humanity
itself as radically, ontologically divided into the unimpeachably
good and the irredeemably bad. You are either one or the other:
either one of the saved, the redeemed, the chosen, or a child of
Satan, the devil's disciple. Pathological dualism is not Gnosticism
or Manichaeism, both of which are about the gods, not humankind. But it is not difficult to see how the one could lead to the
other, because our views of the natural are shaped by our ideas

of the supernatural. To understand how this works we must move from theology to psychology.

A line of thinkers from Sigmund Freud to Melanie Klein have highlighted the processes of splitting and projection. The young child makes a sharp distinction between good objects and bad. Only after maturing is it capable of understanding that people – the mother, the self – can be both good and bad. But there are personality disorders and moments of stress in which this integrated understanding comes under strain or simply never develops. The child is unable to see people, including itself, as both. It may have desires that it is ashamed of and reluctant to acknowledge. What happens then is splitting – a sharp separation between good and bad – and projection, attributing the bad to someone else.

The same can happen to groups. We saw in the last chapter how identity involves dividing the world into two: Us and Them, in-group and out-group, the people like us and the people not like us. Much empirical research has shown that we have a natural tendency to in-group bias. We think more favourably of Us and less favourably of Them. When bad things happen to our group, splitting and projection can occur here as well. The preservation of self-respect may lead us to project the bad onto another group. We are innocent. They are guilty. Good things are failing to happen because someone is preventing them from happening: the devil, Satan, the Prince of Darkness, the evil one, Lucifer, the infidel, the antichrist. It is not theology that is at work here but rather a basic structure of thought that is a legacy of early childhood. We are good. They are bad. And bad things are happening to us because someone bad is doing them.

Consider theology again. Monotheism is not an easy faith. Recall the verse from Isaiah: 'I form the light, and create darkness: I make peace, and create evil.' How can God, who is all-good, create evil? That is the question of questions for the monotheistic mind. Abraham asked: 'Shall the Judge of all the earth not do justice?' Moses asked, 'Why have you done evil to this people?'

The simplest answer is that the bad God does is a response to the bad we do. It is justice, punishment, retribution. That is how Jews coped with the crisis of defeat and exile: 'Because of our sins we were exiled from our land.' The Hebrew Bible is the supreme example of that rarest of phenomena, a national literature of self-criticism. Other ancient civilisations recorded their victories. The Israelites recorded their failures. It is what the Mosaic and prophetic books are about.

But it is not easy to see God as the source of bad as well as good, judgement as well as forgiveness, justice as well as love. The rabbis did this by understanding the two primary names of God in the Bible, *Elokim* (E) and *Hashem* (J), as referring respectively to God-as-justice and God-as-compassion. Niels Bohr, the Nobel Prize–winning physicist, said that he came to his Theory of Complementarity when his son stole something from a local shop. He found himself thinking of his son as a father would do, then as a judge would do, and realised that while he had to think both ways, he could not do both simultaneously. He had to 'switch' from one to the other. That is what monotheism asks of its followers: to think of God as both a father and a judge. A judge punishes, a parent forgives. A judge enforces the law, a parent embodies love. God is both, but it is hard to think of both at the same time.

That explains the human tendency to lapse into dualism even when you belong to a monotheistic faith. *Dualism resolves complexity*. In a recent research study, two American psychologists, Richard Beck and Sara Taylor, found that a belief in Satan as an evil force helps Christians feel more positively about God and less likely to blame him for the pain and suffering in the world. It resolves their ambivalence.[5] But what if monotheism *requires* the ability to handle complexity?

*

Dualism is a dangerous idea, and the mainstream Church and the Synagogue were right to reject it. Pathological dualism, though, is far more serious and appears as a social phenomenon only rarely and under extreme circumstances. It is a form of cognitive breakdown, an inability to face the complexities of the world, the ambivalences of human character, the caprices of history and the ultimate unknowability of God. It leads to regressive behaviour and has been responsible for some of the worst crimes in history: those committed during the Crusades, the pogroms, the witch-hunts, the mass murders in Cambodia, Bosnia and Rwanda, Stalinist Russia and Maoist China. When confined to small sectarian groups, it may not pose a danger. But when it catches fire among larger populations, it is a prelude to tragedy of world historic proportions.

Pathological dualism does three things. It makes you dehumanise and demonise your enemies. It leads you to see yourself as a victim. And it allows you to commit altruistic evil, killing in the name of the God of life, hating in the name of the God of love and practising cruelty in the name of the God of compassion.

It is a virus that attacks the moral sense. Dehumanisation destroys empathy and sympathy. It shuts down the emotions that prevent us from doing harm. Victimhood deflects moral responsibility. It leads people to say: It wasn't our fault, it was theirs. Altruistic evil recruits good people to a bad cause. It turns ordinary human beings into murderers in the name of high ideals.

To understand how it works, it is worth taking an extreme example – Germany from 1933 to 1945. The Nazi ideology was not religious. If anything, it was pagan. It was also based on ideas that were thought at the time to be scientific: the so-called 'scientific study of race' (a mixture of biology and anthropology) and 'social Darwinism', the theory that the same processes operating in nature operate in society also. The strong survive by eliminating the weak.

The point of using it as an example is to show how beliefs that seem from a distance infantile and absurd can be held by very intelligent people indeed. The people who gave Nazism its intellectual gravitas were among Germany's outstanding thinkers:

among them figures like Bible scholar Gerhard Kittel, philosopher Martin Heidegger and legal-political analyst Carl Schmitt.[6] Joseph Goebbels, mastermind of Nazi propaganda, had a doctorate in German literature from the University of Heidelberg. Josef Mengele, the notorious medical superintendent at Auschwitz, had doctorates in anthropology and medicine and was an assistant professor at the Kaiser Wilhelm Institute for Genetics.

There was little or no resistance to the Nazi programme on the part of the German intelligentsia. Academics were among its most zealous supporters, dismissing Jewish colleagues and banning their books without demur. Judges implemented the Nuremberg Laws, depriving Jews of all human rights, without protest. According to Ingo Mueller, even the Supreme Court showed an 'obsessive determination to prosecute all Jews'.[7] Doctors ran the sterilisation and euthanasia programmes. In Auschwitz 'the killing programme was led by doctors from beginning to end'.[8] Half of all German physicians joined the Nazi Physicians' League.[9]

More than half the participants in the January 1942 Wannsee Conference that decided on the 'Final Solution', the complete extermination of Europe's Jews, carried the title 'Doctor', either as medical men or as academics with doctorates,[10] and 41 per cent of the SS Officer Corps were university educated, as opposed to 2 per cent in the population as a whole.[11] In 1927 Julian Benda, in a famous book, *Le Trahison des Clercs*, spoke of how public discourse had turned into 'the intellectual organisation of political hatreds'. This will be, he said, 'one of its chief claims to notice in the moral history of humanity'.[12]

Almost no one is immune to dualism once it takes hold of a culture.

*

Nazism as constructed by Hitler was a perfect pathological dualism. The children of light were the German nation, more specifically the Aryan race. The children of darkness were the Jews.

They were the force of evil, the destroyers of Germany, the defilers of its racial purity, corrupters of its culture and underminers of its morale. Despite the fact that they were less than 1 per cent of the population of Germany, they were said to control its banks, its media and its fate: to be in secret conspiracy to manipulate the world.

As part of the logic of human sociality, the internal cohesion of a group is in direct proportion to the degree of threat it perceives from the outside. It follows that anyone who wants to unite a nation, especially one that has been deeply fractured, must demonise an adversary or, if necessary, invent an enemy. For the Turks it was the Armenians. For the Serbs it was the Muslims. For Stalin it was the bourgeoisie or the counter-revolutionaries. For Pol Pot it was the capitalists and intellectuals. For Hitler it was Christian Europe's eternal Other, the Jews.

To remoralise a nation, leaders often revive memories of former glory. Vamik Volkan, who has applied concepts of splitting and projection to international conflict, emphasises the corollary: the *chosen trauma*, an event that 'has caused a large group to face drastic common losses, to feel helpless and victimized by another group and to share a humiliating injury'. In Bosnia and Kosovo in the 1990s, Slobodan Milosevic and Radovan Karadzic revived memories of the defeat of the Serbs by the Muslims in the Battle of Kosovo six hundred years earlier, in 1389. More recently Osama bin Laden, al-Qaeda and ISIS focused on the Crusades and the break-up of the Ottoman Empire by the West. For Hitler it was the defeat of Germany in the First World War and the humiliating terms of the Treaty of Versailles. For all this – the war itself, Germany's defeat and its subsequent economic travails – Hitler blamed the Jews.

Once you can identify an enemy, reactivate a chosen trauma and unite all factions in fear and hate of a common threat, you activate the most primitive part of the brain, the amygdala with its instant and overwhelming defensive reactions, and render a culture susceptible to a pure and powerful dualism in which you are the innocent party and violence becomes both a justified revenge and the necessary protection of your group. The threefold defeat of morality then follows.

*

The first stage is *dehumanisation*. This is the prelude to genocide. The paradox in the phrase 'crimes against humanity' is that the great crimes are committed against those you do not see as sharing your humanity. To the Hutus, the Tutsis were *inyenzi*, cockroaches. For the Nazis, the Jews were vermin, lice, parasites, a cancer that had to be removed, a diseased limb that had to be amputated. Goebbels spoke of the elimination of the Jews as 'social hygiene', just as 'a doctor takes a bacillus out of circulation'.[13] 'The Jews are the lice of civilised humanity', he said in 1941. 'They have to be exterminated somehow.'[14] Hitler spoke of the Jewish 'racial tuberculosis' and called for Germany to be 'immunised'. We must 'exterminate the poison if we want to recover'.[15] Jews were 'a parasite in the body of other races'[16] and an 'infection of our national ethnic body by blood poisoning'.[17]

Konrad Lorenz, who would later receive the Nobel Prize for his work on animals, wrote in an article for the Nazi Office for Racial Politics that a nation with 'defective members' was like an individual who had a malignant tumour. Surgical removal was necessary in both cases.[18] A Nazi doctor in an extermination camp, when asked how he could have done what he did in the light of his Hippocratic oath as a doctor, replied that 'out of respect for human life, I would remove a gangrenous appendix from a diseased body. The Jew is the gangrenous appendix in the body of mankind.'[19]

Primo Levi, a survivor of Auschwitz, wrote about the crucial interview he had to undergo to be qualified as a scientist to work at a nearby chemical factory, making him necessary enough to the German war effort not to be killed immediately. The examination was conducted by a Doktor Engineer Pannwitz. Levi says that he had 'often wondered about the inner workings' of this man:

> Because the look he gave me was not the way one man looks at another. If I could fully explain the nature of that look – it was as if through the glass of an aquarium directed at some creature belonging to a different world – I would be able to explain the great madness of the Third Reich, down to its very core.
>
> Everything we thought and said about the Germans took shape in that one moment. The brain commanding those blue eyes and manicured hands clearly said: 'This thing standing before me obviously belongs to a species that must be eliminated. But with this particular example, it is worth making sure that he has nothing we can use before we get rid of him.'[20]

Establishing the subhumanity of the Jews was a major part of the Nazi education programme between 1933 and 1939. It was an elaborate, multifaceted effort involving textbooks, children's stories, cartoons in newspapers and periodicals, posters, films, research institutes, learned journals, think tanks and professional bodies. The Education Ministry decreed that 'no student shall graduate unless he has perceived that the future of a Volk depends on race and inheritance'.[21] People had to be educated out of any sympathy for the Jews before the mass murders began. As Rudolf Hess, commandant of Auschwitz, said, 'Look, you can see for yourself. They are not like you and me. They do not behave like human beings. They are here to die.'[22]

*

The second stage is establishing *victimhood*. Just as it is necessary to rob your enemies of their humanity, so you have to find a way of relinquishing responsibility for the evil you are about to commit. You must define yourself as a victim. It follows that you, in committing murder, even genocide, are merely acting in self-defence. It is the victim who is responsible.

This was Hitler's constant and deeply paradoxical claim. As Jeffrey Herf points out, he and his propagandists had to maintain two completely contradictory ideas: 'one rooted in the grandiose idea of a master race and world domination, the other in the self-pitying paranoia of the innocent, beleaguered victim'.[23] In general, as Vamik Volkan notes, dualists tend to combine 'paradoxical feelings of omnipotence and victimization'.[24] On the one hand we are masters of the universe; on the other we are the devil's slaves.

At the 1938 rally at Nuremberg, Hitler accused 'the Jewish world enemy' of 'the attempted annihilation of the Aryan states'.[25] In a broadcast address in April 1942, he explained that 'The hidden powers who drove England in 1914 into World War I were Jews', adding that 'the power that paralyzed us in that war' was 'a Jewish one'.[26]

The Jews, claimed Hitler, were currently responsible for America's opposition to Germany. Roosevelt was a mere puppet of the Jews. 'The Jews in the USA hold power with the help of the Jewish government, bleed the people white, and oppress them.'[27] We know, said Hitler in a radio broadcast in December 1941, 'what power stands behind Roosevelt. It is the eternal Jew.'[28]

The English too were their slaves: 'Today we know who we are facing in England: the world enemy number 1: international Jews and the power-hungry, hate-filled world Jewry.'[29] Goebbels echoed the point, saying about the English that in their 'brutality, lying, pious hypocrisy, and pietistic godliness, they are the Jews among the Aryans and belong to that group of men who must first be smashed in the teeth before one can hope to speak rationally with them'.[30] The lead article in *Der Volkische Beobachter* proclaimed: 'Churchill promises Germany to Jews as Plunder; Solidarity of World Parasite Renewed.'[31]

Jews were also responsible for communism. Hitler told a Nazi gathering in Munich in November 1941, 'The greatest servant of

Jewry is the Soviet Union.'³² As for the question of how Jews could be behind both capitalism *and* communism, the United States *and* the Soviet Union, his answer was simple: 'Regarded superficially, plutocracy and proletarian dictatorship are as different as fire and water. In fact, they are two sides of the same coin. Their common denominator is the Jews.'³³

Hence Hitler's remark, made in the Reichstag on 30 January 1939, and repeated publicly several times, that if the Second World War were to happen, it would be the Jews' fault, and Germany would be performing a service to the world by exterminating them:

> I have very often in my lifetime been a prophet and have been mostly derided . . . I want today to be a prophet again: if international-finance Jewry inside and outside Europe should succeed in plunging the nations once more into a world war, the result will not be the Bolshevization of the earth and thereby the victory of Jewry, but the annihilation [*Vernichtung*] of the Jewish race in Europe.³⁴

Ten days after the German invasion of Czechoslovakia, Goebbels published an essay in which he wrote, 'The Jews are guilty! If in a dark hour war should one day break out in Europe, this cry must resound over our whole part of the earth. The Jews are guilty! They want war, and they are doing everything in their power to drive the peoples into it.'³⁵ In his New Year address, 1 January 1940, Hitler asserted, 'The Jewish-capitalist world enemy that confronts us has only one goal: to exterminate Germany and the German people.'³⁶

On 21 January 1945, with defeat staring Germany in the face, Goebbels published his last major article about the Jews, the claims coming together in a crescendo:

> Who drives the Russians, English, and Americans into the fire, and sacrifices masses of foreign lives in a hopeless struggle against

the German people? The Jews! . . . Who invents new programs of hatred and extermination against us, and in so doing makes this war into an awful act of horrendous self-slaughter and self-annihilation of Europe's life, its economy, education, and culture? The Jews! Who invented, implemented, and jealously watches over the repulsive alliance between England and the USA on the one hand, and Bolshevism on the other? . . . Jews, only the Jews! . . . Wherever you look, you see Jews.[37]

Defining yourself as a victim is a denial of what makes us human. We see ourselves as objects, not subjects. We become done-to, not doers; passive, not active. Blame bars the path to responsibility. The victim, ascribing his condition to others, locates the cause of his situation outside himself, thus rendering himself incapable of breaking free from his self-created trap. Because he attributes a real phenomenon (pain, poverty, illiteracy, disease, defeat, humiliation) to a fictitious cause, he discovers that eliminating the cause does not remove the symptom. Hence efforts must be redoubled. If you kill witches for causing illness, the witches die and the illness remains. So you must find more witches to kill, and still the illness remains. Blame cultures perpetuate every condition against which they are a protest.

They also corrupt others. One of the noblest of all human instincts is compassion. We reach out to help victims even though they are strangers, even though there is no other bond between us other than our shared humanity. But compassion can be exploited. When self-defined victims lay claim to compassion in a less-than-noble cause, they turn people of goodwill into co-dependents. Seeking to assist, they reinforce the pattern of behaviour they wish to cure.

*

When dehumanisation and demonisation are combined with a sense of victimhood, the third stage becomes possible: the commission of evil in an altruistic cause. Nazism presented itself as a profoundly moral movement, designed to purify the nation from alien elements poisoning its bloodstream, restore the greatness of the Aryan race, rid the world of false doctrines like capitalism and communism, and rescue the Volk from degeneracy. From the beginning, Hitler defined his task in moral and aesthetic terms. In *Mein Kampf* he wrote that 'the highest purpose of an ethnic state is concern for the preservation of those original racial elements that bestow culture and create the beauty and dignity of a higher human nature'.[38]

One of the classic texts of altruistic evil is the speech of Reichsführer Heinrich Himmler, leader of the SS, to a conclave in Poland on 4 October 1943:

> I want to make reference before you here, in complete frankness, to a really grave matter. Among ourselves, this once, it shall be uttered quite frankly; but in public we will never speak of it . . . I am referring to the evacuation of the Jews, to the annihilation of the Jewish people. This is one of those things that are easily said. 'The Jewish people is going to be annihilated', says every party member. 'Sure, it's in our programme, elimination of the Jews, annihilation – we'll take care of it.' And then they all come trudging, eighty million worthy Germans, and each has his one decent Jew. Sure, the others are swine, but this one is an A-1 Jew. Of all those who talk this way, no one has seen it happen, not one has been through it. Most of you know what it means to see a hundred corpses lie side by side, or five hundred, or a thousand. To have endured this and – excepting cases of human weakness – to have remained decent, that is what has made us hard. In our history, this is an unwritten and never-to-be-written page of glory.[39]

The first time Himmler visited Auschwitz, the experience made him vomit. Yet he made the same rigorous demands of himself that he made of his subordinates. He steeled himself to return. On that next occasion,

He stopped beside the burning pit and waited for a pair of gloves. Then he put on the gloves, picked one of the dead bodies off the pile, and threw it into the fire. 'Thank God,' he cried with a loud voice. 'At last I too have burned a Jew with my own hands.'[40]

Hitler declared in *Mein Kampf* that in exterminating the Jews, 'I am doing the Lord's work.' He maintained this belief until the very end. His last testament, written on 29 April 1945, a day before he committed suicide, reiterated his claim that neither he nor 'anyone else in Germany' wanted war in 1939. 'It was desired and launched exclusively by those international statesmen who either were of Jewish origin or worked for Jewish interests.' Jews are the 'truly guilty party of this murderous battle'. In the last sentence of his final message to the world, he called on Germans to 'continue in pitiless resistance against the world poisoner of all peoples, international Jewry'.[41]

*

E.H. Gombrich, the great art historian, worked at the BBC during the war, analysing German wartime propaganda. In a lecture after the war he explained that what made it effective was 'less the lie than the imposition of a paranoiac pattern on world events'. Pathological dualism creates a self-contained world which becomes self-confirming. 'Once you are entrapped in this illusionary universe it will become reality for you, for if you fight everybody, everybody will fight you, and the less mercy you show, the more you commit your side to a fight to the finish. When you have been caught in this vicious circle there really is no escape.'[42]

In the light of this we begin to understand the moral force of monotheism. The belief in one God meant that all the conflicting forces operative in the universe were encompassed by a single personality, the God of righteousness, who was sometimes just, sometimes forgiving, who spoke at times of law and at others of love. It was the refusal to split these things apart that made

63

monotheism the humanising, civilising influence that, in the good times, it has been.

Theology creates an anthropology. Discovering God, singular and alone, the first monotheists discovered the human person singular and alone. Monotheism internalises what dualism externalises. It takes the good and bad in the human situation, the faith and the fear, the retribution and the forgiving, and locates them within each of us, turning what would otherwise be war on the battlefield into a struggle within the soul. 'Who is a hero?' asked the rabbis, and replied, 'One who conquers himself.' This is the moral drama that has been monotheism's contribution to the civilisation of the West: not the clash of titans on the field of battle, but the quiet inner drama of choice and will, restraint and responsibility.

Hence the unique mixture of light and shade in all the characters of the Hebrew Bible. Abraham and Isaac pass off their wives as their sisters. Jacob deceives his blind father and takes his brother's blessing. Moses loses his temper. David commits adultery. Solomon, wisest of men, is led astray. The Bible hides none of this from us, and for a deeply consequential reason: to teach us that even the best are not perfect and even the worst are not devoid of merits. That is the best protection of our humanity.

Dualism, as we have noted, comes in many forms: between mind and body, in-group and out-group, and between the higher and lower instincts between which we must constantly choose. It may be that binary opposition is one of the fundamental ways in which we understand the world. But divide humanity into absolute categories of good and evil, in which all the good is on one side and all the evil on the other, and you will see your own side as good, the other as evil. Evil seeks to destroy the good. Therefore your enemies are trying to destroy you. If there is no obvious evidence that they are, this is a sign that they are working in secret. If they deny it, this is proof that the accusation is true, else why would they bother to deny it? And since they are evil and we are good, they are the cause of our present misfortunes and we must eliminate them so that the good to which we are entitled, the honour we once had and the superiority that is our right can be ours again. That is the pathological dualism that leads to altruistic evil with murderous consequences.

Can dualism be as serious as this chapter has suggested? After all, Nazism had nothing to do with religion, and Judaism and Christianity rejected the worldview of the Dead Sea Scrolls and the Nag Hammadi manuscripts. Could dualism really surface in the monotheistic mainstream? If so, how? These are our subjects in the next chapter.

4

The Scapegoat

We have just enough religion to make us hate, but not enough to make us love one another.

Jonathan Swift

ITEM: 26 November 2014. Remarks by Jordanian MP Khalil Attieh after the murder of four rabbis during prayer in a Jerusalem synagogue, broadcast on Roya TV: 'By Allah, it is an honor to incite against the Jews. It is a great accomplishment to provoke and incense them . . . if this is terrorism, we are terrorists. Indeed, I make use of the hatred of the Jews, as all Arabs should, because the Jews respect neither treaties nor human beings. They respect nothing. That accursed ambassador did me a great honor by saying that I hate the Jews. Yes, I hate the Jews. I hate the Jews. I hate the Jews.'[1]

ITEM: 7 November 2014. Friday sermon by Jordanian cleric Sheik Bassam Al-Amoush: 'They [the Jews] are the slayers of peoples. If you study the history of the great wars, you see that the Jews were behind them. If you study anarchy between nations, the Jews were behind them . . . they strive to establish a secret global government through Freemasonry. The Jews are a corrupting people. Even Hitler the racist wrote in *Mein Kampf*, when he killed Jews: "The reason is that they corrupt the German youth, and I need the German youth to turn into real men so that I can take over the world."'[2]

ITEM: 7 September 2014. Remarks by former Jordanian MP Sheik Abd Al-Mun'im Abu Zant, broadcast on Al-Aqsa TV: 'We have to understand the true nature of the Jews, because the entire world is deceived and tormented by them . . . They are liars. They allow cannibalism, and the eating of human flesh . . . On their religious holidays, if they cannot find a Muslim to slaughter, and use drops of his blood to knead the matzos they eat, they slaughter a Christian in order to take drops of his blood, and mix it into the matzos that they eat on that holiday.'[3]

ITEM: 21 January 2010. Former President of Malaysia Dr Mahathir Mohamad: 'Jews have always been a problem in European countries. They had to be confined to ghettoes and periodically massacred. But still they remain, they thrive and they hold whole governments to ransom . . . Even after their massacre by the Nazis of Germany, they survived to continue to be a source of even greater problems for the world.'[4]

ITEM: 17 January 2009. Egyptian cleric Muhammad Hussein Yaqub, broadcast on Al-Rahma TV: 'If the Jews left Palestine to us? Would we start loving them? Of course not. We will never love them . . . They are enemies not because they occupied Palestine. They would have been enemies even if they did not occupy a thing . . . You must believe that we will fight, defeat, and annihilate them until not a single Jew remains on the face of the earth . . . You Jews have sown hatred in our hearts, and we have bequeathed it to our children and grandchildren. You will not survive as long as a single one of us remains.'[5]

ITEM: 12 September 2004. Turkish journalist Ayse Onal reports on the sharp turn to antisemitism in the Turkish press, giving the following examples: '335 children and teachers were murdered in Beslan by the Jews. The barbarism of 9/11 was a Jewish plot. Turkish society and family values are being destroyed by the Jews. It is the Jews who are cutting off heads in Iraq. They [the Jews] are so blinded [with hatred] that in order to conceal the Jewish finger [role] in all of that, they sometimes butcher [their fellow] Jews as well. It was them [the Jews] who bombed their own synagogues. And when their own families died, they shed false tears.'[6]

ITEM: 29 April 2002. Fatma Abdallah Mahmoud, *Al-Akhbar*: 'The Jews are accursed in heaven and on earth. They are accursed from the day the human race was created and from the day their mothers bore them . . . These accursed ones are a catastrophe for the human race. They are the virus of the generation . . . With regard to the fraud of the Holocaust . . . many French students have proven that this is no more than a fabrication, a lie and a fraud . . . But I . . . complain to Hitler, even saying to him from the bottom of my heart, "If only you had done it, brother, if only it had really happened."'[7]

*

On Saturday 14 February 2015, Omar Abdel Hamid El-Hussein opened fire at a cultural centre in Copenhagen where the artist Lars Vilks, who had previously received death threats for his cartoons of the prophet Mohammed, was speaking at a seminar on freedom of expression. One man was killed, and three policemen wounded. Shortly after midnight the same gunman made his way to a Copenhagen synagogue, where a celebration was taking place, and killed a Jewish security volunteer. In Paris on 9 January 2015, Amedy Coulibaly, as part of the terrorist attack in which twelve people working for the magazine *Charlie Hebdo* were killed, made his way to a kosher supermarket where people were shopping for the Sabbath, killing four Jewish customers. In the course of the terrorist attacks in Mumbai in November 2008, four gunmen made their way to a building that contained a Chabad house, a small Jewish religious centre. There they killed six Jews including the rabbi and his six-months-pregnant wife after first sexually assaulting and mutilating them. Indian intelligence picked up radio transmissions in which the attackers were told that 'the lives of Jews are worth 50 times those of non-Jews'. These were strange diversions from what were otherwise clearly focused attacks.

Why the Jews? That is the question of this chapter. It is clear why the terrorists attacked the journalists and cartoonists of *Charlie Hebdo*. They knew whom they were seeking. They wanted to kill the editor and cartoonists. They knew exactly where they would be: at an editorial meeting. *Charlie Hebdo* had been notorious for mocking religion, and among their many targets was Islam. The killings in Paris in January 2015 were part of a pattern that included the attacks on the publishers of Salman Rushdie's *The Satanic Verses*, the *Jyllands-Posten* cartoons in Denmark, and Theo van Gogh. These were precisely targeted assaults. So why Jewish shoppers in a Jewish supermarket?

Equally it is clear why the terrorist attacks on Mumbai in 2008 took place. These were part of the ongoing violence between Muslims and Hindus, Pakistan and India, that includes four wars (1947, 1965, 1971 and 1999), and fifty-eight terrorist incidents since 1984, most notably the Mumbai train bombings of 11 July 2006 that claimed 209 lives. It was clear also why the terrorists chose restaurants and hotels. They wanted to damage the Indian economy, curtail tourism and maximise publicity. So why a young rabbi and his wife, in a country where there are almost no Jews?

It is often said that Islamist attacks on Jews are about the conflict between Israel and the Palestinians. But the Paris supermarket and the Mumbai centre were not Israeli targets, nor were the victims Israelis. As the above quotations show, and as the intercepted message about the lives of Jews being worth fifty times those of non-Jews confirms, this is about Jews. It is antisemitism, not anti-Zionism. This, as we will see, is something new in Islam.

The reason for focusing, in this chapter and the last, on antisemitism is not to draw attention to Jewish suffering. The major casualties, now and in the past, of Christian–Muslim conflict have been Muslims and Christians. It is they who died during the Crusades and they who are dying now in the Middle East, Asia and Africa. Antisemitism is important because it illustrates more clearly than any other phenomenon the psychological and social dynamic of hate. It helps us understand what may be operative in human conflict over and above the normal clash of principalities and powers, nations and interests. Its return within living memory of the Holocaust signals more than a danger to Jews. It is, as it always has been, the first warning signal of a world order in danger of collapse.

Today the Arab and Islamic world is awash with Judeophobia. An Anti-Defamation League study released in May 2014 found 'persistent and pervasive' anti-Jewish attitudes after surveying 53,100 adults in 102 countries and territories worldwide. It found that 74 per cent of those surveyed in the Middle East and North Africa held antisemitic attitudes. The corresponding figure was 24 per cent in Western Europe, 34 per cent in Eastern Europe and 19 per cent in the Americas. In 2011 a Pew Research Center study found that favourable views of Jews were 'uniformly low' in the predominantly Muslim regions it surveyed: 4 per cent in Turkey and the Palestinian territories, 3 per cent in Lebanon, and 2 per cent in Egypt, Jordan and Pakistan.

Three features link today's Islamic antisemitism with its counterpart in Germany in the 1930s. The first is that both represent what historian Robert Wistrich calls an obsession. There are almost no Jews in most of the fifty-six nations that comprise the Organisation of Islamic Co-operation. There were once, but in the 1940s and 1950s almost all left or were driven out. In Germany they comprised 1 per cent of the population. A joke in the 1930s captured the unreality of the situation. Two Germans are discussing the source of their nation's troubles. One says that it is the Jews. The other replies, 'The Jews and the bicycle riders.' 'Why the bicycle riders?' asks the first. 'Why the Jews?' replies the second.

As became clear after the 1935 Nuremberg Laws, which stripped them overnight of all their citizenship rights, the Jews had no influence or power whatsoever, either within Germany or without. Between 1935 and 1939 Hitler, who made no secret of his genocidal intentions towards the Jews, tested the proposition again and again. Were Jews powerful? Did they control Germany? Did they have significant influence over Britain or America? Did they have friends or allies anywhere in the world who would come to their assistance? Only when he had proved to his own satisfaction that Jews were in fact friendless and powerless, could he proceed with safety to accuse them of being so powerful that they controlled the world.

The problems of Germany after the First World War had nothing to do with the Jews. Likewise the problems of Egypt, Syria, Iraq, Iran, Pakistan and Afghanistan had nothing to do with the Jews. They were about internal issues. Could secular nationalism of the kind that emerged in Egypt, Syria and Iraq deliver on its promises of democracy, prosperity and restored national pride? After the Iranian Revolution in 1979 and the Russian withdrawal from Afghanistan in 1989 an alternative gained favour, first set out by Hassan al-Banna and the Muslim Brotherhood in 1928. Might the better way be a return to the pristine Islam of its early centuries, when it conquered large swathes of the Middle East, the Maghreb and al-Andalus (Spain and Portugal) with astonishing speed and bestrode the narrow world like a colossus? This momentous question has nothing to do with Jews, or bicycle riders. Note, however, that the one feature the new Islamism shares with the secular regimes it seeks to replace is antisemitism.

The second aspect that links the new antisemitism with its German forerunner is its irrational, self-contradictory character. Jews were hated in Germany because they were rich and because they were poor, because they were capitalists and because they were communists, because they kept to themselves and because they infiltrated everywhere, because they believed in a primitive faith and because they were rootless cosmopolitans who believed nothing. Hitler believed that Jews were controlling both the United States and the Soviet Union. How could they be doing both? Because they were Jews.

Likewise in the twenty-first century it is impossible both to celebrate the 9/11 attacks and the genius of the al-Qaeda terrorists who planned and executed them, and at the same time say it was the work of Israel and its secret police, the Mossad. Both the cleric who said that Jews are 'cutting off heads in Iraq' and his audience knew that there are no Jews left in Iraq other than a handful of the elderly who cannot move. The Jewish community of Iraq was, outside Israel, the oldest in the world and one of the most distinguished. It was there that Jews were taken captive after the destruction of the First Temple, there by the waters of Babylon that they sat and wept as they remembered Zion, there that, eight centuries later, great rabbinical academies were founded, and there that the masterpiece of rabbinic Judaism, the Babylonian Talmud, was composed. In the 1940s there were 140,000 Jews in Baghdad. By the time the American army arrived in 2003, there were twenty. The Jews cutting off heads in Iraq are figments of the imagination and everyone involved in this pretence knows they are. So by what psychological mechanism do rational human beings come to believe in fantasies?

The third feature the two antisemitisms share is that they are new. The importance of this cannot be sufficiently emphasised. People tend to assume that since there have been instances of hostility to Jews going back to pre-Christian times, its reappearance is simply the old dragon reawakening. The new is just the old reborn. This is not so.

There are indeed negative remarks about Jews in both the New Testament and the Qur'an, just as there are negative remarks about other nations in the Hebrew Bible. As we saw in chapter 2, xenophobia is as old as the human condition. There are evolutionary reasons why we develop favourable attitudes towards our in-group and hostile ones towards others. Antisemitism as such, however, is not ancient. The word itself was only coined in the 1870s, usually attributed to the German journalist Wilhelm Marr in 1879. In the Middle Ages Jews were hated because of their religion. In the nineteenth century they began to be hated for their race. That is what was new.

The case of Islam is slightly different. The distinguished historian of Islam, B.S. Lewis, has argued that historically Islam had contempt for Jews but not hate.[8] You do not die from contempt, but you do from hate. The myths that shaped the new antisemitism entered Islam from the outside, as we will see. They are not indigenous to it. So we are dealing with a phenomenon that is obsessive, irrational and, if not entirely new, then at least a significant mutation of previous forms of hostility.

Chapter 2 argued that violence is born, together with the better angels of our nature, in the phenomenon of human groupishness. We are altruistic to members of our group, and hostile to members of other groups. This gives rise to xenophobia. But xenophobia, though it may cause wars, does not in and of itself give rise to the demonisation of opponents, a sense of victimhood and the resultant altruistic evil. You do not go around murdering women and children because of some biological imperative of survival. That requires culture, and as we saw in chapter 3, the specific form that disables the moral sense and leads otherwise ordinary individuals to commit bestial crimes is pathological dualism – itself a mutant form of the theological dualism of ancient Iran and Greece that infected sectarian groups within Judaism and Christianity in the late pre-Christian and early Christian times. Pathological dualism emerged in Germany after the First World War. A not dissimilar dualism, between the faithful on the one hand and the Greater and Lesser Satan on the other, dominates Islamist and Iranian discourse today.

What turns dualism into a pathology? The Gnostics were dualists, but they were not violent. Manichaeism, another form of dualism, won enormous popularity between the third and seventh centuries, spreading from Rome to China and beginning to rival Christianity as a world force. But its adherents were persecuted, many were killed, and by the fourteenth century it had almost disappeared. The Qumran sect and the Christians of the Nag Hammadi manuscripts tended to retreat from the mainstream of society to pursue their mystical speculations and wait for the true God to defeat his earthly impostor. So what was this further factor?

*

The scholar who did more than most to provide an answer was the French literary theorist and cultural anthropologist René Girard, in his book *Violence and the Sacred* (1972).

Together with Freud, a deep influence on his work, Girard reversed conventional wisdom. It is not religion that gives rise to violence. It is violence that gives rise to religion. Freud argued that the primal act of violence in prehistoric times came when the children of the tribe combined to murder their father, whose monopolisation of the females of the tribe they resented. They were then haunted by guilt: what Freud called *the return of the repressed*. God, for Freud, was the voice of the dead father, internalised by the children as the voice of conscience.

Girard had a less fanciful explanation. Early societies, he argued, did not yet have a legal system – laws, courts, prisons and punishments – to enforce order. Instead they practised reciprocity, the rule of Tit-for-Tat that, as we saw, was the first principle to emerge from computer simulations of the Iterated Prisoner's Dilemma. They acted generously to others until they encountered a hostile response. They then did to the others what the others had done to them.

The trouble with this strategy – as biologists also noted when they began creating computer programmes that outperformed Tit-for-Tat – is that it gives rise to potentially endless cycles of retaliation. It begins with a single act of murder. This sets in motion a blood feud, vendetta or clan war. It is one of the oldest and most familiar themes in fiction: the Montagues versus the Capulets, the Jets against the Sharks, the Tattaglias versus the Corleones. Short of mass assassination, there is no natural end to the cycle of retaliation.

Girard's thesis is that *the most effective way by which the two groups can end the cycle is by killing a third party*, one who is neither a Montague nor a Capulet, who stands outside the feud, and whose death will not lead to another cycle of retaliation. The victim must be, in other words, an outsider, someone either not protected by a group, or the member of a group not in a position to inflict its own retaliatory violence.

By sacrificing the outsider, a revenge killing has taken place, so both sides can feel that justice has been done, but in such a way as to stop the cycle since the victim is not a member of either of the contending groups. Hence Girard's contentions that, first, the primal religious act is human sacrifice; second, the primal sacrifice is the scapegoat; and third, the function of religion is *to deflect away internal violence that would otherwise destroy the group*.

This, for Girard, is a statement not merely about the ancient past but about the present and future also. All societies generate internal conflict that can become violent and self-destructive. Therefore all societies require religion, which performs the task of 'casting out' the violence, deflecting it away from the group itself by placing it on an external victim, thus turning violence outwards instead of allowing it to turn destructively inwards.

As a social phenomenon, the system works only when there is a generally agreed scapegoat. The victim must be sufficiently *like* or close to the feuding parties to be a plausible substitute. You could not end a feud between two Italian families in Verona by going off to China to kill someone there. The victim must also be capable of being portrayed as the *cause* of the present troubles, otherwise killing him would make no sense. Between the fourteenth and seventeenth centuries, witches were blamed for diseases, crop failures and other mishaps. The Illuminati, an eighteenth-century German sect, and the Freemasons have both been accused of secretly plotting to rule the world. In his novel *The Da Vinci Code*, Dan Brown imagined a conflict between two shadowy Christian groups, the Priory of Sion and Opus Dei, the former a secret society, the latter a Catholic sect. Conspiracy theories have flourished for centuries.

However, the particular combination of conspiracy theory and substitute victim involved in the creation of a scapegoat requires a difficult mental feat. You have to be able to believe at one and the same time that the scapegoat is *both* all-powerful *and* powerless. *If the scapegoat were actually powerful, it could no longer fulfil its essential function as the-victim-of-violence-without-risk-of-reprisal.* You do not choose a lion or a crocodile as your sacrificial victim, since if you do, you are more likely than it is to land up as the victim. *But if the scapegoat were believed to be powerless, it could not plausibly be cast as the cause of our present troubles.* You could not, for example, choose a group of illiterate, unemployed migrants as your scapegoat. You could kill them without fear of reprisal, but you could hardly portray them successfully as controlling the banks, the media and the White House. The simultaneous presence of contradictory beliefs is a sure sign of the active presence of a scapegoat mechanism within a culture.

*

For a thousand years the scapegoat of choice in Europe and the Middle East has been the Jews. They were the most conspicuous outsiders: non-Christians in a Christian Europe, non-Muslims in an Islamic Middle East. But this chapter is not primarily about antisemitism. It is about what gives rise to it. Antisemitism is only contingently about Jews. Jews are its *victims* but they are not its *cause*. The cause is *conflict within a culture*. It is the potential internal violence that, if expressed, has the power to destroy a society.

Recall Girard's point: the scapegoat is the mechanism by which a society deflects violence away from itself by focusing it on an external victim. Hence, *wherever you find obsessive, irrational, murderous antisemitism, there you will find a culture so internally split and fractured that if its members stopped killing Jews they would start killing one another.* That is what happened in Europe in the seventeenth century and again in two world wars in the twentieth, and it is what is happening today in Syria, Iraq, Afghanistan and other war-torn regions in the Middle East, Asia and Africa.

To understand the emergence of the Jew-as-scapegoat we must focus on certain key historic moments. The first is 1095 when Pope Urban II delivered his call for the First Crusade. In 1096 some of the Crusaders, on their way to liberate the holy city of Jerusalem, paused to massacre Jewish communities in northern Europe: in Cologne, Worms and Mainz. Thousands died. Many Jews committed suicide rather than be seized by the mob and forcibly converted to Christianity. It was a traumatising moment for European Jewry, and the portent of worse to come.

From this point onwards Jews in Christian Europe began to be seen by many not as human beings at all but as a malevolent force, an evil presence, a demonic and destructive power that mysteriously yet actively sought the harm of others. Jews were accused of desecrating the host, poisoning wells and spreading the plague. They were held responsible for the Black Death, the epidemic that in the fourteenth century cost many millions of lives. It was an age in which Jews lived in fear.

That period added to the vocabulary of the West such ideas as public disputation, book burning, forced conversion, Inquisition, auto-da-fé, expulsion, ghetto and pogrom. In duration and intensity it ranks among one of the most sustained chronicles of hatred in history. It was dualism of the most stark and devastating kind.

Eventually Europe moved on, but not before two events that were to have significant consequences centuries later. The first took place in Spain, where, under threat of persecution, Jews had been living in fear from 1391, Spain's Kristallnacht when synagogues were burned and Jews massacred, until their expulsion in 1492. Many, under threat, had converted. Some were suspected of maintaining Jewish practice in private and became victims of the Inquisition. Others, though, embraced the new faith and achieved positions of prominence in Spanish society.

It was then that a new phenomenon appeared: the persistence

of prejudice after its overt cause had been removed. The 'new' Christians were still hated by some, now not for their religion but for their race. Legislation was introduced to protect *Limpieza de sangre*, 'purity of blood'. The first such statute appeared in Toledo in 1449. Originally opposed by the Church, it received the approval of Pope Alexander VI in 1496 and lasted well into the nineteenth century. It was the first appearance in history of the racial antisemitism that would flow through mainland Europe four and a half centuries later.

The second significant development was Martin Luther. Initially favourably disposed to Jews, he believed that the reason they had not converted was the ineptitude and cruelty of the Catholic Church. Approached with love, he thought they would become Christians en masse. When they did not, his anger knew almost no bounds. In 1543 he published a pamphlet entitled *On the Jews and their Lies* that became a classic in the literature of hate. Synagogues should be burned. Jewish homes should be destroyed. Jews should be made to live in a single room or stable to know that they were no more than 'miserable captives'. Their prayer books and Talmuds should be confiscated and their rabbis forbidden to teach. They should be forbidden to travel and given no legal protection until the world was rid of what he called 'our plague, pestilence and misfortune'. The pamphlet was reprinted several times during the Nazi era, and its suggestions paralleled by the Nuremberg Laws.

Luther's outburst ensured that hostility to the Jews would persist after the Reformation, and it left a lasting impression in countries where Lutheranism held sway. The striking Christian exception was John Calvin, who held the Hebrew Bible in high regard and was less inclined than most to denigrate the Jews. This had a lasting effect on Holland in the sixteenth century and England in the seventeenth, as well as on the Pilgrim Fathers in America. These were among the first places to develop religious liberty.

It is at this point that the story takes a remarkable and tragic twist. Western Europe in the eighteenth century turned to

Enlightenment in the belief that reason could overcome the prejudices of the past. In the nineteenth century this was followed by Emancipation, through which minority religious groups, among them the Jews, were granted civil rights in the new nation states, held together not as in the past by religion but by citizenship and civil law. Yet prejudice persisted, as it had done in post-expulsion Spain.

Among its practitioners were some of Europe's leading minds. Voltaire called Jews 'an ignorant and barbarous people, who have long united the most sordid avarice with the most detestable superstition and the most invincible hatred for every people by who they are tolerated and enriched'. He added, generously, 'Still, we ought not to burn them.'[9]

Immanuel Kant spoke of Jews as 'the vampires of society' and called for 'the euthanasia of Judaism'.[10] Georg Hegel saw Jews and Judaism as paradigms of a 'slave morality', unable to conceive or practise a religion of love.[11] By rejecting Christianity, Jews had been stranded by history and were left as a 'fossil nation', a 'ghost-race'.

Johann Gottlieb Fichte believed Jews were the enemy of freedom: 'As for giving [the Jews] civil rights,' he wrote, 'I see no other way than that of some night cutting off their heads and attaching in their place others in which there is not a single Jewish idea.' Alternatively they should be 'packed off' to 'their promised land'.[12] Arthur Schopenhauer spoke of Jews as 'no better than cattle', as 'scum of the earth', and as a people to be expelled. Friedrich Nietzsche castigated Judaism as the 'falsification' of all natural values. His great originality is that, instead of criticising Jews for rejecting Christianity, he blamed them for giving birth to it in the first place.

Anyone who blames religion for creating hate should consider these examples and think again. Philosophical antisemitism from Voltaire to Heidegger is a little-known phenomenon but a devastating one. As European culture became secularised and religious anti-Judaism mutated into racial antisemitism, the consequences were lethal. Christians could work for the conversion of the Jews, because you can change your religion. But you cannot change your blood or your genes. Antisemites could therefore only work for the elimination of the Jews. The result was the Holocaust.

Over the course of this period from 1095 to 1945, a number of myths emerged, two of which are of unusual interest. The first was the Blood Libel. In Norwich in 1144 a child named William was discovered stabbed to death. A rumour circulated that Jews were responsible. No one took it seriously at the time, but it became a *cause célèbre* five years later when an account appeared, written by a monk named Thomas of Monmouth.[13] It claimed that Jews killed Christian children to use their blood to make matza, the 'unleavened bread' eaten on the festival of Passover. It was patently absurd: if anything is abhorrent to Jews, it is blood (a single speck found in food renders it inedible in Jewish law) and child sacrifice. The Blood Libel was officially condemned by several popes – among them Innocent IV, Gregory X, Martin V, Paul III and Nicholas V – as well as by Emperor Frederick II. That did not stop the accusation spreading throughout Europe. There were more than 150 recorded cases, many leading to massacres of the local Jewish population.

The second, some 750 years later, was *The Protocols of the Elders of Zion*. Devised by members of the Russian Secret Police based in Paris, it was a document that purported to be the minutes of a secret Jewish conspiracy to achieve world domination by controlling the press and economies of the world. Fabricated from works of fiction and conspiracy theories, none of which was originally about Jews,[14] it was exposed as a forgery by *The Times* in 1921. It nonetheless sold widely, first in Russia, then in Germany, where its use in Nazi propaganda turned it into, in Norman Cohn's phrase, a 'warrant for genocide'.[15]

What makes these two myths fascinating is the way they exemplify the splitting-and-projection that gives dualism its unique psychological hold. The Blood Libel is a Christian projection (that is not to say that Christianity embraced it or was responsible for it: recall the papal rejection of it). It makes no sense within the framework of Judaism. But it made sense to some believers in transubstantiation, the idea that the bread and the wine used in the Eucharist are not symbolically but actually the body and blood of the Son of God. The term 'transubstantiation' was first used by Hildebert de Lavardin, Archbishop of Tours, around 1079, and the doctrine itself was formalised by the Fourth Lateran Council in 1215. It is precisely between these dates that the Blood Libel appears.

Likewise, the *Protocols*. They were first published in Russia in 1903 when the Jews were undergoing the trauma of the Kishinev pogrom. Following the pogroms that had broken out throughout Russia in 1881 and the antisemitic May Laws of 1882, millions of Jews from the Pale of Settlement were in flight to the West. A pamphlet written at that time by an assimilated Jew, Leon Pinsker, gave full and poignant expression to what it felt like to be Jewish in Eastern Europe at that time. 'Among the living nations of the earth,' he wrote, 'the Jews are as a nation long since dead.' They are 'a living corpse, a people without unity or organisation, without land or other bonds of unity, no longer alive yet walking among the living'.

That such a people, rightless refugees, could be engaged in secretly running the world was self-evidently preposterous. Yet if understood as a repressed and projected desire on the part of its fabricators, it made eminent sense. These were the last dreamers of Russian imperial grandeur before the revolutions of 1905 and 1917 ended their world for ever. It explains why Hitler, with his dreams of world domination, was so taken by the *Protocols*, though he was well aware of their exposure as a forgery (the fact that Jews denied their veracity was, for him, perfect proof that they were true). 'No one could be so brilliant', Hitler said to Goebbels on 13 May 1943, 'as to describe the Jewish striving for world domination as well as the Jews themselves.'[16]

What makes these myths relevant today is that they were both subsequently introduced into the Middle East and Islam. The

Blood Libel was introduced to the Middle East in the early nineteenth century by Christians, in Aleppo (1811, 1853), Beirut (1824), Antioch (1826), Hamma (1829), Tripoli (1834), Dayr al-Qamar (1847), Damanhur (1877) and Damascus (1840, 1848 and 1890). Until that time, charges of ritual murder levelled against Jews were virtually unknown within Islam. The most famous case was the Damascus Blood Libel of 1840. A Capuchin monk in Damascus disappeared. His fellow monks, assisted by a local French diplomat, accused the Jews of killing him for ritual purposes. Heads of the Jewish community were imprisoned and tortured. Some died. Others confessed. The case became widely publicised in Europe and provoked protests until the Ottoman authorities investigated the charge and admitted that the accusations were false. This did not stop the libel spreading elsewhere and there were further notorious cases in Algeria in 1897–8 and Cairo in 1901–2.

In 1983 the Syrian defence minister Mustapha Tlass wrote a book, *The Matza of Zion*, arguing that the original charge in the Damascus affair was in fact true, and that Jews continue to kill Gentile children to use their blood in making matza for Passover. The book has been translated into English and reprinted several times. On 8 February 1991, according to the Jewish Telegraph Agency, the Syrian delegate to the U.N. Human Rights Commission praised this 'valuable book,' saying it 'unmasked the racist character of Zionism.'[17] In 2001 the Egyptian newspaper *Al Ahram* reiterated the charge, adding, 'The bestial drive to knead Passover matzahs with the blood of non-Jews is [confirmed] in the records of the Palestinian police where there are many recorded cases of the bodies of Arab children who had disappeared being found, torn to pieces without a single drop of blood.'[18]

The Protocols of the Elders of Zion was introduced, along with *Mein Kampf* in Arabic translation, into the Middle East in the 1930s by, among others, the Grand Mufti of Jerusalem, Muhammed Amin al-Husayni, who had spent the Second World War in Berlin, producing Arabic broadcasts for the Nazis and recruiting Bosnian Muslims for the Waffen SS. It continues to be reprinted and widely sold and read. In 2002 a forty-one-part television dramatisation of the *Protocols*, entitled *Horseman without a Horse*, was shown on a Lebanon-based satellite television network owned by the terrorist organisation Hezbollah during Ramadan.[19] In 2003 a similar series, *Al-Shatat* ('Diaspora'), was shown on Syrian television.[20]

The *Protocols*, despite widespread knowledge that they are a forgery, figure prominently in the discourse of the Islamists and appear in the Hamas Charter. In this context an observation made by several recent writers is worth noting. They refer to a discovery made by the FBI in 2007 in the course of preparing for the Holy Land Foundation terrorism-financing trial (on 24 November 2008, five former officials of the Foundation were found guilty of conspiring to provide material support to terrorists).

During their search they came across a document dated 22 May 1991 prepared by Mohamed Akram, leader of the Muslim Brotherhood in the United States. Entitled 'Explanatory Memorandum on the General Strategic Goal for the Group in North America', it included the following passage: 'The Ikhwan (i.e. the Brotherhood) must understand that their work in America is a kind of grand Jihad in eliminating and destroying the Western civilization from within and "sabotaging" its miserable house by their hands and the hands of the believers so that it is eliminated and God's religion is made victorious over all other religions.'[21] When people accuse others of seeking to control the world, it may be that they are unconsciously projecting what they themselves want but do not wish to be accused of wanting. *If you seek to understand what a group truly intends, look at the accusations it levels against its enemies.*

Which brings us to the present. At the very time Europe was attempting to ensure that the Holocaust could never happen again, antisemitism in the form of its two most effective myths was being reborn in the Middle East, and from there has spread to parts of Islam. As early as 1986, Bernard Lewis issued this warning:

At this time there are some signs that the anti-Semitic virus that has plagued Christianity almost since the beginning may at last be in process of cure; by a sad paradox, the same profound religious hatred has now attacked the hitherto resistant body of Islam. It may be that the moment of choice has gone, and that the virus has already entered the bloodstream of Islam, to poison it for generations to come as Christendom was poisoned for generations past. If so, not only Arab but also Jewish hopes will be lost in the miasma of bigotry. The open democracy that is the pride of Israel will be polluted by sectarian and ethnic discrimination and repression, while the free institutions that are the best hope of the Arabs will be forgotten, as the Middle East sinks under the rule of the cynics and fanatics who flourish in the soil of hatred.[22]

This chapter has been about how dualism moves from being theological or metaphysical to become pathological and a source of violent hate. It happens when a victim – an individual or group – is turned into a scapegoat as a way of projecting outwards the violence that would otherwise destroy a society from within. The paradigm case in the history of the past thousand years has been the Jews. What makes antisemitism central to the argument of this book is that when it becomes violent it represents the first and clearest sign of a civilisation in crisis. With few exceptions, Jews were not massacred during the first thousand years of Christianity, or in Western Europe in the nineteenth century, or classically within the nations of Islam, where Jews often fared better than they did in Christendom.

Dualism becomes lethal when a group of people, a nation or a faith, feel endangered by internal conflict. This happened in Christianity in the eleventh century in the wake of the Great Schism of the Church, in 1054, when the state Church of the Roman Empire divided into its Eastern (Greek) and Western (Latin) branches. It happened in Germany after defeat in the First World War, the punitive conditions of the Treaty of Versailles, the hyperinflation of the 1920s and the weakness of the Weimar system. It began within Islam after its last major bastion of power, the Ottoman Empire, fell in 1924. The tensions then generated between secular and religious approaches to politics, between different groups within the national boundaries arbitrarily imposed by Britain and France, as well as historic tensions between Sunni and Shia, and moderate and radical interpretations of the faith, still reverberate today.

At work in this whole process is the basic principle of group dynamics. We saw in chapter 2 that we are naturally inclined to favour members of our group and fear members of another group. One result is that *in almost any group, the greater the threat from the outside, the stronger the sense of cohesion within.* People who lived through the Blitz, the aerial attack on London in the Second World War, say they felt a sense of kinship between strangers they never experienced before or after. Our most primal instincts of bonding within the group occur when it confronts an external enemy.

That is why ruthless politicians, threatened by internal discord, focus on and sometimes even invent external enemies. Paranoia is the most powerful means yet devised for sustaining tyranny and repression. If tyrants can invoke religion – persuading people that it is their faith, their values and their God that are under attack – it becomes more powerful still, since religion evokes our most self-sacrificial instincts. The classic instance is antisemitism, and where you find it at its most virulent, there you will find despotism and denial of human rights. The murder of Jews is only one result. The real victims are the members of the host society itself. The hate that begins with Jews never ends with them. No free society was ever built on hate.

The trouble with the use of scapegoats is that it is a solution that compounds the problem. It makes internal tension bearable by turning the question 'Why has this happened?' into the question 'Who did this to me?' If it is someone else's fault, not mine, I can preserve my self-respect intact. For at least a thousand years a narrative has been available that blames the Jews. So powerful is the rapid-response emotional brain that, under stress, it can entirely overwhelm the slower-moving prefrontal cortex, the distinction- and decision-making mind, turning otherwise ordinary human beings into Crusaders in one age, perpetrators of genocide in another, and suicide bombers and jihadists in a third.

And when the violence is over, the problems remain, since the scapegoat never was the cause of the problem in the first place. So people die. Hope is destroyed. Hate claims more sacrificial victims. And God weeps.

5

Sibling Rivalry

A little more than kin, and less than kind.

Shakespeare, Hamlet *(Act 1, scene 2, line 65)*

Yet we are still missing a piece of the puzzle. The phenomena we have described thus far – identity, splitting, projection, pathological dualism and the scapegoat – are general. They could affect anyone. They have no special connection with Judaism, Christianity and Islam. They help us understand violence but not the fraught relationship between the Abrahamic faiths. There must be some additional cause to explain the Crusades, jihads, forced conversions, inquisitions, burnings at the stake, pogroms and suicidal terrorism in religions dedicated to love, forgiveness and compassion. What is it that brought Jews, Christians and Muslims, spiritual children of a common father, to such animosity for so long? I want, in this chapter, to track down that factor, the puzzle's last piece. It begins with a powerful Freudian insight whose significance Freud himself seems to have repressed.

Recall that Freud and René Girard argued that it is not religion that leads to violence. It is violence that leads to religion. We saw in the last chapter how that led to Girard's theory of the scapegoat as the primal religious rite. However, he went on to ask how violence begins in the first place. Freud consistently claimed that the initiating violence, in both individual and group psychology, arises from the tension between fathers and sons, the Oedipus complex. Girard cast his net wider. Violence is born in what he called *mimetic desire* (from *mimesis*, meaning 'imitation').

Mimetic desire is wanting what someone else has because they have it. This is behaviour we often see in children. When one child is given a new toy, the others suddenly discover that they want it. They may never have wanted it before, but they do now because someone else has it. Mimetic desire is not just wanting to *have* what someone else has. Ultimately it is wanting to *be* what someone else is. Desiring 'this man's art, and that man's scope', we wish we were them. This is mimetic desire. Often it leads to violence, because if I want what you have, sooner or later we will fight. Girard then suggested that one of the prime sources of strife is not between father and son but between brothers: sibling rivalry.

Myth and religious narrative bear this out. Genesis is full of such relationships: Isaac and Ishmael, Jacob and Esau, Joseph and his brothers. The first murder is a fratricide: Cain killing Abel. In Egyptian myth there are Set and Osiris. The Greek equivalents are Atreus and Thyestes. The story of Hamlet begins with a fratricide: Claudius kills his brother, Hamlet's father, and takes his throne.

The founding myth of Rome is a story of two brothers, Romulus and Remus, who argue over where the city should be built. Romulus kills Remus and in a famous poem, Horace says that a curse has lain over the city ever since:

> A bitter destiny dogs the Romans
> The guilt of a brother's murder
> Since Remus' innocent blood poured on the ground,
> A curse on Rome's posterity.[1]

The irony is that Freud himself knew the significance of sibling rivalry and felt it deeply, but seems to have been so obsessed with the Oedipus complex that he failed to give it its due weight. It was his colleague Alfred Adler who focused on sibling rivalry. Yet whenever Freud spoke about it, he did so with blazing intensity. In *The Interpretation of Dreams* he writes, 'The elder child ill-treats the younger, maligns him and robs him of his toys; while the younger is consumed with impotent rage against the elder, envies and fears him, or meets his oppressor with the first stirrings of a love of liberty and a sense of justice.'[2]

In a letter to the novelist Thomas Mann, he says about Napoleon's relationship with his older brother Joseph, 'The elder brother is the natural rival; the younger one feels for him an elemental, unfathomably deep hostility for which in later life the expressions "death wish" and "murderous intent" may be found appropriate. To eliminate Joseph, to take his place, to become Joseph himself, must have been Napoleon's strongest emotion as a small child.'[3]

In a lecture on 'Femininity' he said, 'But what the child grudges the unwanted intruder and rival is not only the suckling but all the other signs of maternal care. It feels that it has been dethroned, despoiled, prejudiced in its rights; it casts a jealous hatred upon the new baby and develops a grievance against the faithless mother . . . we rarely form a correct idea of the strength of these jealous impulses, of the tenacity with which they persist and of the magnitude of their influence on later development.'[4]

We know that Freud felt intensely hostile towards his younger brother Julius, born in 1857 when Freud was seventeen months old. Julius died before his first birthday. Freud admitted to a lifelong feeling of guilt for wishing to be rid of him.[5] Did he displace these feelings by focusing instead on fathers and sons?

What Freud would not have known, since it is a relatively recent biological finding, is that sibling rivalry is not confined to humans. Douglas Mock has assembled the animal behavioural evidence in *More than Kin and Less than Kind*.[6] In the Galapagos Islands young fur seals attack their newborn siblings, seizing them by the throat and tossing them into the air, killing them unless the mother seal intervenes.

In many species the urge for dominance is part of the instinct for survival. Food supplies are scarce, and the competition to be first in the queue may spell the difference between life and death. Egrets, for example, give birth to multiple young who hatch out at different stages. The first two, born earlier and with an advantage of size and strength over their younger siblings, peck at them aggressively until a mere gesture – stretching the neck – is sufficient to induce submission.

Among birds, chicks quickly establish a hierarchy of their own – the origin of the phrase 'pecking order'. The older use their strength to get the first bite of food. Some animals, like spade-foot tadpoles, eat their own siblings if starved of other nutrition. Others like the black stork have been seen throwing the youngest of a brood out of the nest, the better to ensure the survival of those that remain.

This is the first point. The primal act of violence is fratricide not parricide. Sibling rivalry plays a central role in human conflict, and it begins with mimetic desire, the desire to have what your brother has, or even be what your brother is.

*

The second stage of the journey takes us to the post-Holocaust years when a French historian, Jules Isaac, who survived the war but lost his wife and daughter at Auschwitz, began to assemble the evidence of the long history of Christian anti-Jewish teachings that he called 'the teachings of contempt'. His work came to the attention of Pope John XXIII, and the two met in 1961. This may have been one of the factors that led the pope and his successor Paul VI to institute the process that culminated in Vatican II in 1965, and the document *Nostra Aetate* that transformed the relationship between the Catholic Church and other faiths, especially the Jews.[7]

Beginning around this time, a group of courageous Christian theologians began themselves to explore the roots of Christian anti-Judaism. They included figures like Rosemary Radford Ruether, Gregory Baum, Edward Flannery, Paul Van Buren, R. Kendall Soulen, Mary Boys and the novelist James Carroll.[8] The question hovering in the background of their work was: how was the Holocaust possible in the heart of Christian Europe?

The Holocaust was *not* the result of Christianity; it is important to state this categorically at the outset. As Yosef Hayim Yerushalmi pointed out, Christianity had an interest in the *preservation* of Jews, not their destruction.[9] The history of Christian–Jewish relations is not one of unrelieved darkness.[10] There were bishops who defended Jews at times of persecution, and popes who rejected anti-Jewish myths like the Blood Libel. And though there were massacres, there were also times when Jews flourished under Christian rulers.

While the Holocaust was taking place, there were Christians who saved Jews, among them the members of the French village of Le Chambon-sur-Lignon who, under the inspiration of Lutheran pastor André Trocmé, gave shelter to five thousand Jews. Quakers and Jehovah's Witnesses helped Jews to safety. There were Christian opponents of Hitler like Dietrich Bonhoeffer and Martin Niemöller. There were the more than twenty-five thousand individual heroes, memorialised in Yad Vashem, the Holocaust Memorial in Jerusalem, who saved lives. There were collective acts of heroism like the members of the Danish Resistance who saved most of Danish Jewry from death. And it is important to note also that many Jews were saved by Muslims during these years, a story told by Robert Satloff in his book *Among the Righteous*.[11]

More than a century before the Holocaust, the poet Heinrich Heine made a remarkable prophecy:

> Christianity – and that is its greatest merit – has somewhat miti-gated that brutal German love of war, but it could not destroy it. Should that subduing talisman, the Cross, be shattered, the fren-zied madness of the ancient warriors, that insane Berserk rage of which Nordic bards have spoken and sung so often, will once more burst into flame . . . Then . . . a play will be performed in Germany which will make the French Revolution look like an innocent idyll.

It was Christianity that prevented tragedy, thought Heine, by standing between Germany and its pagan roots. Lose it and the dark gods of blood and brutality would return.

What the post-Holocaust theologians searched for were the

roots of the Church's hostility to Jews. That is not my concern here: in any case, it is an internal conversation within Christianity. My argument in this chapter will be simple. It has to do with narrative and identity: the stories we tell ourselves to explain who we are. It turns out that Judaism, Christianity and Islam all define themselves by a set of narratives about the factor identified by Girard and felt by Freud to lie at the root of violence, namely, sibling rivalry. This is where we need to focus our attention if we are to understand and heal the hate that leads to violence in the name of God.

Sibling rivalry is, as we noted, a central motif of the book of Genesis: Cain and Abel, Isaac and Ishmael, Jacob and Esau, Rachel and Leah, and Joseph and his brothers. It is a key theme of Judaism. However, during the early years of Christianity it became a theme there as well, most notably in the writings of Paul. Something similar happened later with the birth of Islam.

*

Paul is one of the most complex figures in the history of religion. Thousands of books have been written about him, and there are major differences of opinion about his personality, his theology, and especially his relationship with Jews and Judaism. It is not my intention here to advance any view about these issues, but simply to reflect on his use of the Genesis sibling rivalry narratives.

Paul was a Jew, originally named Saul, who was at first strongly opposed to the first Christians and had been one of their persecutors. He was on one such mission to Damascus when he experienced a conversion experience that changed his life, turning him into Christianity's first and greatest theologian. Paul never met Jesus: his conversion took place some years after Jesus' death. Yet his writings, mainly in the form of letters to Christian communities, form the first Christian texts, preceding the Gospels.

Paul took a controversial stand on the nature of the new faith. Many of the early Christians, like Paul himself, were Jews.

Initially they differed from their co-religionists only in their belief that the Messiah had come. Most believed that Jesus' mission was primarily to the Jews. Accordingly, they kept Jewish law, including circumcision, the prohibition of work on the Sabbath and Judaism's strict dietary restrictions. Led by Jesus' brother James, they are known as the Jerusalem church.

Paul thought otherwise. To understand why, we have to set him in context. Israel at the time was under Roman rule. We know from several sources of the period that many Gentiles in the wider Roman Empire were attracted to various aspects of Judaism. To some they were known as the 'God-fearers'. Josephus speaks about them. So does the New Testament. So do Roman writers, among them Tacitus, Juvenal and Celsus. Seneca saw the irony in non-Jews adopting Jewish ways: 'The vanquished have given their laws to the victors', he said. The God-fearers were not full converts. They were drawn to some elements of Judaism, not all. Then as now, the concept of Jewish identity had fuzzy edges. There were people who were not fully Jewish according to Jewish law, but who identified with the people and its faith.

It was among this group that Paul's teachings resonated, especially when he showed that to be a Christian it was not necessary either to be circumcised or to keep the full Mosaic code with its multiple (613) commands. In fact, he argued, the new dispensation changed the very terms of the covenant. It was no longer a matter of law but of faith. In essence, Paul had founded the Gentile, or de-ethnicised, church. As a result he was faced with an immense problem. How could Christianity be at one and the same time a continuation of Judaism and yet a radically transformed faith – in the people it addressed, the life it espoused and the story it told? This tension haunted Paul and everything he set in motion.

Often he reminded his listeners that he was a Jew. What then was his attitude to his fellow Jews? On this he is notoriously ambiguous. On the one hand, understandably, he was often critical of them. He believed he had seen the light, they had not. He was convinced that something decisive had occurred to change the relationship between God and the world, but they did not. On the other hand, he was clearly attached to his people and said so. They had been the first to hear the call of God and to enter into a covenant with him. In Romans 9–11, he says that to the Jews belong 'the adoption, and the glory, and the covenants, and the giving of the law, and the service of God, and the promises' (KJV, 9:4). Theirs is the tree onto which a new olive branch had been grafted (11:16–24). A measure of ambivalence was inevitable, given the path he had taken. In any case, Paul himself said that he spoke differently to different audiences (1 Cor. 9:20–21), as if to remind his listeners and those who read his writings that context mattered in understanding what he was saying.

It is hard to read Paul without being distracted by the immense burden of history, of all that has happened to Christianity and Judaism and their followers in the intervening centuries. He lived a tempestuous life in tempestuous times. During his lifetime, there was no such thing as 'Christianity' as we now understand it. The decisive break with Judaism had not yet taken place. There was an intense argument within the Church itself as to what the new faith required, and even if it was a new faith at all. The Gospels had not yet been written. There was as yet no 'New Testament'. Doctrine had not yet been formulated. The Jewish world was in ferment, chafing under sometimes harsh and arbitrary Roman rule. Jewry was itself divided into Sadducees, Pharisees and Essenes. We know from rabbinic sources that there was intense internecine rivalry. Trying to reconstruct those times, we see as through a glass darkly.

One detail only of the Pauline letters will concern us in this chapter, namely sibling rivalry itself, for it was Paul who introduced the theme into Christianity. Here is how he puts the argument in Galatians, a document most historians agree to be among the earlier of his writings in the New Testament:

Tell me, you who want to be under the law, are you not aware of what the law says? For it is written that Abraham had two sons, one by the slave woman and the other by the free woman. His son by the slave woman was born in the ordinary way; but his son by the free woman was born as the result of a promise.

These things may be taken figuratively, for the women represent two covenants. One covenant is from Mount Sinai and bears children who are to be slaves: this is Hagar. Now Hagar stands for Mount Sinai in Arabia and corresponds to the present city of Jerusalem, because she is in slavery with her children. But the Jerusalem that is above is free, and she is our mother . . .

Now you, brothers, like Isaac, are children of promise. At that time the son born in the ordinary way persecuted the son born by the power of the Spirit. It is the same now. But what does the Scripture say? 'Get rid of the slave woman and her son, for the slave woman's son will never share in the inheritance with the free woman's son.' Therefore, brothers, we are not children of the slave woman, but of the free woman. (Gal. 4:21–31)

Recall the story to which Paul is referring. God had promised Abraham and Sarah a child. Yet the years pass, and there is no child. We sense Abraham's torment in his first recorded words to God: 'Lord God, what will you give me, since I continue to be childless?' (Gen. 15:2). Eventually Sarah proposed that Abraham should have a child by her servant Hagar. She would become, as it were, a surrogate mother. Hagar conceives and has a child named Ishmael. Eventually Sarah does indeed have a son, Isaac, and she then insists that Abraham send Hagar and Ishmael away. It is a difficult story, and we will examine it in greater depth in a later chapter.

What Paul is doing in his letter to the Galatians is to reverse Jewish self-understanding. Jews are, we say in our prayers several times daily, the children of Abraham, Isaac and Jacob. That is constitutive of Jewish memory, history and identity. Paul argues otherwise. For him, Sarah represents Christianity while Hagar is Judaism. Christians are free, Jews are slaves. Christians are Isaac, Jews are Ishmael. Christians belong, while Jews are to be driven away.

It may be hard for a Christian to understand how a Jew feels when he or she reads these texts. It feels like being disinherited, violated, robbed of an identity. This is my past, my ancestry, my story, and here is Paul saying it is not mine at all, it is his and all who travel with him.

Context matters if we are to understand Paul. He was addressing a community that had come under the influence of those who believed that Christians entering the Abrahamic covenant had to keep the Mosaic law with all its strenuous demands. This, for Paul, was completely to misunderstand what Christianity was. The new dispensation bound people to God through faith, not law. Paul had somehow to convince his listeners that they, not the people who kept the law of Moses, were the true children of Abraham. That is what he is doing in this speech. Paul is talking not to Jews but to Christian Judaisers. It was one of the main struggles of his life and he had not yet won. He was fighting, as he saw it, for the soul of the Church.

Paul continued the argument in his letter to the Romans. By now, though, older and more reflective, he testified to his fondness for the Jewish people into which he had been born and whose refusal to accept the new dispensation caused him such distress. But he insisted nonetheless that it is the followers of Jesus, not those of Moses, who are the true children of Abraham:

> [N]ot all who are descended from Israel are Israel. Nor because they are his descendants are they all Abraham's children. On the contrary, 'It is through Isaac that your offspring will be reckoned.' In other words, it is not the natural children who are God's children, but it is the children of the promise who are regarded as Abraham's offspring. For this was how the promise was stated: 'At the appointed time I will return, and Sarah will have a son.' (NIV, Rom. 9:6–9)

Again Paul's point is simple. Abraham was biologically the father of both Isaac and Ishmael. But it was Isaac, not Ishmael, who continued the covenant. It follows, argues Paul, that biological descent from Abraham is not enough to make you a child of the promise. For that, you need something else: in Paul's view, faith in Jesus. Those who have it are the true children of Abraham, and those who do not, are not. He continues:

> Not only that, but Rebekah's children had one and the same father, our father Isaac. Yet, before the twins were born or had done anything good or bad – in order that God's purpose in election might stand: not by works but by him who calls – she was told, 'The older will serve the younger.' Just as it is written: 'Jacob I loved, but Esau I hated.' (NIV, Rom. 9:10–13)

Now the claim becomes stronger still. Esau and Jacob had the same parents. They were twins. Yet Jacob was heir to the covenant, while Esau was not. Indeed, as Paul reads the text, this fact was announced by God before they were born. It follows that it was nothing that Jacob or Esau did that determined their fate. They had done nothing as yet, not even emerged into the world. God causes to inherit or disinherit whom he chooses. Merely claiming Jewish parenthood, says Paul, is not enough. It is not even relevant. Those who follow Jesus are Jacob. Those who do not, even if they are Jews, are like Esau. What is more, says Paul, quoting Malachi (1:3), God *hates* Esau. Paul is suggesting that the Jews who remain true to their faith have been not just rejected, but *hated*, by God himself.[12]

The argument was taken further still by the Church Fathers. In the third century Cyprian developed a new contrast between Jacob's two wives, Leah and Rachel: 'Also Jacob received two wives: the elder Leah, with weak eyes, a type of the Synagogue; the younger, the beautiful Rachel, the type of the Church . . .'[13]

Rosemary Ruether notes the persisting afterlife of this contrast:

> This image of the 'weak-eyed Leah' could be mingled with the Pauline image of the 'veil' that lies over the eyes of the Jews,

blinding them to the truth, to provide an image of the 'blind-ness' of the Synagogue. Medieval cathedrals were commonly to use this image of two wives, the Church and the Synagogue, one beautiful and triumphant, the other dejected, with a blind over her eyes.[14]

Maximinus, Tertullian, John Chrysostom and Aphrahat made the final, devastating move: that the Jews are Cain who, having murdered their brother, are now condemned to permanent exile. As the fourth-century writer Prudentius put it: 'From place to place the homeless Jew wanders in ever-shifting exile . . . This noble race [is] . . . scattered and enslaved . . . It is in captivity under the younger faith.'[15] It was an analogy much taken up by Augustine, and it served eventually to justify the expulsions of Jews from one country after another in the Middle Ages, begin-ning in England in 1290 and culminating in Spain in 1492.

The historic irony is that two centuries later Islam did for Christianity something not dissimilar to what Paul had done for Judaism. It said that Abraham, Moses and Jesus were all prophets preparing the way for the final revelation whose expression was Islam itself. The Abrahamic succession passed through Ishmael, not Isaac. The Hebrew Bible says otherwise only because Jews had falsified it. Christians had misrepresented Jesus. He was merely a prophet like others, not the Son of God. Jews and Christians should therefore, in principle, convert, but if they did not do so, they were to be spared as 'people of the Book', and allowed to live as *dhimmi*, citizens with less than full civil rights under Islamic rule and protection.

*

It is now clear why Judaism, Christianity and Islam have been locked in a violent, sometimes fatal embrace for so long. Their relationship is sibling rivalry, fraught with mimetic desire: the desire for the same thing, Abraham's promise.

Judaism, Christianity and Islam are not just three different religions or civilisations. Had this been so, the devotees of each might still consider themselves a chosen people. More generously, each might have come to Niels Bohr's conclusion that the opposite of a trivial truth is a falsehood, but the opposite of a profound truth may be another profound truth. There is more than one way of being-in-the-world under the sovereignty of God. More probably they would simply have ignored one another. Their differences would not have led to centuries of bloodshed and animosity.

When civilisations are merely different, each stands on its own ground. They are incommensurable. Pauline Christianity, however, claims that it is heir to the Abrahamic covenant. Islam is built on the incorporation of Judaism and Christianity into its own scheme of salvation. Despite their structural differences and internal complexities, all three Abrahamic faiths seek to build their home on the same territory of the mind – one reason why they have so often competed for the same territory on earth: the Holy Land and the sacred city of Jerusalem. They are competing brothers. Each must therefore see the other as a profound existential threat.

At the heart of all three faiths is the idea that within humanity there is one privileged position – favoured son, chosen people, guardian of the truth, gatekeeper of salvation – for which more than one candidate competes. The result is conflict of the most existential kind, for what is at stake is the most precious gift of all: God's paternal love. One group's victory means another's defeat, and since this is a humiliation, a dethronement, it leads to revenge. So the strife is perpetuated. Its most famous biblical expression is the oracle granted to Rebekah while suffering pain in her pregnancy. She went 'to seek the Lord', and was told:

> Two nations are in your womb,
> And two peoples will separate from within you;
> One people will be mightier than the other,
> And the elder will serve the younger. (Gen. 25:23)

The message seems clear. Her children are not merely struggling in the womb. They are destined to do so for all time (I say 'seems' because my argument will depend on showing that this translation is fatefully misconstrued; I explain this in chapter 7). Their relationship is agonistic, conflictual. One can only prevail by subjugating the other. 'The elder will serve the younger.'

Such has been the history of the relationship between Judaism, Christianity and Islam. The younger believes it has prevailed over the elder. Christianity did so to Judaism. Islam did so to both. Between them is not simply a conflict between different systems of thought and ways of life. It is, rather, an intense sibling rivalry. Each regards itself as *the* heir to the covenant with Abraham. Strife is written into the script. It may lie dormant for centuries, but its seeds lie intact, ready to spring to life once circumstances favour religious revival. Each defines and defends itself by negating the others.

This is the final piece of the puzzle. It explains why the three Abrahamic faiths have, from time to time, felt so threatened by one another. Recall the words Freud used to describe sibling rivalry: 'impotent rage . . . elemental, unfathomably deep hostility . . . death wish . . . murderous intent . . . jealous hatred'. This is the language of violence. Remember, too, his judgement that 'We rarely form a correct idea of the strength of these jealous impulses, of the tenacity with which they persist and of the magnitude of their influence on later development.' Freud knew this from his own experience, and it haunted him for a lifetime.

*

We can now sum up the argument. Violence exists because we are social animals. We live and find our identity in groups. And groups conflict. They fight over the same resources: food, territory, other scarce goods. That is our nature and it leads to all that is best and worst about us: our altruism towards other members of our group, and our suspicion and aggression towards members of other groups. Religion plays a part in this only because it is the most powerful source of group identity the world has yet known.

Every attempt to find a substitute for religion has resulted in even more violence. Nationalism led to two world wars. Political ideology led to Lenin and Stalin. Race led to Hitler and the Holocaust. The result was the bloodiest century in human history. The idea that we can abolish identity altogether by privileging the individual over the group is the West's current fantasy and it has led to the return of religion in its most belligerent form. So, four centuries have led us in a complete circle back to where we were in the last great era of religious war.

Group identity need not lead to violence, but there is a mutant form, pathological dualism, that divides the world into two – our side, the children of light, and the other side, the children of darkness. If there is evil in the world, it is because of Them, not Us. This mode of thinking leads to some of the worst crimes in history because it causes people to demonise their opponents, see themselves as victims and convince themselves that evil committed in a good or sacred cause is justifiable, even noble. If there are internal resistances to such murderous and suicidal simplifications, they can be overcome by the invention of the scapegoat. Paranoia will do the rest. This is the politics of hate, and large parts of the world in the twenty-first century are awash with it.

And much of it is religious. There is nothing intrinsically religious about dualism. It existed in Nazi Germany, Stalinist Russia, Mao's China and Pol Pot's Cambodia. However, for several centuries it surfaced in Christianity in the Middle Ages, and it has made its appearance in some forms of Islam today. We have seen in this chapter why. Built into their self-definitions are a series of sibling rivalries drawn from the early narratives of the Hebrew Bible. According to Freud and Girard, sibling rivalry is a primal source of violence, and what makes Judaism, Christianity and Islam unusual is that their narratives of identity are stories of sibling rivalry that assign a secondary, subordinate role to the others. This means that however rare violence between them is, it is always waiting in the wings.

*

But this has brought us to an astonishing conclusion. Theologians have usually assumed that this tension arose with the birth of Christianity. After all, until then, there was only one Abrahamic monotheism, Judaism, and its battle was not with siblings, faiths that were part of the family, but with idolatry. Only with the birth first of Christianity, then of Islam, was the tension born out of the competition for 'most favoured faith in the eyes of Abraham's God'.

It turns out, however, that the tension was there from the very beginning, long before there was a Christianity or Islam. The key narratives are in the book of Genesis. It is there that the drama of choice began: Isaac but not Ishmael, Jacob but not Esau. It was not some late development, two thousand years ago. It existed before then within Judaism itself. It must therefore be a problem in Jewish, not just Christian and Islamic, theology. This is quite unexpected.

What is more, as soon as we state the problem, we begin to discern, hazily in the distance, the glimmerings of a solution. For can it really be true that the God who created the world in love and forgiveness, setting his image on every human being, loves me but not you? Or you but not me? Sibling rivalry exists in nature because food is in short supply. It exists in human society because material goods – wealth and power – are, at any given moment, zero-sum games. It exists within the family because we are human, and sometimes parents have favourites. But can the same possibly be said about God's love or forgiveness or grace? Are these in short supply, such that if he gives them to you he must take them from me? There is something odd, discordant, about such an idea.

Yet the Hebrew Bible does talk about sibling rivalry. It is the dominant theme of the book of Genesis. The point could not be made more forcefully. *The first religious act, Cain and Abel's offerings to God, leads directly to the first murder.* God does seem to have favourites. There does seem to be a zero-sumness about the stories. It is no accident that Jews, Christians and Muslims read these stories the way they did.

But what if they do not mean what people have thought them to mean? What if there is another way of reading them? What if this alternative reading turned out, on close analysis, to be how they were written to be read? What if the narratives of Genesis are deliberately constructed to seem to mean one thing on the surface, but then, in the light of cues or clues within the text, reveal a second level of meaning beneath?

What if the Hebrew Bible understood, as did Freud and Girard, as did Greek and Roman myth, that sibling rivalry is the most primal form of violence? And what if, rather than endorsing it, it set out to undermine it, subvert it, challenge it, and eventually replace it with another, quite different way of understanding our relationship with God and with the human Other? What if Genesis is a more profound, multi-levelled, transformative text than we have taken it to be? What if it turned out to be God's way of saying to us what he said to Cain: that violence in a sacred cause is not holy but an act of desecration? What if God were saying: *Not in My Name*?

Such a suggestion sounds absurd. Jews, Christians and Muslims have been reading these stories for centuries. Is it conceivable that they do not mean what they have always been taken to mean? Yet perhaps this is not as absurd as it sounds, because until now each tradition has been reading them from its own perspective. But the twenty-first century is summoning us to a new reading by asking us to take seriously not only our own perspective but also that of the others. The world has changed. Relationships have gone global. Our destinies are interlinked. Christianity and Islam no longer rule over empires. The existence of the State of Israel means Jews are no longer homeless as they were in the age of the myth of the Wandering Jew. For the first time in history we can relate to one another as dignified equals. Now therefore is a time to listen, in the attentive silence of the troubled soul, to hear in the word of God for all time, the word of God for our time.

Part I has offered an explanation of the fraught, often violent relationship between the three Abrahamic faiths, and it has found, at its tormented heart, a series of stories about sibling rivalry and mimetic desire. Part II offers a radically different reading of these narratives, seeing in them signposts to a world in which brothers, with all their differences and dissonances, can at last dwell together in peace.

PART TWO

Siblings

6

The Half-Brothers

Though my father and mother might forsake me,
The Lord will hold me close.

Psalm 27:10

It is the first story of sibling rivalry in Abraham's family, and
it begins with heartache. Abraham, still known at this time as
Abram, had been promised countless children. He would, said
God, become a great nation. His descendants would be as many
as the stars. Yet the years pass and still he and Sarah have no child.
In despair, Sarah proposes an arrangement. Let Abram sleep with
her handmaid Hagar. Perhaps she will bear him a child. She is
proposing that Hagar become a surrogate mother. Then as now it
is a procedure fraught with potential conflict.

Hagar does conceive, and this alters the relationship between
the two women. Hagar 'no longer respected her mistress' (Gen.
16:4). As the bearer of Abraham's child, she is no longer content
to be treated as a servant. Sarah notices the change and reacts
angrily. She says to Abraham, 'You are responsible for the wrong
I am suffering. I put my servant in your arms, and now that she
knows she is pregnant, I have lost her respect. Let the Lord judge
between you and me' (16:5).

Uncharacteristically, Abraham shrugs off the dilemma. 'Your
servant is in your hands. Do with her as you please' (16:6). Sarah
ill-treats Hagar, who flees into the desert. There she is met by an
angel who tells her to go back. He adds that she will give birth
to a son, whom she should call Ishmael. She returns and Ishmael
is born.

In the next chapter, God appears to Abraham and reaffirms his covenant with him, adding for the first time a command: circumcision. Abraham is to undergo this operation. So is Ishmael. It will become the sign of the covenantal family.

The revelation, however, contains a twist. Despite the fact that Abraham now has a son, God tells him he will have another, born to him by Sarah. At this, Abraham 'fell on his face and laughed, saying in his heart, Will a son be born to a man a hundred years old? Will Sarah bear a child at the age of ninety?' (17:17). Nonetheless, God insists that it will be so. They will have a son whom they will name Isaac, and he rather than Ishmael will be the bearer of the covenant into the future. There is an ominous sound to this. It is a situation fraught with the possibility of conflict.

A year later, Isaac is born. Sarah is overjoyed, but again there is a note of discord. Sarah is troubled by the presence of Ishmael. The tension rises to a height at the celebration the couple make on the day Isaac is weaned:

> Sarah saw that the son whom Hagar the Egyptian had borne to Abraham was mocking, and she said to Abraham, 'Send this slave woman away with her son, for this slave woman's son shall not be an heir with my son Isaac.' (Gen. 21:9–10)

Abraham is 'greatly distressed', but God tells him to listen to Sarah and do as she says. The next morning he sends Hagar and Ishmael away with food and water for the journey. They go, the water runs out, and Hagar realises that, dehydrated in the blazing desert sun, Ishmael will die. She places him under a bush for shade, and weeps. Again an angel appears and reassures her. The child will live. She opens her eyes and sees a well. She gives Ishmael a drink. They continue their journey. Ishmael grows to become an archer. Hagar finds an Egyptian wife for him and the story closes, or so we think.

This is a key narrative, the first of several we are about to analyse. Identity is based on narrative, the stories we tell about who we are, where we came from, and what is our relationship to others. The real theological work of this book lies here, in close reading of biblical texts, especially those whose theme is sibling rivalry. This is what led to the strife between Jews, Christians and Muslims and it is here, if anywhere, that we will find the solution.

We have just read the story of Abraham's two sons, and the message seems clear. Just as Abraham was chosen out of all humankind, so is Isaac. But this is not a straightforward story. Isaac is not the firstborn. Ishmael is. What we seem to have here is a *displacement narrative*. In almost all societies where birth order has a bearing on rank, the oldest (usually male) child succeeds to the role occupied by the father. Here the order is reversed. The older Ishmael is displaced by his younger half-brother. The result, happy for Sarah and Isaac, is tragic for Hagar and Ishmael. We can sense the incipient tension. This sounds like the beginning of a story that will end in resentment and revenge.

Historically, as we saw in chapter 5, it had a fateful afterlife. Paul, in the epistle to the Romans, performs a second reversal, arguing that it is the younger religion, Christianity, that has replaced the elder, Judaism, as heir to the covenant. In Islam the story was turned around yet again, in a different way, saying that it was Ishmael who was chosen, not Isaac. He, after all, was the first of Abraham's children to be circumcised and carry the sign of the covenant. Muslims accused Jews of falsifying the biblical text, rewriting it to make Isaac the hero. Once these faiths had taken the decision to see themselves as heirs of the Abrahamic covenant, re-reading was inevitable. One might call it *the revenge of the rejected*.

But all this is on the surface. If we now peel away the layers of this complex and subtle text, we will discover another story altogether. We will discover how the rabbis heard discordant notes in the narrative, and realised that it is conveying a different and surprising message. Only a superficial reading yields the conclusion: Isaac chosen, Ishmael rejected. In fact, at this strategic point, the first generational succession in the Abrahamic covenant, the Hebrew Bible contains not only a narrative but also a counter-narrative.

*

The first thing to note is the extraordinary length to which the text goes to insist that *Ishmael will be blessed by God*. This is stated four times, the first and last to Hagar, the second and third to Abraham himself.[1] The first occurs when Hagar, still pregnant, flees into the desert:

> Then the angel of the Lord said to her, 'Return to your mistress and submit to her authority.' The angel added, 'I will so increase your descendants that they will be *too numerous to count*.' (Gen. 16:9–10)

This *repeats to Hagar the promise God made to Abraham*, that his children would be too numerous to count (Gen. 15:5). The handmaid will be blessed just as Abraham, the 'knight of faith', will be.

On the second occasion God speaks to Abraham:

> 'As for Ishmael, I have heard you. I have blessed him and will make him fruitful and will multiply him exceedingly. He will be the father of twelve rulers, and *I will make him into a great nation*.' (Gen. 17:20)

Again the language is suggestive. The promise of 'twelve rulers' reminds us of Jacob's twelve sons, each of whom becomes a tribe. The phrase 'a great nation' echoes God's promise to Abraham (12:2), as does the doubled 'greatly, greatly' (17:2, 6). Abraham is being promised by God that, although Isaac will continue the covenant, Ishmael will, in worldly terms, be no less great, perhaps greater. Certainly he will have a share in Abraham's blessing.

The third occurs when Sarah proposes sending Hagar and Ishmael away. God says to Abraham:

'Listen to whatever Sarah tells you, because it is through Isaac
that descendants will bear your name. I will make the son of
the maidservant into a nation also, because *he is your offspring*.'
(Gen. 21:12–13)

God recognises that Ishmael *remains Abraham's son and will be
blessed accordingly*. The text makes a fine distinction between
biological and ascribed identity. Ishmael, says God to Abraham,
'*is* your offspring', while Isaac will be '*called* your offspring'.
The former promises worldly greatness, the latter covenantal
responsibility.

The final scene recapitulates the setting of the first. Once again
we are in the desert, with Hagar running out of water. Her son
Ishmael is about to die:

> God heard the boy crying, and the angel of God called to Hagar
> and said to her, 'What troubles you, Hagar? Fear not, for God
> has heard the cry of the boy where he is. Help the boy up and
> take him by the hand, for I will make him into a great nation' . . .
> God was with the boy as he grew up. He lived in the desert and
> became an archer. (Gen. 21:17–20)[2]

Note first that God does not reject Hagar. He hears and heeds
her distress. He saves her and Ishmael from death. Next, he
repeats to Hagar what he had already said to Abraham, that
Ishmael will become 'a great nation'. Third, note the name
the child bears. Ishmael means 'God has heard', the name the
angel had commanded Hagar to give him, 'for *God has heard*
of your misery' (16:11). It turns out that what we have here is
not a simple drama of choice and rejection at all. Isaac has been
chosen for a specific destiny, but *Ishmael has not been rejected*
– at least not by God.

*

Next, we note the characterisation of the key figures, especially Abraham and Sarah. No reader can fail to sense the harsh light in which Sarah is portrayed in her relationship with Hagar and Ishmael. Having proposed the idea of Hagar sleeping with Abraham, she later blames Abraham: '*You* are responsible for the wrong I am suffering' (16:5). There is nothing in the narrative to suggest this was in fact the case. To the contrary, Abraham seems caught helplessly in the tension between the two women.

The Hebrew text uses a significant word to describe Sarah's treatment of Hagar. She 'afflicted' her. The Hebrew verb is the same as will later be used to describe the Egyptians: they 'afflicted' the Israelites (Exod. 1:11–12). It also appears in Deuteronomy in the text of remembrance to be recited by the Israelites on bringing firstfruits to the Temple ('The Egyptians ill-treated and *afflicted* us . . . and God saw our *affliction*, toil and oppression', Deut. 26:6–7). Hagar was herself an Egyptian (Gen. 16:3). There is a subtle hint here that to some degree the experience of the Israelites at the hands of the Egyptians will mirror the Egyptian Hagar's experience at the hands of Sarah. This too is surprising, and qualifies the simple stereotype: Israelites good, Egyptians bad.

Later, when Sarah insists that Abraham sends Hagar and Ishmael away, she becomes dismissive: 'Send this *slave woman* away with her son, for this slave woman's son shall not be an heir with my son Isaac' (Gen. 21:10). Not only does she not dignify either mother or child by calling them by name; her language has changed since the earlier scene. Then she called Hagar a 'maid' (*shifchah*). Now she has become 'a slave' (*amah*).

The most enigmatic feature of the text is what exactly provoked Sarah's anger at the feast for Isaac's weaning. The text states that she saw Ishmael *metzachek*, translated above as 'mocking', but which literally means 'laughing'. The verb *z-ch-k* is a recurring motif in the story of Abraham and Sarah. It appears seven times in the narrative,[3] and in the Pentateuch the sevenfold repetition of a word is always significant. It signals a keyword around which the text is thematised.[4] Abraham 'laughs' when he hears the news that he and Sarah will have a son (17:17). So does Sarah (18:12), for which she is rebuked by God. The name Isaac itself means 'he will laugh'. When he is born, Sarah says, 'God has given me laughter, and everyone who hears this will laugh for me' (21:6). It has a whole range of senses, from *joy* to *disbelief* to *disdain*. In a later chapter it even has sexual undertones, 'acting familiarly' (26:8). At this point the text is deliberately ambiguous, leaving it to us, the readers, to decide whether Sarah is right to take offence (Ishmael is mocking) or wrong (he is sharing in the general celebration).

The portrait of Sarah in these scenes is so unsympathetic that the thirteenth-century Spanish commentator Nahmanides writes about the first episode in which Sarah mistreats Hagar, causing her to flee:

> Our mother [Sarah] transgressed by this affliction, and Abraham did likewise by permitting her to do so. And so God heard her [Hagar's] affliction and gave her a son who would be 'a wild donkey of a man', to afflict the seed of Abraham and Sarah with all kinds of affliction.[5]

This is a most unusual comment in two respects. First, the medieval Jewish commentators – Nahmanides among them – were loath to criticise the patriarchs and matriarchs, and almost always interpreted the text to cast them in the best possible light. This criticism is therefore exceptional. Even more so is the implication he draws from it. He is saying that Sarah's mistreatment of Hagar was a reason why Sarah's children would one day be persecuted by the descendants of Hagar, that is, by the people of Islam.

Spanish Jewry had suffered from Islamic persecution, especially after the rise of the Almohads in the twelfth century. This had forced the family of Nahmanides' great predecessor, Moses Maimonides (1135–1204) to flee from Cordoba in 1148, wandering for several years before settling in Fostat, Egypt. Jews, like Muslims themselves, identified Ishmael as the precursor of

Islam. Nahmanides' comment is thus pointedly self-critical. Do not believe, he is telling his Jewish readers, that we are entirely without blame.

The portrayal of Abraham is more complex. It was not he but Sarah who proposed having a child by Hagar. Yet once Ishmael is born, he is attached to him. He is acutely distressed when God first tells him that his mission will be continued by Isaac, not Ishmael: 'Abraham said to God, If only Ishmael might live in Your presence!' (Gen. 17:18). Later, when Sarah insists that he send the boy away, we read, 'The matter distressed Abraham greatly because of his son' (21:11). Abraham accedes to Sarah's request, the first time of his own accord, the second at God's insistence: 'In all that Sarah says to you, listen to her voice' (21:12). Yet the love between father and son is unmistakable. As we will soon see, this theme was taken much further by rabbinic Midrash.

*

What of the emotional tonality of the Hagar-Ishmael episodes?[6] One feature is particularly noticeable. In general, the Hebrew Bible is highly reticent in telling us about people's emotional states. We do not know, for example, what Noah's reaction was when he heard that all life was about to be destroyed by a flood, or Abraham's feelings when told to leave his land, birthplace and father's house. By contrast, both scenes involving Hagar are etched with drama. The first paints a vivid scene of Hagar alone in the desert, close to despair, then comforted by an angel. The second is unmatched for its emotional intensity.

To understand the significance of this, we have to realise that Genesis 21, the sending away of Ishmael, is a parallel passage to Genesis 22, the binding of Isaac. In both, Abraham undergoes a trial involving the potential loss of a son. Ishmael and Isaac, the two children, are both only dimly aware of what is happening. In both, they are about to die until heaven intervenes, in the first case by providing a well of water, in the second, a ram to be offered as a sacrifice in Isaac's place. The similarities serve to highlight the differences.

The story of the binding of Isaac is notable for its complete absence of emotion. God commands, Abraham obeys, Isaac joins him on the journey, Abraham prepares the altar, binds his son and lifts his knife, then an angel says, 'Stop.' Throughout the ordeal Abraham says nothing to God except for one word at the beginning and the end: *hineni*, 'Here I am' (22:1, 11).

By contrast, the episode involving Hagar and Ishmael is saturated with emotion. Hagar weeps: 'Then she went off and sat down nearby, about a bow-shot away, for she said to herself, "Let me not see the child die." As she sat, she lifted up her voice and wept' (21:16). Ishmael weeps: 'God heard the boy crying' (21:17). There is a pathos here that is rare in biblical prose. There can be no doubt that the narrative is written to enlist our sympathy in a way it does not in the case of Isaac. We *identify* with Hagar and Ishmael; we are *awed* by Abraham and Isaac. The latter is a religious drama, the former a human one, and its very humanity gives it power.

None of this is as we would expect. Ostensibly the hero of the story is Isaac. He is the chosen. But our sympathies are not drawn to Isaac, nor, in these episodes at least, to Sarah. Isaac has been singled out to carry the covenantal destiny. God has said so repeatedly. But we are left in no doubt that Abraham is attached to Ishmael, that our sympathies are drawn to him and Hagar, that Ishmael will be blessed, that God hears his tears and is 'with him' as he grows up. It is not that Ishmael is evil that disqualifies him from being heir to the covenant. The only term that might cast him in a negative light – that he was 'laughing' while Sarah was celebrating – is, as we saw, ambiguous.

Why then was Ishmael not chosen? The answer suggested by the text is instructive. It is because, like Esau in the next generation, he has physical strength and cunning. He is 'a wild donkey of a man, his hand against every man, and every man's hand against him' (16:12). Eventually he becomes 'an archer' (21:20).

We now begin to sense the subtlety of the biblical narrative. This is not the world of myth with its simple plots and two-dimensional characters. In myth, Ishmael would be a tragic hero, strong, resourceful, combative but defeated by implacable fate. Abraham would have sent him away, fearing that he would one day become a threat. Ishmael might return unexpectedly, killing Abraham not realising that he is his father, and we would then have a biblical version of *Oedipus*.

Instead – and this is fundamental to understanding Genesis – what we have is a *subversion* of myth, a consistent frustration of narrative expectation. God's promise does *not* come true in the way we expect. Abraham's fortunes are not suddenly transformed. Promised children, he remains childless. Eventually given a son, he is told by God that this is *not* the son. Abraham – unlike Laius, Oedipus' father – does *not* want to send Ishmael away. He does so against his will. The only vivid image we are given of Ishmael is not as a man of strength, the epic hero, but as a child, abandoned and about to die.

More significantly still, the conflicts in the story are not what they are in myth – between the personal and the impersonal, human aspiration and blind fate, hubris and nemesis. Instead, the conflict is *within the minds of the protagonists*. Sarah is torn between her desire for a child and her envy of the pregnant Hagar. Abraham is torn between his love of Ishmael and his obedience to God. As Jack Miles puts it, '*Tanakh* [the Hebrew Bible] is more like *Hamlet* than it is like *Oedipus Rex*'.[7]

Myth belongs to a universe bounded by nature. The gods live within, not beyond, the world. What counts in myth is strength, power, force. What makes myth tragic is its realisation that nature ultimately defeats the strongest. We are dwarfed in its presence, undone by its caprice. The choice of Isaac instead of Ishmael has many dimensions, but they all share one feature: they are a refusal to let nature have the final word.

Sarah, like other biblical heroines – Rebekah, Rachel, Hannah and others – is unable naturally to have children. She is infertile,

116

ninety years old and post-menopausal: 'Sarah had stopped having the periods of women' (18:11). Nor is destiny conferred by fatherhood as it was in the ancient world, but by motherhood: Ishmael is Abraham's child but not Sarah's. It is the latter point – anticipating later Jewish law that Jewish identity is matrilineal, not patrilineal – that is crucial. Most fundamentally, Isaac has none of the attributes of a mythic hero. Unlike Ishmael, he is *not* strong, physical, at home in the fields and forests. The same contrast will later be played out by Esau and Jacob. Throughout the narrative Isaac remains a shadowy figure, passive rather than active, done-to rather than doing. If, in myth, character is proved in heroic action, Isaac is the non-hero, the figure of quiet obedience who exemplifies Milton's line, 'They also serve who only stand and wait.'[8]

Intimated here is one of the most striking themes of the Pentateuch. God chooses *those who cannot do naturally what others take for granted*. Abraham, Isaac and Jacob, all promised the land of Canaan/Israel, own none of it and have to beg or pay to bury their dead, pitch their tent or draw water from wells they themselves have dug. Moses, bearer of the divine word, is the man who says, 'I am not a man of words . . . I am slow of speech, and of a slow tongue' (Exod. 4:10). Israel is the people whose achievements are transparently God-given. What for others is natural, for Israel is the result of divine intervention. Israel *must be weak if it is to be strong*, for its strength must come from heaven so that it can never say, 'My power and the strength of my hands have achieved this wealth for me' (Deut. 8:17). It is Ishmael's natural strength that disqualifies him.

Yet *Ishmael is not vilified*. That is the masterstroke of the narrative. Despite the fact that Abraham, Sarah and Isaac are the heroes of the story as a whole, in the two crucial scenes in the desert our imaginative sympathies are with Hagar and her child. That is what gives the story its counter-intuitive depth.

There is a moral reason for this and it is fundamental. We saw in chapter 2 that violence begins in the in-group/out-group dichotomy. I identify with my side, and am suspicious of the other side. In situations of stress, sympathy for the other side can come to seem like a kind of betrayal. It is this that the Ishmael story is challenging. At the first critical juncture for the covenantal family – the birth of its first children – we feel for Sarah and Isaac. She is the first Jewish mother, and he the first Jewish child. *But we also feel for Hagar and Ishmael.* We enter their world, see through their eyes, empathise with their emotions. That is how the narrative is written, to enlist our sympathy. We weep with them, feeling their outcast state. *As does God.* For it is he who hears their tears, comforts them, saves them from death and gives them his blessing. Ishmael means 'he whom God has heard'.

*

Nor is this the end of the story. After the close of the biblical canon, reflection on Israel's destiny passed from the prophets to the sages, and from revelation to interpretation – the genre known as Midrash through which the sages filled in the many gaps in biblical narrative.[9] In the case of Abraham, they noticed several tantalising clues, which eventually led them to piece together an extraordinary sequel to the story. The first clue appears in the announcement of the death of Abraham:

> Then Abraham took his last breath and died at a good old age, old and full of years; and he was gathered to his people. *His sons Isaac and Ishmael* buried him in the cave of Machpelah near Mamre, in the field of Ephron son of Zohar the Hittite. (Gen. 25:8–9)

What is Ishmael doing here, standing next to Isaac at their father's grave? Until now, we have assumed that from early childhood they had lived separate lives. Isaac grew up with Abraham and Sarah, Ishmael with Hagar. There was, as far as we know, no contact between them. How then did they come together for Abraham's funeral? What was their relationship? Did Ishmael bear a grudge at being sent away? These are questions bound to arise for anyone who has been attending carefully to the story. Yet the text offers no answers. It does not even seem to be aware of the questions.

The second anomaly: throughout Abraham's long journey, he has been accompanied by Sarah. The text emphasises their faithfulness to one another and to God. Sarah dies and Abraham buys a field with a cave in which to bury her – his first share in the Promised Land. In the next chapter, he sends his servant to find a wife for Isaac. The story seems to have reached closure. Abraham has seen, if not the fulfilment of the divine promises, at least a beginning. He has a son, his son is married, and he has a fragment of the land. We expect, in the next scene, to see him die in peace. At this point, however, the text takes a digression that seems to make no sense at all:

> Abraham took another wife, named Keturah. She bore to him Zimran, Jokshan, Medan, Midian, Ishbak and Shuah. Jokshan was the father of Sheba and Dedan; the descendants of Dedan were the Asshurites, the Letushites and the Leummites. The sons of Midian were Ephah, Epher, Hanoch, Abida and Eldaah. All these were descendants of Keturah. (Gen. 25:1–4)

What is happening here? Why, after the protracted drama of Abraham's wait for a child, do we suddenly read that, in old age, Abraham has six more sons by a new wife? Who is Keturah, of whom we have heard nothing until now and of whom we will hear nothing again?

Genesis is a highly purposeful narrative. It tells us nothing merely because it happened. It is not 'history' in the conventional sense. It is *covenantal* history, the working out of truth through time. It discloses a pattern, and nothing extraneous to that pattern is allowed to divert our attention. It may be that the story of Abraham's other children is there to supply the background to certain nations who will later play a part in Israel's story – Midian, for example, or Asshur (Assyria). Alternatively it may be telling us that this is how Abraham became, as God said he would, 'the father of many nations'. Neither, though, seems likely. No weight is later placed by the Bible on the fact that the Midianites and Assyrians were children of Abraham. Nor does it emphasise, as it does in the case of Ishmael, that they were to become 'great nations'. Who was Keturah, and why does this episode appear just before the end of Abraham's story?

The third oddity is location. After the binding of Isaac, Abraham returned to Beersheba. The death and burial of Sarah take place at Hebron. We would expect to find Isaac at one or other of these two places. However, two episodes locate him elsewhere. When Abraham's servant returns, bringing Rebekah to become Isaac's wife, we read: 'Isaac had just come from *Beer Lahai Roi*, for he was living in the Negev' (24:62). After Abraham's funeral we read again: 'After the death of Abraham, God blessed his son Isaac. At that time, Isaac was living near *Beer Lahai Roi*' (25:11). What is this place and what was Isaac doing there?

It was this that gave the rabbis the key to unlock all three mysteries. Looking back, we discover that *Beer Lahai Roi* appears in Genesis 16 when Hagar first fled into the desert. Having been met and blessed by an angel, she gave the place a name:

> So she called the name of the Lord who spoke to her: 'You are the God of seeing', for she said, 'Did I not have a vision after He saw me?' That is why the well was called *Beer Lahai Roi* ['the well of the living One who sees me']; it is still there, between Kadesh and Bered. (Gen. 16:13–14)

Beer Lahai Roi is *the place of Hagar*. Teasing out the implications of this unexpected turn in the plot, the sages said: 'On seeing that his father had sent to fetch him a wife, Isaac said, Can I live with her while my father lives alone? I will go and return Hagar to him.'[10] Isaac had been on a mission of reconciliation to reunite Hagar and Abraham.

The rabbis made a further interpretive leap. One device of Midrash is to identify unknown with known biblical characters.[11] Who then was Keturah? Said the rabbis: Hagar herself! Why then was she called Keturah? Because, said the sages, 'her acts were as fragrant as incense [*ketoret*]'.[12]

A complete counter-narrative is taking shape. Whether of his own accord or at the prompting of Isaac, Abraham took Hagar back and gave her a place of honour in his household. What does this Midrash tell us about how the rabbis read the text?[13] It tells us that they felt there was something morally amiss about the story as it stood. Hagar, obedient to her mistress's wishes, was sent away. So too was Ishmael, the child born at Sarah's request.

The story beneath the story, hinted at by these three discrepant details, is that neither Abraham nor Isaac made their peace with the banishment of handmaid and child. As long as Sarah was alive, they could do nothing about it, respecting her feelings as God had commanded Abraham to do. But once Sarah was no longer alive, they could engage in an act of reconciliation. That is how Isaac and Ishmael came to be together when Abraham died.

Only against this background can we understand a rabbinic tradition remarkable both for its psychological insight and for its astonishing interfaith implications:

He [Ishmael] lived in the desert of Paran (Genesis 21:21). Ishmael sent for and married a woman named Ayesha from the plains of Moab. Three years later Abraham went to see his son Ishmael. He arrived at midday and found his wife at home. 'Where is Ishmael?' he asked. 'He has gone to fetch dates from the desert', she replied. 'Give me a little bread and water', he asked. 'I have none', she replied. He said to her, 'When Ishmael comes, tell him that an old man from the land of Canaan came to see him and said, "The threshold of the house is not good."' When Ishmael returned his wife told him this, and he divorced her.

His mother then sent to her father's house and took for him a wife named Fatimah. Three years later, Abraham again went to see his son. He arrived at midday and found Ishmael's wife at home. 'Give me a little bread and a little water, for my soul is weary from the road', he asked. She took out [bread and water] and gave them to him. Abraham stood and prayed before the Holy One, blessed be He, and Ishmael's house became filled with all good things.

When Ishmael came, his wife told him about it, and Ishmael then knew that his father still loved him.[14]

What an extraordinary rewriting of the story! Now it transpires that Abraham, despite the fact that he had sent Ishmael away, did not cease to love or care for him. He made a visit to see him. Discovering that he had married an ungracious wife, he left a coded message. 'Tell him that an old man from Canaan came to see him' was his way of announcing his identity. 'The threshold of the house is not good' was a way of hinting, 'This is not the woman you should have married.' He pays a further visit three years later and finds that Ishmael has remarried, this time to a woman who gives hospitality to strangers. He blesses their home.

The passage ends on a marvellous note: 'Ishmael then knew that his father still loved him.' When he had been sent away, Ishmael was too young to understand what had happened. He must have thought that his father had disowned him. Now he knew this was not so. Whatever the reason for his exile, he had forfeited neither his father's love nor his blessing that his home be 'filled with all good things'.

What gives the Midrash its unique significance is the names it ascribes to Ishmael's wives. *Both are references to the Qur'an and Islam.* Ishmael's first wife, Ayesha, bears the name of the prophet Mohammed's child-bride. Fatimah is the name of the prophet's daughter. Neither are Hebrew names. This dates the passage to an early period in the history of Islam, probably the era of the Umayyads. It is astonishing in what it implies. Yes, Ishmael *is* the central figure in Islam. He *is* a beloved and blessed child of Abraham. Fatimah is a figure of grace and kindness. Nor is this mere apologetics. The proof is that long before the birth of Islam, many rabbis in the Mishnaic and Talmudic periods, from the first century CE onwards, were called Ishmael, hardly likely – indeed impossible – if Ishmael were a rejected figure in Judaism. The force of the Midrash is greater still in light of one striking fact: that in the Bible, Abraham *does not bless Isaac*. God does, after Abraham's death, but he himself does not. One ancient Jewish tradition states explicitly: 'Abraham did not bless Isaac because he did not want Ishmael to feel resentment against him [Isaac].'[15]

Less important to the story of Ishmael but central to the theme of this book is the *test* by which Abraham judges the worthiness of Ishmael's wives, namely, *did they show kindness to strangers?* – the criterion by which, in the Bible, Abraham's servant chooses a wife for Isaac. At the core of the Bible's value system is that cultures, like individuals, are judged by their willingness to extend care *beyond* the boundary of family, tribe, ethnicity and nation.

*

On the surface, the story of Isaac and Ishmael is about sibling rivalry and the displacement of the elder by the younger. Beneath the surface, however, the sages heard a counter-narrative telling the opposite story: *the birth of Isaac does not displace Ishmael*. To be sure, he will have a different destiny. But he too is a beloved son of Abraham, blessed by his father and by God. He becomes a great nation. God is 'with him' as he grows up. God stays with him to ensure that his children flourish and become 'twelve rulers'. Abraham and Isaac both make a journey of reconciliation. The two half-brothers stand together at their father's grave. There is no hostility between them. Their futures diverge, but there is no conflict between them, nor do they compete for God's affection, which encompasses them both. This reading becomes all the more powerful when, in the Midrash, it is extended to the relationship between Judaism and Islam.

This is the first indication of what will, in the next few chapters, emerge as a systemic feature of the biblical text. In each narrative of apparent choice-and-rejection, there is a counter-narrative that subverts the surface story and presents a more nuanced, generous picture of divine (and, by implication, human) sympathy. It is never blatant. It never unequivocally announces itself. But it is unmistakably there in the text. The counter-narrative is not an interpretation imposed by a modern or postmodern sensibility. The proof is that early rabbinic Midrash heard the nuances and drew attention to them, *despite* the fact that they preclude any clear, black-and-white, good-versus-bad reading of the text.

The surface narrative is itself revolutionary. It asserts that the hierarchy of the ancient world – where the elder is destined to rule, the younger to serve – was about to be overthrown. The counter-narrative is more radical still, because it hints at the most radical of monotheism's truths: that God may choose, but *God does not reject*. The logic of scarcity – of alpha males and chosen sons – has no place in a world made by a God whose 'tender mercies are on *all* his works' (Ps. 145:9). Perhaps it needed the twenty-first century, with its ethnic and religious conflicts, to sensitise our ear to the texts' inflections and innuendoes.

Brothers *can* live together in peace, so the counter-narrative implies. But if this is true of Isaac and Ishmael, can it really be true of the supreme instance of displacement: the story of Jacob and Esau?

7

Wrestling with the Angel

Wishing me like to one more rich in hope,
Featur'd like him, like him with friends possessed,
Desiring this man's art, and that man's scope,
With what I most enjoy, contented least . . .

Shakespeare, Sonnet 29

Nowhere are narrative and counter-narrative more subtly interwoven than in the story of Jacob and Esau. It is a work of awesome brilliance, so surprising in its effect that we cannot doubt, once we have understood its hidden message, that it is intended as *the* refutation of sibling rivalry in the Bible. Its significance, set at the very centre of Genesis, is unmistakable. Once we have decoded the mystery of Jacob, our understanding of covenant and identity will be changed for ever.

The surface narrative is a paradigm – almost a caricature – of displacement. The first time we see the twins, at their birth, the younger Jacob is already clinging to the heels of the firstborn Esau. They are different types, Esau a hunter, Jacob 'a plain man staying with the tents' (Gen. 25:27). The tension is heightened by parental attachment. Isaac loves Esau, Rebekah favours Jacob. In the first dramatic scene between the two brothers, Esau comes in exhausted from the hunt, smells the stew Jacob is making and asks for some. Jacob drives a hard bargain: my stew for your birthright. Esau agrees and in a staccato succession of five consecutive verbs – 'he ate, drank, rose, left, and despised his birthright' – reveals his character: mercurial, impetuous, no match for the subtle Jacob.

The story rises to a crescendo in the great scene of the deception.

Isaac, by now old and blind, asks Esau to hunt him some venison and prepare a meal so that 'my soul may bless you before I die' (27:2–4). Rebekah, overhearing, decides that Jacob must take the blessing. Jacob has his doubts. What if Isaac feels him to check his identity? Esau is hairy, Jacob smooth-skinned. Rebekah, ever resourceful, has an answer. She takes Esau's goatskin clothes and puts them on Jacob, covering his hands and neck. The disguise works, despite Isaac's repeatedly expressed doubts and misgivings. The blessing is bestowed. Isaac says to Jacob:

> May God give you
> Of the dew of the heavens,
> And the richness of the earth,
> And abundant grain and wine.
> May nations serve you
> And peoples bow down to you.
> Rule over your brothers,
> And may your mother's sons bow down to you. (Gen. 27:28–29)

Jacob leaves. Soon after, Esau arrives with the food he has prepared. Father and son slowly realise what has happened. Isaac trembles. Esau lets out 'a long and bitter cry', adding, 'Is he not rightly called Jacob seeing that *he has supplanted me* these two times' (27:36). Here, displacement is explicit. The younger has usurped the place of the elder. Conflict has yielded tragedy – a blind man misled, a son robbed of his blessing, a trust betrayed, a family divided, and violence waiting in the wings: 'Esau said in his heart: The days of mourning for my father are approaching. Then I will kill my brother Jacob' (27:41).

Nor is this unexpected. In a unique scene, the theme of sibling rivalry is announced even before the children are born. Rebekah, hitherto infertile, becomes pregnant but suffers agonising pain. She goes 'to enquire of the Lord', who tells her that she is carrying twins already contending for dominance:

126

Two nations are in your womb,
And two peoples will separate from within you;
One people will be mightier than the other,
And the elder will serve the younger. (Gen. 25:23)

The brothers' fate is to clash, their destiny to conflict. Nowhere else does the Bible come so close to Greek tragedy. The scene reminds us of the Delphic oracle in *Oedipus Rex* who tells Laius that he will be killed by his son. The story begins with the end, and the tension lies in waiting to see how it comes to pass. Fate and tragedy belong together, which is what makes this passage so unexpected, so *unbiblical*. The Hebrew Bible rejects the idea of inescapable fate, a pre-ordained future. Yet the verse sets up an expectation, shaping the way we interpret all that follows. The story begins with the words, 'The elder will serve the younger', and ends with Isaac's blessing to Jacob, 'Rule over your brothers, and may your mother's sons bow down to you.' The prediction has come true. Jacob has been granted dominance, his apparently predestined fate. A simple tale.

Yet something is amiss. Reading the passage in which Jacob takes the blessing, it is impossible not to notice how often Isaac doubts that the son in front of him is really Esau:

He went to his father and said, 'My father.'

'Yes,' he answered. 'Who are you, my son?'

Jacob said to his father, 'I am Esau, your firstborn. I have done as you asked. Please sit up and eat some of my venison so that you may give me your blessing.'

. . . Then Isaac said to Jacob, 'Come near so that I can touch you, my son. Are you really my son Esau or not?'

Jacob went close to his father Isaac, who touched him and said, 'The voice is the voice of Jacob, but the hands are the hands of Esau.' He did not recognise him, for his hands were hairy like those of his brother Esau; so he blessed him.

'Are you really my son Esau?' he asked.

'I am,' he replied. (Gen. 27:18–24)

Three times, Isaac expresses doubts – giving Jacob three opportunities to admit the truth. He does not. Far from glossing over the morally ambiguous nature of Jacob's conduct, the text goes out of its way to emphasise it.

Jacob leaves. Esau enters. The power in this scene is not just what happens, but how the Bible describes it:

After Isaac finished blessing him, and Jacob had just left his father's presence, his brother Esau came in from his hunt. He too had prepared some tasty food and brought it to his father. Then he said to him, 'My father, sit up and eat some of my game, so that you may give me your blessing.'

His father Isaac asked him, 'Who are you?'

'I am your son,' he answered, 'your firstborn, Esau.'

Isaac *trembled violently* and said, 'Who was it, then, that hunted game and brought it to me? I ate it just before you came and I blessed him – and indeed he will be blessed!'

When Esau heard his father's words, he *burst out with a loud and bitter cry* and said to his father, 'Bless me – me too, my father!'

But he said, 'Your brother came deceitfully and took your blessing.'

Esau said, 'Is he not rightly named Jacob, for he has supplanted me these two times: he took my birthright, and now he's taken my blessing.' Then he asked, 'Haven't you reserved any blessing for me?'

Isaac answered Esau, saying, 'But I have made him lord over you and have made all his brothers his servants, and I have supported him with corn and new wine. What is left for me to do for you, my son?'

Esau said to his father, 'Do you have only one blessing, my father? Bless me too, my father.' Then Esau *wept aloud*. (Gen. 27:30–38)

Reading this passage, we cannot but identify with Isaac and Esau, not Jacob. We feel the father's shock – 'Isaac trembled violently' – as he realises that his younger son has deceived him. We empathise with Esau, whose first thought is not anger against his brother but simple love for Isaac: 'Bless me – me too, my father.' Then comes Isaac's helplessness – 'So what can I possibly do for you, my son?' – and Esau's weeping, all the more poignant given what we know of him, that he is strong, a hunter, a man not given to tears. The scene of the two together, robbed of what should have been a moment of tenderness and intimacy – son feeding father, father blessing son – is deeply affecting. There is only one other scene like it in the Pentateuch: Hagar and Ishmael, alone in the heat of the desert, without water, about to die. The comparison is deliberate. Just as there, so here, our sympathies are being enlisted on behalf of the elder son.

There is another discrepant note. Unexpectedly, Isaac *does* manage to give Esau a blessing:

> The fat places of earth can still be your dwelling.
> [You can still have] the dew of heaven.
> But you shall live by your sword.
> You may have to serve your brother,
> But when your complaints mount up,
> You will throw his yoke off your neck. (Gen. 27:39–40)

The 'fat places of earth' and the 'dew of heaven' are plentiful enough, Isaac implies, for there to be enough for both sons. More significant is his qualification of Jacob's supremacy. It will last, he says, only as long as he does not misuse it. If he acts harshly, Esau will 'throw his yoke off' his neck. For the first time, a doubt enters our understanding of the brothers' respective fates. Until now we had been led to believe that the narrative had reached closure. The elder (Esau) will serve the younger (Jacob). So Rebekah was told; so Isaac said in his first blessing. Now, it is suddenly less clear. Perhaps Esau will not serve Jacob after all. Perhaps Jacob will misuse his power and Esau will rebel – a small incongruity, but a significant one.

The real doubt, however, lies in the way the text describes Jacob's conduct. Whatever else the covenant is, we feel, it cannot be *this*: a blessing taken by deceit, a destiny acquired by disguise. Did God not say of Abraham, 'I have known him so that he may instruct his children and his household after him to keep the way of the Lord, doing what is right and just' (Gen. 18:19)? Righteousness, justice, integrity, truth – these are key words of covenantal ethics, and we strain to see how they could be applied to Jacob's conduct towards his blind father. Besides which, Isaac may have been deceived, but was God? The idea is absurd. Had God wanted the blessing to go to Jacob, not Esau, he would have told Isaac, as he told Abraham about Isaac and Ishmael. There is just enough discord to make us wonder if we have read the story correctly. In the end we will discover that our unease was justified and that nothing in the story is as it seems – but only at the end. The suspense is maintained until the final scene. Even then, only the most careful listening reveals the unexpected truth, because of yet another brilliant literary device. The final scene almost passes without notice because of the drama that precedes it. It is to this we must now turn.

*

The story of Jacob's wrestling match with an unnamed adversary alone at night is the supreme enigma of the Bible.[1] Told by Rebekah that Esau is planning to kill him, Jacob flees to his uncle Laban and stays there for some twenty years. Returning home, he hears that Esau is preparing to meet him with a force of four hundred men. He is terrified: 'Jacob became exceedingly afraid and distressed' (Gen. 32:7).[2] He makes every possible preparation. He sends emissaries to Esau with large gifts of cattle and sheep. He prays. He divides his camp into two so that if one is killed, the other may survive. There then takes place the defining scene of Genesis, the episode in which Israel, the covenantal people, gets its name.

Alone at night Jacob wrestles with a stranger (32:22–32). As dawn is about to break, the man asks to be released. Jacob refuses to do so until the stranger has blessed him. He does so by giving Jacob a new name: 'No longer will it be said that your name is Jacob, but Israel, for you have striven with God and men and have prevailed' (32:28). The episode is cryptic almost to the point of unintelligibility.

Who was Jacob's unnamed adversary? The text calls him 'a man' (32:24). According to the prophet Hosea, it was an angel (Hos. 12:5). For Judaism's sages, it was Esau's guardian angel.[3] Jacob had no doubt that it was God himself. He calls the place of the encounter Peniel, 'because I *saw God face to face*, yet my life was spared' (Gen. 32:30). The stranger implies as much when he gives Jacob the name Israel, 'because you have striven *with God and men and have prevailed*' (32:28). The clues seem to point in all directions at once, yet we cannot doubt that the episode holds the key to the identity of the people known to eternity as 'the children of Israel'. Names in the Bible, especially when given by God, are not labels but signals of character or calling. Israel, later known as the Jews, are *the people who struggle with God and men and yet prevail*. What does this mean? The clue must lie in what happened next. But it is here that we encounter a succession of surprises.

Everything we have read thus far – Jacob's fear, his frantic preparations, his nocturnal struggle – prepares us for a tense meeting. The last time we saw the brothers together, twenty-two years earlier, Esau had vowed to kill Jacob. We know that Esau is hasty, hot tempered, physical, violent. Yet when he finally appears, all the fears turn out to be unfounded. Esau runs to meet Jacob, throws his arms around his neck, kisses him and weeps. He shows no anger, animosity or threat of revenge. Suddenly we understand Esau's character. He is, we now realise, an impulsive man who lives in the mood of the moment, quick to anger, quick to forget.

He has none of Cassius's 'lean and hungry look' or Iago's cold calculation. The scene is pure anti-climax.

So overpowering is the sense of tension aroused, then released, that at first reading we miss two extraordinary details in *Jacob's* behaviour when the brothers meet. The first is that he 'bowed down to the ground seven times' (33:3), prostrating himself before Esau. Each of his family members does likewise: 'Then the maidservants and their children approached and bowed down. Leah and her children also came and bowed down. Finally, Joseph and Rachel came, and they too bowed down' (33:6–7). The threefold repetition is emphatic. No less strange is Jacob's use of language. Five times he calls Esau 'my lord', *adoni*. Twice he calls himself Esau's 'servant', *eved*. As with the physical gesture of sevenfold prostration, so with his sevenfold use of the words 'my lord' and 'your servant' – this is the choreography of self-abasement.

But this makes no sense at all in the context of the wrestling match of the previous night. Jacob had just won a *victory* over his adversary. At the very least he had refused to let him go until he blessed him. The new name implied that henceforth Jacob should have no doubts about his ability to survive any conflict. A man who has 'wrestled with God and with men and has overcome' is not one who needs to bow down to anyone or call him 'my lord'. We would expect Jacob to show a new-found confidence, not this wholly surprising servility.

Nor does it accord with everything else we had been led to believe until now. Rebekah had been told while the twins were still in the womb that 'the elder will *serve* the younger'. Isaac had blessed Jacob, saying, '*Rule* over your brothers, and may your mother's son *bow down* to you.' If either the prophecy or the blessing were true, it should have been Esau who bowed down to Jacob, Esau who called him 'my lord' and himself 'your servant'. Yet when the encounter takes place, the roles are reversed.

Nor is this all. Esau at first refuses the massive gifts of cattle Jacob had sent the previous day by his emissaries. 'I have plenty,' he says. 'Let what is yours be yours.' Jacob replies in the following significant words:

'No, please, if I have found favour in your eyes, accept this gift [*minchah*] from my hand, for to see your face is like seeing the face of God, now that you have received me favourably. Please accept my blessing [*birkhati*] that was brought to you, for God has been gracious to me and I have everything.' (Gen. 33:10–11)

There are three puzzling features of this speech. Why does Jacob change his language, speaking first of a 'gift', then a 'blessing'?[4] In what conceivable way is seeing the face of Esau like 'seeing the face of God'? And why, when Esau says, 'I have plenty', does Jacob say, 'I have everything'?[5]

The most striking feature of the passage is its repeated use of the word 'face', *panim*. Jacob's words to Esau, 'to see your *face* is like seeing the *face* of God', echo his statement after the wrestling match: 'He called the place Peniel, saying, "It is because I saw God *face* to *face*, yet my life was spared."' Altogether, chapters 32 and 33 (the preparations for the meeting, the night-time struggle, and the meeting itself) echo time and again with variants of the word *panim*. This is almost entirely missed in translation, because *panim* has many forms in Hebrew not apparent in English. To take one example, verse 32:20:

[Jacob said to his servants], 'You shall say, Your servant Jacob is coming behind us,' for he thought, 'I will pacify him with these gifts I am sending on ahead; later, when I see him, perhaps he will receive me.' (Gen. 32:20)

The word 'face' does not appear once in this translation, yet in the Hebrew it appears *four times*. Literally, it reads:

'You shall say, Your servant Jacob is coming behind us,' for he thought, 'I will wipe [the anger from] his *face* with the gift that

133

goes ahead of my *face*; afterwards, when I see his *face* perhaps he will lift up my *face*.'

There is a drama here and it has to do with faces: the face of Esau, of Jacob, and of God himself.[6] What is it?

It cannot be coincidence that when Jacob had earlier taken Esau's blessing, Isaac was blind. The deception was possible only because Isaac could not see. The text at that point is almost an essay on the senses. Deprived of one (sight), Isaac uses the other four. He *tastes* the food, *touches* Jacob's hands (which Rebekah has covered with goatskins) and *smells* his clothes ('Ah, the smell of my son is like the smell of a field the Lord has blessed'). He *hears* his voice ('The voice is the voice of Jacob, but the hands are the hands of Esau'). Eventually, Isaac trusts the evidence of taste, touch and smell over sound, and gives Jacob the blessing. He does so only because *he cannot see Jacob's face*. Somehow, the idea of a face connects the earlier and later scenes.

We have before us an extraordinary literary phenomenon. On the surface, this is a simple tale of sibling rivalry in which the younger supplants the elder. Everything points in this direction, from the prophecy before the twins were born to the deception itself. Esau, the strong, loses to Jacob, the quick-witted. The younger will prevail. Yet the discrepancies mount up. We identify with Esau, not Jacob. Isaac qualifies the blessing: Jacob may not always dominate. Then, after the wrestling match, Jacob unexpectedly reverses the roles. It is he, not Esau, who prostrates himself, calling himself a servant and Esau 'my lord'. We tend to miss this because everything in the narrative directs our attention to *Esau's* behaviour. Will he attack Jacob? If so, who will win? So surprising is his conduct – the embrace, the warmth – that we hardly notice that Jacob's behaviour is stranger still. Only when we have noticed these discords do we go back and read the story again, in the light of all we have discovered subsequently. That is when we make the discovery that changes everything.

*

There was a second blessing. That is the detail whose significance we miss on the first reading. *After* the deception, Rebekah realises that Jacob is in danger because Esau is planning to kill him. She arranges for Jacob to escape. Her pretext is the fact that Esau had married two Hittite women. This was 'a source of grief to Isaac and Rebekah' (Gen. 26:35). This is her opportunity. She tells Isaac that it is imperative for Jacob to leave and go to her brother Laban, where he will find a non-heathen wife. Isaac agrees, and as Jacob is about to leave, he blesses him in these words:

> May God Almighty bless you, make you fruitful and increase your numbers so that you become a community of peoples. May he give you and your descendants the blessing of Abraham, so that you may take possession of the land where you now live as a foreigner, the land God gave to Abraham. (Gen. 28:3–4)

This is a completely different blessing from the one Isaac had given Jacob thinking him to be Esau. The earlier blessing spoke of *wealth* ('the dew of the heavens and the richness of the earth') and *power* ('Rule over your brothers'). The later blessing speaks of *children* ('make you fruitful and increase your numbers') and a *land* ('the land God gave to Abraham'). This is what transforms our entire reading of the story.

Children and a *land* are the covenantal blessings. They are what God promised Abraham. They dominate the book of Genesis.[7] Time and again God blesses the patriarchs – but always and only in terms of children and a land. He never promises them 'the richness of the earth', or that they will 'Rule over their brothers'. Wealth and power have nothing to do with the covenant. They are not part of Israel's destiny. What Isaac is doing in the second blessing is handing on to Jacob the legacy of Abraham, saying in effect: it will be you who will continue the covenant into the future.

This second blessing was given by Isaac to Jacob knowing that

135

he was Jacob. There never was a need for deception. Isaac did not intend to disinherit Jacob, nor did he mean to hand on the covenant to Esau. The blessing he had reserved for his elder son was the one he knew to be right for him. Esau was a man of nature, physical, strong, a hunter – and Isaac loved him. That love is unmistakable and mutual throughout the narrative. The rabbis knew it. 'No one', they said, 'ever honoured his father more than Esau honoured Isaac.'[8] Isaac loved Esau even though he knew that the covenant would be continued by Jacob. Why? *Because that is what it is to be a father*. Isaac loved Esau for what he was, not for what he was not. He wanted to give him the blessings appropriate to him: wealth and power. These are natural, not spiritual, goods. Isaac knew that his children were different. Their paths would diverge. They warranted different blessings. The blessing Jacob took was never meant for him. Isaac had reserved for Jacob another benediction, given later: that he would continue the covenant of Abraham. To receive *that* blessing Jacob had no need for disguise.

*

Recall René Girard's thesis, set out in chapter 5, that the root cause of violence is *mimetic desire*, the wish to have what someone else has, which is ultimately the desire to be what someone else is. Nowhere in all of literature is this more clearly the case than with the biblical Jacob.

One fact stands out about Jacob's early life. *He longs to be Esau*. He desires to occupy Esau's place. He struggles with him in the womb. He is born holding on to Esau's heel (hence the name *Jacob*, 'heel-grasper'). He buys Esau's birthright. He dresses in Esau's clothes. He takes Esau's blessing. When the blind Isaac asks him who he is, he replies, 'I am Esau, your firstborn.'

Why? Because Esau was everything Jacob was not. He was the firstborn. He emerged from the womb red and covered in hair (Esau means 'fully made'[9]). He was strong, full of energy, a skilled

136

hunter, a man of the fields. More importantly, *he was the child his father loved*. Esau was a force of nature. He knew that *homo homini lupus est*, 'man is wolf to man'. He had the strength and skill to fight and win in the Darwinian struggle to survive. These were his natural battlegrounds and he relished the contest.

Esau is the archetypal hero of a hundred myths and legends. He is not without dignity, nor does he lack human feelings. His love for his father is genuine, as is Isaac's love for him. Rabbinic Midrash, for educational reasons, turned Esau into a bad man.[10] But that is not how he is portrayed in the Bible. He is a *natural* man, celebrating the Homeric virtues and the Nietzschean will to power.

It is not surprising that Jacob's first desire was to be like him.[11] The keywords of the Jacob story – *face*, *name* and *blessing* – are all about identity. Jacob wanted to be Esau. He experienced, as Freud thought all siblings do, mimetic desire. It was Esau's face he saw in the mirror of his imagination. It was as Esau he took his blind father's blessing. But Jacob was not Esau, nor was the blessing he took the one destined for him. The true blessing was the one he received later *when Isaac knew he was blessing Jacob*, not thinking him to be Esau.

Jacob's blessing had nothing to do with wealth or power. It had to do with the children he would teach to be heirs of the covenant, and the land where his descendants would seek to create a society based on the covenant of law and love. To receive that blessing Jacob did not have to dress in Esau's clothes. Instead *he had to be himself*, not a man of nature but one whose ears were attuned to a voice beyond nature, the call of God to live for something other than wealth or power, namely, for the human spirit as the breath of God and human dignity as the image of God.

It is now clear exactly what Jacob was doing when he met Esau twenty-two years later. *He was giving back the blessing he had taken all those years before.*[12] The herds and flocks he sent to Esau represented *wealth* ('the dew of the heavens and the richness of the earth'). The sevenfold bowing and calling himself 'your servant' and Esau 'my lord' represented *power* ('Be lord over your brothers, and may the sons of your mother bow down to you'). Jacob no longer wanted or needed these things. His statement 'I have *everything*' means 'I no longer need wealth or power to be complete'. He says explicitly what he is doing. He says, 'Please take [not just my *gift* but also] my *blessing*.' He now knows the blessing he took from Esau was never meant for him, and he is giving it back.

It is equally clear what happened in the wrestling match the night before. It was Jacob's battle with existential truth. Who was he? The man who longed to be Esau? Or the man called to a different destiny, the road less travelled? 'I will not let you go until you bless me,' he says to his adversary. The unnamed stranger responds in a way that defies expectation. He does not give Jacob a conventional blessing (you will be rich, or strong, or safe). Nor does he promise Jacob a life free of conflict. The name *Jacob* signified struggle. The name *Israel* also signifies struggle, but in a different way.

In effect, the stranger said to him, 'In the past you struggled to be Esau. In the future you will struggle not to be Esau but to be yourself. In the past you held on to Esau's heel. In the future you will hold on to God. You will not let go of him; he will not let go of you. Now let go of Esau so that you can be free to hold on to God.' The next day, Jacob did so. He let go of Esau by giving him back his blessing. And though Jacob had now renounced wealth and power, and though he still limped from the encounter of the previous night, the passage ends with the words, 'And Jacob emerged *complete*' (Gen. 33:18). He no longer wanted Esau's blessings. In the past, when he had mimetic desire, he was divided within himself and thus prey to anxiety and fear. The truth at which Jacob finally arrived, to which the name *Israel* is testimony, is that to be complete we need no one else's blessings, only our own. The face that is truly ours is the one we see reflected back at us by God. That is the meaning of the priestly blessing 'May God *turn his face* towards you and grant you *peace*' (Num. 6:26).

Peace comes when we see our reflection in the face of God and let go of the desire to be someone else.

*

What then of the words with which the story of the brothers began, namely that 'the elder shall serve the younger' (in Hebrew, *ve-rav ya'avod tsa'ir*)? Here the Bible delivers a masterstroke. At first sight, the words mean what they say. Only in retrospect – and only in the original Hebrew – do we discover that they contain multiple ambiguities.

The first, noted by several medieval Jewish commentators,[13] is that the word *et*, which signals the object of the verb, is conspicuously missing. Normally in biblical Hebrew the subject precedes, and the object follows, the verb, but not always. Especially in Hebrew poetry (and the prophecy about Rebekah's children is constructed as a four-line poem), the order may be reversed: object-verb-subject. There are only two ways of resolving the ambiguity, either by context (in Job 14:19, for example, the sequence *stone-wear-water* must mean 'water wears away stones', not 'stones wear away water') or by the syntactic marker *et*. In the case of Rebekah's prophecy, both are missing. Thus the phrase may mean 'the elder shall serve the younger', *but it may equally mean the opposite*: 'the younger shall serve the elder'.

The second is that the Hebrew terms *rav* and *tsa'ir* are not opposites. *Tsa'ir* means 'younger', but its opposite is *bechir* ('older' or 'firstborn').[14] *Rav* does *not* mean 'older'. It means 'great' or 'numerous' or possibly 'chief'. This linking together of two terms as if they were polar opposites, which they are not, further destabilises the meaning. Who was the *rav*? The elder? The leader? The more numerous? The word might mean any of these things.

The third ambiguity is not in the biblical text itself but was added by later tradition. The Pentateuch is not *read* in the synagogue, but *sung*, and there is a precise musical notation which also serves as a form of punctuation (biblical Hebrew has neither vowels nor punctuation marks). We would have expected the three words to be notated as a single sequential phrase. In fact, however, they are sung in such a way as to place the musical equivalent of a comma after the first word: 'the older, shall the younger serve' – again, precisely the opposite of the conventional reading.

Re-reading the text, we now discover that the words with which the Jacob-Esau story begins are deliberately ambiguous. They may mean *either* 'the elder shall serve the younger' *or* 'the younger shall serve the elder'. This is remarkable in its own right, but its real significance can only be grasped if we reflect on what this implies about the form of the message itself. *An ambiguous supernatural message is not a prophecy but an oracle.* This is the meaning of God's statement about Moses (Num. 12:8): 'With him I speak mouth to mouth, plainly and not in *dark speeches*' – that is to say, not in oracles, whose message is ambiguous and obscure ('oracular').

The medieval commentators were puzzled about the remark that Rebekah 'went to seek the Lord'.[15] To whom was Rebekah going? A prophet? Were there prophets in those days, other than Abraham and Isaac? Besides which, the phrase 'to seek the Lord' means, in the Bible, to pray, not to enquire.[16] God communicates in Genesis either in simple, unambiguous speech or through visions or dreams, but never – except in this one instance – in oracles. Oracles do not belong in Israelite religion. They belong to the world of myth, the world the Hebrew Bible rejects.

This is not a small point but a fundamental one. Oracles and prophecies belong to two different types of civilisation. Oracles belong to the cluster of ideas – fate, hubris, nemesis – that yield tragedy in the classic, Greek sense. In tragedy the outcome is signalled in advance, and the more the characters fight against their fate, the more enmeshed in it they become. Prophecy, by contrast, belongs to open, non-predetermined, historical time, the time that makes its first appearance in the Hebrew Bible, and constitutes one of its most original contributions to human thought. The prophet *warns*; he does not *predict*. Tomorrow is made by our choices today. Time, for the prophets, is not the inexorable unfolding of destiny but the arena of human freedom in response to the call of God.

We are now in a position to understand the full scope and ingenuity of the literary unit that is the Jacob-Esau story.[17] It is two narratives in one. The surface narrative tells the story as if it were a Greek tragedy – a story of sibling rivalry (Romulus-Remus) of a kind found in all mythological cultures. The cunning younger brother outwits and displaces his stronger, elder sibling, only to find himself threatened by revenge. This is a basic form of myth. A father, usually the king, dies, and his sons contend for the succession. One wins, only to be defeated in turn. This is mimesis, Girard's source of human violence.[18] The entire Jacob-Esau story, from oracle to victory to fear of revenge, is written to be heard, at first reading, like myth.

The counter-narrative, suddenly revealed at the end, is a totally unexpected subversion and rejection of myth. Mimesis, rivalry, displacement, anger, violence, revenge – these are what the Bible challenges at their very roots. Jacob was wrong to seek Esau's blessing. In the wrestling match at night, Jacob fights, not Esau, but himself-in-the-presence-of-God.[19] That is what he means when he says he has seen God face to face. He now knows who he is, not the man holding on to his brother's heel, but the man unafraid to wrestle with God and with man because he has successfully wrestled with himself. The next morning he gives back to Esau what he had taken from him twenty-two years before. He now knows that his true blessing was quite different and to obtain it he had no need of disguise.

Sibling rivalry is defeated the moment we discover that we are loved by God for what we are, not for what someone else is. We each have our own blessing. Brothers need not conflict. Sibling rivalry is not fate but tragic error. As a young man, Jacob had lived 'desiring this man's art, and that man's scope', wanting to be what he was not. Alone at night, wrestling with the angel, he discovered the rivalry-dissolving truth that it is *for what we uniquely are that we are loved.*

Not by accident was this episode the point at which the covenantal people acquired its name. For Israel is summoned to a different destiny than the pursuit of wealth and power. It would never know the wealth of ancient Greece or Rome, Renaissance Italy or aristocratic France. It would never be an imperial power. When it longed for these things, as in the days of Solomon, it lost its way. Israel's strength lay not in its own power but in the power that transcends all earthly powers, and the wealth that is not physical but spiritual, a matter of mind and heart.

No less interesting is the Bible's attitude to Esau and his descendants. Moses commands, 'Do not hate an Edomite [a descendant of Esau], for he is your brother' (Deut. 23:7). God instructs the Israelites:

> You are passing by the borders of your brothers, the descendants of Esau, who live in Seir. Although they fear you, be very careful not to provoke them. I will not give you even one foot of their land, since I have given Mount Seir as Esau's inheritance. (Deut. 2:4–5)

Something of deep consequence is being intimated here. *The choice of Jacob does not mean the rejection of Esau.*[20] Esau is not chosen, but neither is he rejected. He too will have his blessing, his heritage, his land. He too will have children who become kings, who will rule and not be ruled. Not accidentally are our sympathies drawn to him, as if to say: not all are chosen for the rigours, spiritual and existential, of the Abrahamic covenant, but each has his or her place in the scheme of things, each has his or her virtues, talents, gifts. Each is precious in the eyes of God.

To be secure in my relationship with God does not depend on negating the possibility that others too may have a relationship with him. Jacob was loved by his mother, Esau by his father; but what of God, who is neither father nor mother but both and more than both? We can only know our own relationships; we can never know another's. Am I loved more than my brothers or sisters?

Less? Once asked, the question must lead to sibling rivalry, but *it is the wrong question and should not be asked*. Love is not quantifiable: not a matter of more or less. Jacob is Jacob, heir to the covenant. Esau is Esau, with his own heritage and blessing. The people of the covenant must wrestle, as did Jacob, in the depths of the soul to discover the face, the name and the blessing that is theirs. Before Jacob could be at peace with Esau and with himself, he had to overcome mimetic desire, abandon sibling rivalry and learn that he was not Esau but Israel – one who wrestles with God and never lets go.

8

Role Reversal

Do not judge your fellow until you have been in his place.

Mishnah[1]

With the story of Joseph and his brothers, sibling rivalry becomes high drama. No other narrative in the Pentateuch is as long – it occupies almost a third of Genesis – and none is as tightly constructed. Like the last movement of a great symphony, it focuses all the tensions that have gone before and wrestles with them until it reaches resolution.[2]

The final scene in which Joseph assures his brothers that he has forgiven them – 'Am I in place of God? You intended evil against me but God has turned it to good' (Gen. 50:19–20) – is Genesis' serene and unexpected closure. In retrospect it is as if the entire book, from Cain's murder of Abel, has been leading to this denouement, where brothers learn what it is to resolve conflict, be reconciled, make space for one another and forgive. Only now can the story move forward to the book of Exodus. Genesis was about the birth of the covenantal *family*. Exodus is about the birth of the covenantal *nation*. The unstated but implicit message of Genesis is this: not until families can live in peace can a nation be born.

The Joseph narrative is not merely longer than the others. It is also significantly different. In the case of Isaac and Ishmael, it was God and Sarah who chose; with Jacob and Esau, it was Rebekah. Both times, the father is attached to the elder: Abraham to Ishmael, Isaac to Esau. In the Joseph story, however, the roles are reversed. This time it is Jacob who loves the younger. Indeed Jacob favours the younger three times, preferring Rachel to her elder sister Leah, Joseph to his older sons, and the younger

144

Ephraim over Manasseh, Joseph's children. The entire life of Jacob is a set of variations on the danger of favouritism, and the grief to which it gives rise.

The Joseph story is the most searching of all Genesis' studies of sibling rivalry and its consequences. It is so because of its narrative technique. God, who has been in the forefront of the action until now, steps back, allowing us to focus on the human drama as it unfolds. It is a tense and enthralling tale – doting father, spoiled child, envious brothers, jealousy and its unforeseen outcomes. No other passage in the Pentateuch is so literarily constructed; none reads so much like a novel. That is no coincidence. In the Bible, form follows function. Having given us several dramas of sibling rivalry, it now invites us to deepen our understanding of the theme by identifying with the characters, empathising with their emotions, understanding for ourselves what goes wrong when one child is favoured over others. God is not absent. To the contrary, nowhere else does he control the action so tightly, but always obliquely – through a dream here, a conveniently placed stranger there, by making Joseph successful in all he does, and giving him the power to interpret the dreams of others. The outcomes are divine, the emotions all too human.

And it happens because of love. Nowhere in Genesis do we read that Abraham loved Sarah. Once we hear that Isaac loved Rebekah.[3] *Three times* we read that Jacob loved Rachel,[4] and three times that he loved Joseph.[5] The Hebrew Bible is a book of love: love God with all your heart, soul and might (Deut. 6:5); love your neighbour as yourself (Lev. 19:18); love the stranger (Lev. 19:34). But love is not unproblematic. Given to one but not another, to one *more* than another, it creates tensions that can turn to violence. More than any other character in Genesis, Jacob loves, but the result is conflict between Leah and Rachel, and between Joseph and his brothers. The message of Genesis is that love is necessary but not sufficient. You also need sensitivity to those who feel unloved.

The Joseph story begins on an ominous note which tends to be lost in translation: 'Jacob dwelt [*vayeshev*] in the land in which his fathers sojourned [*megurei aviv*]' (Gen. 37:1). The contrast between the two verbs, 'to dwell' and 'to sojourn', to live securely and insecurely, suggests that Jacob wanted what Abraham and Isaac did not have: tranquillity. Having fled twice, once from his brother Esau, a second time from his father-in-law Laban, he longs for a quiet life. He will not achieve it. The sages said: 'Jacob sought to dwell in peace; immediately there broke upon him the storm of Joseph.'[6]

In a few deft strokes, the Bible sketches a picture of tension within the family. Jacob loves Joseph, the youngest-but-one of his twelve sons. The reason stated in the text is that Joseph 'was a son of his old age' (37:3). The more significant, unstated reason is that he was the son of his beloved Rachel. The first glimpse we have of him is when he is tending the flocks with the sons of the handmaids Bilhah and Zilpah. Already there is tension between him and the sons of Leah. They keep a distance from one another.

Three incidents orchestrate the conflict. The first is that he brings his father a 'bad report' about his brothers (37:2). He tells tales. The second is the visible sign of his father's favouritism, the 'coat of many colours' or richly ornamented robe (37:3). This acts as a constant provocation to his brothers. The third is that he dreams dreams: first that his brothers' sheaves will bow down to his, then that the sun, moon and stars will bow down to him. Worse: he tells his brothers about them. At this stage we have no idea whether the dreams are auguries of the future, or merely the vaulting ambition of a child. At this point, the Bible withholds from us the one piece of information that would resolve the ambiguity. Not until much later (41:32) do we discover that a repeated dream is a divinely sent prophecy. Had we known this at the outset, the Joseph story would have lost its tension, its capacity to make us identify with both sides of the conflict. At this stage we have no idea how to evaluate Joseph. All we know is how others see him.

His father loves him; his brothers hate him. We are told this repeatedly with cumulative force. First, 'they hated him and could not speak peaceably to him' (37:4). Communication had broken down, and in the Bible where words fail, violence follows. A second time, after the first dream, 'they hated him all the more' (37:5). Then after the second dream, 'his brothers were jealous of him' (37:11). The hostility is palpable and about to explode.

The text sets up a contrast between love and hate. Twice we read that Jacob loved Joseph, twice that his brothers hated him. They hated him *because* their father loved him. As we will see in the next chapter, the same pair of verbs, 'to love' and 'to hate', have already appeared in the story of Jacob's wives, the sisters Rachel and Leah (Gen. 29:30–31). This is a crucial point, the core of the problem Genesis is intent on exploring. To create a universe, Genesis implies, is easy. It takes up no more than a single chapter (Gen. 1:1–2:3). To create a human relationship is difficult. Jacob's love for Joseph – innocent, human, benign – generates envy and hate. It is this honest confrontation with complexity that makes Genesis so profound a religious text. It refuses to simplify the human condition.

The climax comes when Jacob sends Joseph off to see his brothers who are tending sheep near Shechem. For the first time they are about to be together, alone and far from home. The brothers see Joseph approaching, recognising him by his robe. The text at this point is powerfully ironic. 'They *saw him in the distance* and before he reached them they plotted to kill him' (37:18). This sentence, like so many others in the Joseph narrative, has two meanings. On the surface, it means what it says: they saw him approach, and they planned murder. At another level, however, it is a philosophical statement about love and hate. They were able to contemplate fratricide because 'they saw him at a distance'.[7] They refused to allow him to come close. He was a threat rather than a person. They could see his cloak, but in Emmanuel

Levinas's terminology, they could not yet see his 'face', his alterity, his reality as a person.[8] Distant physically, they would not let him come close emotionally.

In case we doubt whether this double meaning is really there in the text, the next verse but one resolves the doubt. The brothers say, 'Come, let's kill him and throw him into one of these wells . . . *then we'll see what comes of his dreams*' (37:20). Here, the irony could not be more explicit. The words mean one thing to the brothers, the opposite to us, the listeners.[9] Once we have reached the end of the story and go back to read it a second time, we realise that the very act intended to frustrate the dreams by killing the dreamer is the beginning of a sequence of events that will make the dreams come true. We have here a Hebraic counterpart of the story of Oedipus. Laius, Oedipus' father, is told by the Delphic oracle that he will be murdered by his son. To prevent this, he leaves him as a baby, nailed to a rock to die. This too is the first of a sequence of events that leads to the oracle being fulfilled. The irony is the same in both cases. The difference is that the Greek story is tragic, the biblical one non-tragic.

From this point on the story moves rapidly forward through a series of reversals and unexpected shifts of fortune. Persuaded by Reuben, the brothers refrain from killing Joseph. Instead, throwing him into one of the cisterns, they leave him to die (Reuben had intended to rescue him, but does not, in the end, have the opportunity). Then Judah proposes selling him into slavery. He is taken to Egypt. There he becomes head of the household of Potiphar, one of Pharaoh's officials. Potiphar's wife conceives a fancy for him, but he refuses to betray his master. Instead he himself is betrayed. Potiphar's wife accuses him of attempted rape. He is thrown into prison, where once again he shows talent as an administrator.

He is also an interpreter of dreams, and successfully deciphers the dreams of two of his fellow prisoners, Pharaoh's erstwhile butler and baker. Two years later Pharaoh himself has a pair of dreams. Troubled by them, he asks the court magi to explain their significance, but is satisfied with none of their explanations. At this point the butler, restored to office, remembers Joseph, who is brought out from the prison and gives Pharaoh an interpretation that makes sense: there will be seven years of plenty, followed by seven of famine. Without pausing, Joseph then proceeds to solve the problem he has diagnosed: take a fifth of the harvest during the years of plenty, store it, and there will then be food during the years of drought.

Impressed, Pharaoh appoints Joseph as his second-in-command and dresses him in royal robes. He gives him a new name, Zaphenath-Paneah. Joseph marries an Egyptian wife, Asenath, daughter of an Egyptian priest. The years pass, the plenty comes and the drought begins. Jacob, facing famine in Canaan, sends the ten sons to Egypt to buy food. There they enter the presence of the man in charge of Egypt's economy and prostrate themselves before him. He tells them he is their long-lost brother Joseph and asks them to bring the rest of the family to Egypt. They arrive. Jacob and Joseph, his beloved son, are reunited. The family settle in Egypt under Joseph's aegis.

End of story. The dreams have come true. Joseph has risen to great heights. As he foresaw, his family has bowed down to him. Not merely in his father's affections but also in terms of worldly estate, the younger has succeeded; the older brothers have not. We have yet another typical displacement narrative – except that *this isn't the story at all*. It should have been, had the Bible followed narrative convention. But the Bible does not. Instead it subverts it, for profoundly moral reasons. Rarely is this done more subtly than in the Joseph story, the last and most explicit of Genesis' treatments of sibling rivalry.

*

What actually happens when the brothers arrive in Egypt is wholly counter-intuitive:

Now Joseph was the governor of the land, the one who sold grain to all its people. So when Joseph's brothers arrived, they bowed down to him with their faces to the ground. As soon as Joseph saw his brothers, he recognised them [*vayakirem*], but he pretended to be a stranger [*vayitnaker*] and spoke harshly to them. 'Where do you come from?' he asked.

'From the land of Canaan,' they replied, 'to buy food.'

Although Joseph recognised [*hikir*] his brothers, they did not recognise him [*hikiruhu*]. (Gen. 42:6–8)

This is unexpected. The story is nearing closure. Joseph has become a ruler. His brothers have bowed down to him. All that remains is for Jacob and Joseph's young brother Benjamin to be brought to Egypt. There they will make their obeisance and the end foretold at the beginning will be complete. We cannot but expect this to happen, given the story thus far.

It does not. Instead Joseph accuses the brothers of being spies. He places them in custody for three days. He then tells them that to verify their story – that they have come to buy food – they must bring him their youngest brother. This is illogical. The existence of another brother has nothing to do with whether or not they are spies. Indeed, were they to bring a child, there would be no way an Egyptian ruler would be able to tell whether he was their brother or not. The strangeness of the request does not, however, raise doubts in the minds of the brothers. They know they are in trouble; that is all. One of their number, Simeon, is put in prison as a hostage against their return. On the journey back, they discover that the silver they have paid for the grain has been returned to them in their sacks. They tremble: 'What is this that God has done to us?' (42:28).

They go back and tell Jacob what has happened. There is a sense of foreboding. Jacob has now lost two of his sons, and no longer trusts the brothers. The demand that Benjamin go with them to Egypt touches Jacob's most sensitive nerve. Benjamin was the other son of Jacob's beloved wife Rachel. She had died giving birth to him. How can he let him go and risk losing him? But how can he not let him go when they are facing starvation? Reuben offers to leave his own two sons with Jacob as hostages. It is a pointless offer, and Jacob rejects it. Eventually Judah says that he will personally accept responsibility for Benjamin's safe return. Jacob agrees.

They arrive in Egypt. Seeing them, Joseph orders one of his men to escort them to his house. They are terrified, suspecting that some evil fate awaits them. Instead, Joseph treats them with lavish hospitality. Simeon is brought out of prison to join them. They eat, buy their grain, and leave. No sooner have they left the city, however, than one of Joseph's officers overtakes them, accusing them of stealing a goblet (it had been placed there deliberately on Joseph's instructions). He searches their sacks, one by one, and finds it in the last, Benjamin's. They return ignominiously to the palace and declare that they are all now the ruler's slaves. But Joseph tells them: No, you are free. 'Only the one in whose sack the cup was found must stay as a slave' (44:17). This is the moment of crisis, and Judah rises to it. In an impassioned, eloquent speech he says he cannot go home without his youngest brother. He has personally guaranteed his safe return, and besides, his father loves him so much that were Judah to return without him, Jacob would die. 'Let me', he says, 'be your slave, and let the child go free' (44:33). At this point, Joseph finally reveals his identity. The brothers are speechless with surprise, but Joseph insists that they should not feel guilty:

'I am your brother Joseph, whom you sold into Egypt! Now, do not be distressed or feel guilty for selling me here, because it was to save lives that God sent me ahead of you. For two years now there has been famine in the land, and for the next five years there will be no ploughing and harvest. God sent me ahead of you to preserve for you a remnant on earth and to save your lives by a great deliverance. So then, it was not you who sent me here, but God. He made me father to Pharaoh, lord of his entire household and ruler of all Egypt.' (45:4–8)

What is going on in this strange and apparently pointless diversion? Why Joseph's false accusation? Why the deception and intrigue? Why force the brothers to bring Benjamin? How does it advance the narrative or tell us something we need to know? In terms of the dreams, it delays their fulfilment rather than hastens it.

The first explanation that comes to mind is revenge. The text, however, explicitly rules this out. At every stage of the stratagem, Joseph weeps. He weeps at their first meeting (42:24), again at the second (43:30), and a third time at the end of Judah's speech (45:2). People taking revenge do not weep. Joseph is doing something he finds personally painful yet morally necessary. He bears them – as he says when he reveals his identity – no malice. He has forgiven them. Why then does he put them through such fear and subject them to such a trial?

*

I argued in chapter 2 that the source of violence lies in our need to exist in groups, which leads to in-group altruism and out-group hostility. The pathological form of this, as we saw in chapter 3, is the dualism that divides humanity into children of light and children of darkness, the one all-good, the other all-evil. *It follows that the most profound moralising experience, the only one capable of defeating dualism, is to undergo role reversal.* Imagine a Crusader in the Middle Ages, or a German in 1939, discovering that he is a Jew. There can be no more life-changing trial than finding yourself *on the other side.*

That, in essence, is what Joseph is forcing his brothers to do. He is putting them through the intensely painful yet morally transformative ordeal of role reversal. They suspected him of ambition. Now they learn what it is to be under suspicion. They planned to sell him as a slave. Now they know what it feels like to face enslavement. They made Jacob go through the grief of losing a son. Now they must witness that grief again, this time through no fault of their own. Above all, they treated their brother as a stranger. *Now they must learn that the stranger*, Zaphenath-Paneah, ruler of Egypt, *is actually their brother.*

What is at stake in this role reversal? One concept is implicit throughout the Bible, essential to the message of the prophets and made explicit in the book of Jonah. Yet it was only in the rabbinic period, following the destruction of the Second Temple, that it became the subject of systematic reflection. It is the idea of *teshuvah*, usually translated as 'repentance'.[10] Literally it means 'return' – in Christianity *metanoia*, in Islam *tabwa*, in secular terms moral change and growth.

We know from the writings of Paul, especially the letter to the Romans, that he wrestled long and hard with the phenomenon of guilt.[11] What we know we ought to do, he said, we often fail to do. The body does not obey the promptings of the soul. The result is guilt, all the more so in a religion like Judaism, full of commands. The very fact of command, he argues, generates its own resistance. Tell someone not to do something and he will immediately be tempted to do it. How can one live under such a burden of conscience?

The answer Paul gave was to construct, in essence, a Judaism without commands: a religion of the soul rather than the body, of faith rather than deeds. The answer given by the Jewish sages, however, was different. To be sure, we sin. Each of us has a *yetser*, an impulse to evil,[12] but as God said to Cain, sin 'desires to have you, but you must master it' (Gen. 4:7). He does not ask for perfection. The whole thrust of Genesis is that God scales down his demands to the point where they become live-able, rather than a code for saints. When we sin, all we have to do is acknowledge that we have sinned, express remorse, and resolve to act better in future – in short, that we repent. This is how Maimonides defines it:

What is repentance? It consists in this, that the sinner abandon his sin, remove it from his thoughts, and resolve in his heart never to repeat it, as it is said, 'Let the wicked forsake his way, and the man of iniquity his thoughts' (Isaiah 55:7) . . . it is also necessary that he make oral confession and utter the resolutions he made in his heart.[13]

Repentance is an attitude to the past and a resolve for the future. What, though, shows that the remorse is genuine? The answer lies in the concept of 'perfect repentance' (*teshuvah gemurah*), which is not purity of heart but a simple, demonstrable change of deed. Maimonides again:

What is perfect repentance? It occurs when an opportunity presents itself for repeating an offence once committed, and the offender, while able to commit the offence, never the less refrains from doing so, because he is penitent and not out of fear or failure of strength.[14]

Perfect repentance comes about when you find yourself in the same situation but this time you act differently. That is proof in action of a change in heart.

What Joseph is doing is, in effect, taking his brothers through the experience of *teshuvah*, change of heart. So in their first encounter, after he has accused them of being spies, they undergo the first stage of repentance:

They said to one another, 'We deserve to be punished because of our brother. We saw how distressed he was when he pleaded with us for his life, but we would not listen. That is why this distress has come upon us.' (Gen. 42:21)

This is regret, remorse, confession. The text adds that, at this point, Joseph turned aside and wept, and that the brothers did not know what was happening. Not only did they not recognise the Egyptian ruler as their brother. They did not even know he understood their language.

The scene is now set for the second act of the drama. They had sold their brother into slavery. How would they act if placed in the same situation again? Joseph plans the scene with meticulous care. He must create a situation in which they can purchase their freedom by leaving one of their number as a slave. It cannot be one of the brothers chosen at random. It must be one of whom they are jealous, as they were of Joseph. That is why he chooses Benjamin, the other son of Rachel, his father's favourite wife. He has to add one further element. What provoked them to rage many years earlier was the physical emblem of favouritism, the richly embroidered cloak. That is why, in an otherwise inexplicable detail, when the brothers return with Benjamin and sit to eat their meal, 'When the portions were served to them from Joseph's table, Benjamin's portion was *five times as much* as anyone else's' (43:34).

In effect, Joseph has constructed a controlled experiment in 'perfect repentance'. When the cup is found in Benjamin's sack and the brothers say, 'We are all your slaves,' Joseph replies, 'Far be it from me to do such a thing! Only the man who was found to have the cup will become my slave. The rest of you, go back to your father in peace' (44:17). He gives them the chance to walk away in freedom if they are willing to leave Benjamin as a slave. This is the moment of trial, and it is crucial that Judah rises to it, because it was Judah who had initially proposed selling Joseph as a slave (37:26–27). His long and emotive speech reaches a climax when he says, 'Now please, let your servant remain here as my lord's slave, and let the boy return with his brothers' (44:33). As soon as Judah has shown that, placed in the same situation, he has changed – he is now willing to sacrifice his own freedom rather than let his brother be enslaved – the trial is over and Joseph can reveal his identity. Judah has fulfilled exactly the requirements of perfect repentance.

That is why Joseph can tell them their sin is forgiven. He does so a second time, when Jacob dies. The brothers fear the possibility that Joseph may simply have delayed taking revenge as

long as their father was still alive.[15] Joseph reassures them with
majestic grace:

> Joseph said to them, 'Don't be afraid. Am I in the place of God?
> You may have intended to harm me, but God intended it for good so
> that it would come about as it is today, saving many people's lives.
> So then, don't be afraid. I will provide for you and your children.'
> And he reassured them and spoke kindly to them. (50:19–21)

On this serene note, Genesis ends.

*

The three dramas of sibling rivalry have all ended on a note of
reconciliation, each time at a more profound level. With Isaac and
Ishmael, it is implied. The text merely speaks of them standing
together at Abraham's funeral. The rabbis had to piece together
the rest of the story from the text's cues and clues. With Esau
and Jacob, the brothers meet and embrace as friends, but they
part and go their separate ways. With Joseph and his brothers, the
entire process of reconciliation is told in painstaking detail. The
issue is not *forgiveness*: Joseph forgives his brothers without their
asking for it, without their apology, and long before he tells them
who he is. The issue is *repentance*. Forgiveness is easy, repentance
– true change of character – is difficult. Yet it is repentance, moral
growth, on which the biblical vision depends.

By making the human person 'in his image' God has given
us freedom: the freedom to do good, which also necessarily
entails the freedom to do evil. In the early chapters of Genesis
we feel God's pain and disappointment as first Adam and Eve,
then Cain, then the generation of the Flood use their freedom to
bring chaos to God's universe of order. Yet there is never a hint
that God might create Homo sapiens without freedom. The free
God desires the free worship of free human beings. The idea that
God might create a billion computers programmed to declare his

praise is, in biblical terms, absurd. Only a being with freedom is a true 'Other', and the freedom and dignity of otherness is central to the divine project.

Few things have been denied more often, and more variously, than human freedom. Fate, the Greek concept of *ananke*, is in the hands of the gods or the stars: so thinkers have argued since the birth of time. Later, it was attributed to divine (Calvin) or physical (Spinoza) determinism, economic forces (Marx), the experiences of early childhood (Freud), or genetic endowment (the neo-Darwinians). The Hebrew Bible argues, contrarily, that if our acts are no more than the effects of causes over which we have no control, then we inhabit a tragically configured universe, and time is no more than a cycle of eternal recurrences. Against this the Bible predicates its faith – God's faith – in freedom. If we can change, then the future is not destined to be an action replay of the past. Repentance is the proof that we can change. The Judah who offers to sacrifice his freedom so that Benjamin can go free is not the same man he was twenty-two years earlier. And if we can change ourselves, together we can change the world. The Hebrew Bible is the West's key text of human freedom – and more than it tells the story of man's faith in God, it tells the story of God's faith in humankind.

The Joseph story brings Genesis to closure by showing that sibling rivalry is not written indelibly into the human script. We can change, repent and grow. The brothers show that they have changed when they demonstrate that they are no longer willing to let Benjamin – the Joseph-substitute – be enslaved. Joseph, by his act of reconciliation, shows that he is not captive to the past and its resentments. His statement, 'You intended to harm me, but God intended it for good', shows the power of a religious vision to reframe history, liberating ourselves from the otherwise violent dynamic of revenge and retaliation. In a real sense, then, freedom extends to more than our ability to choose between alternative futures. It includes the freedom to reshape our understanding of the past, healing some of its legacy of pain. The point could not be more significant in the context of the sibling rivalry between

Judaism, Christianity and Islam. The past does not dictate the future. To the contrary, a future of reconciliation can, in some measure at least, retroactively redeem the past.

The length and weight of the Joseph story testifies that, within the highly structured book of Genesis, it is resolving the tension not of that generation alone, but of all that went before. Genesis is about failure and learning from failure, discovering that we can change. Jacob discovers this after a long night of wrestling with the angel. His sons discover it after a long period of suspense and fear. In learning, they enact the greatest of biblical themes: the defeat of tragedy in the name of hope.

It happens through role reversal. The most fundamental fact about consciousness is that I cannot feel someone else's pain. I can only feel my own. This is the source of the human tendency to divide the world into brothers and others, kin and non-kin, friends and strangers, the 'Us' to whom I belong, and the 'Them', the Other, to whom I do not belong. That is why the covenantal family, the children of Israel, begin their collective life as a nation in Egypt, as slaves, so that they will know from the inside what it feels like to be on the other side.

That is what Joseph is forcing his brothers to do. He is educating them in otherness through role reversal. They must undergo what he went through when he was sold as a slave to a strange land far from home. This is not revenge, for which Joseph has neither desire nor need. It is, rather, the only way they will understand what evil feels like from the other side, not as perpetrator but as victim. That is the necessary prelude to repentance, itself the most compelling proof that we are free. Cain is able to commit murder because, he says, 'Am I my brother's keeper?' He does not feel Abel's pain. He feels only his own at having his offering rejected. *The way we learn not to commit evil is to experience an event from the perspective of the victim.* Judah's repentance – showing that he *is* his brother Benjamin's keeper – redeems not only his own earlier sin, but also Cain's.

*

There is a masterstroke in the Joseph narrative, completely missed in translation. It occurs in the crucial scene, quoted above, where the brothers come before Joseph for the first time, not knowing who he is, thinking him to be an Egyptian. There is a rare linguistic phenomenon known as a *contronym,* one word with two contradictory meanings. In English, the word 'sanction' can mean both a permission and a prohibition. 'Fast' can mean immovably stuck or moving quickly. 'Cleave' can mean to cut in two or to join together.[16] In Hebrew the root *n-k-r* is a contronym. It can mean 'to recognise' or the opposite, 'to be a stranger', someone who is *not* recognised.

If we now re-read the text cited above, we see that it uses the root *n-k-r* four times in two verses, three in the sense of recognition, one in the sense of estrangement. 'Joseph *recognised* his brothers but they did *not recognise* him', and Joseph '*recognised* them but *acted as a stranger*'.

The power of this contronym is intense. The central question of Genesis is: are human beings friends or strangers, brothers or others? That has been hammering at our consciousness since Cain and Abel, the first human children. Judah, in proposing the sale of Joseph, utters the devastatingly ironic words, 'Come, let us sell him to the Ishmaelites and not lay our hands on him; *after all, he is our brother*, our own flesh and blood' (37:27). This is close to Cain's 'Am I my brother's keeper?' Genesis is about recognition and non-recognition in the deepest sense, about the willingness to accord dignity to the other rather than see the other as a threat.

The irony of Joseph is that his siblings did not recognise him, in Egypt, as their brother. *They recognised him only as a stranger*, an Egyptian ruler called Zaphenath-Paneah, who wore Egyptian robes of office and whom they assumed could not even speak their language. Eventually Joseph forced them to recognise that just as a brother can be a stranger (when kept 'at a distance'), so a stranger can turn out to be a brother.

The dual meaning of the verb *n-k-r* gathers into itself the whole force and dramatic conflict of Genesis as a sustained exploration of recognition and estrangement, closeness and distance. It tells us that if only we were to listen closely to the voice of the other, we would find that beneath the skin we *are* brothers and sisters, members of the human family under the parenthood of God. When others become brothers and conflict is transformed into conciliation, we have begun the journey to society-as-a-family, and the redemptive drama can begin.

9

The Rejection of Rejection

The Lord is near to all who call on him,
to all who call on him in truth.

Psalm 145:18

The Hebrew Bible was a document meant to be *heard* rather than read. It came into being at the critical juncture between orality and literacy. When it was first written, the alphabet had only recently been invented. The world's first alphabets were semitic.[1] The word 'alphabet' itself comes, via Greek, from the first two letters of Hebrew script, *aleph-bet*. The biblical verb *likro*, which later came to mean 'to read', primarily means 'to call'. The Hebrew name for the Bible, *Mikra*, means a summons, a proclamation.[2] To this day, every Sabbath, and in a shorter form three times during the week, a section of the Pentateuch is read aloud from the handwritten Torah scroll in the synagogue. To understand the Bible you sometimes have to *listen* to it rather than read it.

There is a fundamental difference between reading and hearing in the way we process information. Reading, we can see the entire text – the sentence, the paragraph – at one time. Hearing, we cannot. We hear only one word at a time, and we do not know in advance how a sentence or paragraph will end. Some of the most powerful literary effects in the Bible occur when the opening words of a sentence lead us to expect one ending and instead we encounter another.

There is a stunning example in Genesis, and it sheds powerful light on the entire subject we have been studying: sibling rivalry. In this case, however, the conflict is not between brothers but between sisters: the two daughters of Laban, Rachel and Leah.

Jacob, in flight from Esau's anger, has travelled to the house of Laban. Arriving, he meets Laban's younger daughter Rachel and falls in love with her. Laban proposes a deal: work for me for seven years and I will give her to you in marriage (Gen. 29:18–19). Jacob does so, but on the wedding night Laban substitutes Leah for Rachel. The next morning, Jacob discovers the deception and protests, 'Why did you deceive me?' Laban replies with massive irony, 'It is not done *in our place* to give the younger before the elder' (29:26). This is a reference back to Jacob's deception of Isaac, when the younger took the blessing of the elder, Esau. Measure for measure, the deceiver has been deceived.

Laban then agrees that in return for a further seven years' labour, Jacob may marry Rachel. He does not have to wait seven years, but he must at least wait seven days until Leah's wedding celebrations have ended. The days pass. Jacob marries Rachel. We then read:

> He also [*gam*] married Rachel, and he also [*gam*] loved Rachel . . . (Gen. 29:30)

Freezing the text at that point, we are led to believe that the two sisters are equal in Jacob's eyes. That is what the repeated word *gam*, 'also', signifies. The deception has – so we must suppose at this point – a happy ending after all. Jacob has married both sisters. He loves them both. It seems that for the first time there will be no sibling rivalry. It is possible to love two women equally. The next word sends this expectation crashing to the ground:

> . . . *more* than Leah.

This is the negative counterpart of a joke. It is meant to make us cry, not laugh. The surprise, though, is unmistakable. Jacob, fleeing from one sibling rivalry, has just unintentionally created another. The sentence is deliberately ungrammatical. The words 'also' and 'more than' cannot co-exist side by side in the same sentence. Either one loves X *and also* Y, or one loves X *more than* Y. The emphasis cannot be on both. The discord is strident and arresting. Jacob does not love the two sisters equally. He may love them both, but his real passion is for Rachel. The next verse contains an even sharper discord:

God saw that Leah was hated [*senuah*] . . . (Gen. 29:31)

This is a phrase that *cannot* be understood literally. The previous verse has just said that Leah was not hated but loved. The commentators wrestled with this difficulty: they read *senuah* not as 'hated' but as 'less loved'.[3] Yet, though the text is semantically impossible, it makes psychological sense. Leah, less loved, *felt rejected*. The words 'God saw' mean that God identified with her sense of humiliation. Laban's deception had tragic human consequences. Leah weeps inwardly for the husband she acquired by her father's wiles, whose love is for someone else.

Only now, in retrospect, do we understand the significance of the Torah's first description of Leah:

Now Laban had two daughters; the name of the older was Leah, and the name of the younger was Rachel. The eyes of Leah were weak [*rakot*], but Rachel was lovely in form, and beautiful. (Gen. 29:16–17)

The word *rakot* could mean many things: beautiful,[4] weak,[5] or sensitive.[6] But the word is more significant than that. It means – as Rashi, Kimche and midrashic tradition[7] explain – 'Leah was easily moved to tears.' She was emotionally vulnerable, with none of the resilience that might have carried her through her husband's attachment to her younger sister. Thin-skinned, sensitive, easily hurt, she knew she was Jacob's lesser love, and it caused her pain. The subtlety with which this is conveyed is remarkable. The text has sketched Leah's situation and character in a few deft strokes, each of which we only notice if we are listening carefully.

The story does not end there. Over the next few verses, the Bible makes us hear Leah's pain in the names she gives her children. Her first she calls Reuben, saying, 'It is *because the Lord has seen my troubles.* Surely my husband will love me now.' The second she calls Shimon, '*Because the Lord heard that I am unloved.*' The third she calls Levi, saying, 'Now *at last my husband will become attached to me*' (Gen. 29:32–34). There is sustained anguish in these words.

We hear the same tone later when Reuben, Leah's firstborn, finds mandrakes in the field. Mandrakes were thought to have aphrodisiac properties, so he gives them to his mother hoping that this will draw his father to her. Rachel, who has been experiencing a different kind of pain, childlessness, sees the mandrakes and asks Leah for them. Leah then says, 'Wasn't it enough that you took away my husband? Will you take my son's mandrakes too?' (Gen. 30:15). The misery is palpable.

The final denouement occurs centuries later, in the days of Moses, in the book of Deuteronomy, and in a legal context:

> If a man has two wives, one loved, the other unloved [*senuah*], and both bear him sons but the firstborn is the son of the unloved one, when he wills his property to his sons, he must not give the rights of the firstborn to the son of the loved one in preference to his actual firstborn, the son of the unloved one. He must acknowledge the son of his unloved wife as the firstborn by giving him a double share of all he has. That son is the first sign of his father's strength. The right of the firstborn belongs to him. (Deut. 21:15–17)

In the Hebrew, this passage is saturated with linguistic evocations of Genesis and the rivalry between Leah and Rachel and their respective sons. The same key word, *senuah*, 'unloved', appears in both, and these are the only occurrences of the word in the Pentateuch. The phrase 'first sign of his father's strength' is the same as that used by Jacob on his deathbed, referring to Reuben,

Leah's (and his) firstborn (Gen. 49:3–4). The reference to 'double share' recalls Jacob's words to Joseph, firstborn of his beloved Rachel, 'To you I gave one portion more than to your brothers' (48:22). He does this by giving Joseph's two sons, Manasseh and Ephraim, the status of tribes in their own right (48:5). The intertextuality of the two passages is unmistakable.

So is the implication: Jacob's behaviour is *not* to become normative for his descendants. What he did then, is now forbidden.[8] *There are to be no more dramas of chosen and rejected sons, preferential treatment, favouritism, and the psycho-dynamics of sibling rivalry.* Deuteronomy brings belated closure to the narratives of Genesis. No more will the younger usurp the older.

*

This drama between Leah and Rachel encapsulates the entire extended drama of which Genesis has been a set of variations. *It all begins with love.* As we noted earlier, the religion of Abraham is supremely based on love – three loves. 'You shall love the Lord your God with all your heart, with all your soul and with all your might' (Deut. 6:5). 'You shall love your neighbour as yourself' (Lev. 19:18). And 'You shall love the stranger, for you were once strangers in a strange land' (see Lev. 19:34).

But love is not enough, and the story of Leah tells us why. Jacob loved Rachel. He loved her at first sight. There is no other love story quite like it in the Torah. Abraham and Sarah are already married by the time we first meet them. Isaac had his wife chosen for him by his father's servant. But Jacob loves. He is more emotional than the other patriarchs. That is the problem. Love unites but it also divides. It leaves the unloved, even the less loved, feeling rejected, abandoned, forsaken, alone. That is why you cannot build a society, a community or even a family on love alone.

If we look at the eleven times the word 'love', *ahavah*, is mentioned in the book of Genesis, we make an extraordinary discovery. *Every time love is mentioned, it generates conflict.* Isaac loved Esau but Rebekah loved Jacob. Jacob loved Joseph, Rachel's firstborn, more than his other sons. From this came two of the most fateful sibling rivalries in Jewish history.

Even these pale into insignificance when we reflect on the first time the word 'love' appears in the Bible, in the opening words of the trial of the binding of Isaac: 'Take now your son, your only one, the one you love . . .' (Gen. 22:2). Rashi, following Midrash, itself inspired by the obvious comparison between the binding of Isaac and the book of Job, says that Satan, the accusing angel, said to God when Abraham made a feast to celebrate the weaning of his son, 'You see, he loves his child more than you.'⁹ That, according to the Midrash, was the reason for the trial: to show that Satan's accusation was untrue.

Abrahamic monotheism is predicated on love for profound theological reasons. In the world of myth the gods were at worst hostile, at best indifferent to humankind. In contemporary atheism the universe and life exist for no reason whatsoever. We are accidents of matter, the result of blind chance and natural selection. The Hebrew Bible by contrast tells us that we are here because God created us in love. God's love is implicit in our very being.

But love is not enough. You cannot build a family, let alone a society, on love alone. For that you need justice also. Love is partial, justice is impartial. Love is particular, justice is universal. Love is for this person not that, but justice is for all. Much of the moral life is generated by this tension between love and justice. Justice without love is harsh. Love without justice is unfair, or so it will seem to the less loved. That is what the Bible is forcing us to understand when we read the words, 'And God saw that Leah was hated.'

'And God saw': recognising her humiliation, he gave her children instead – one of whom, Levi, would eventually beget Israel's three great leaders, Moses, Aaron and Miriam, as well as its future priests; another of whom, Judah, would be the ancestor of Israel's kings.

We now understand why the book of Genesis ends as it does, with the reconciliation between Joseph and his brothers. The story of Joseph brings to a climax the drama that began when Jacob married two sisters, Leah and Rachel, the second of whom he loved more than the first. What happened between the sisters then occurred between their children. The love which involves choice, favouring one over the other, is experienced as rejection by the unloved:

> Now Israel *loved* Joseph more than all his other sons . . . When his brothers saw that their father *loved* him more than any of them, they *hated* him and could not speak to him in peace. (Gen. 37:3–4)

The less loved feel hated, and therefore hate. The story of Joseph and his brothers almost takes us back to the world of Cain and Abel as the brothers plot to kill Joseph and eventually sell him as a slave. This is the end of the road that begins with sibling rivalry. *From here on there will be no more choice*, no more dramas of elder and younger sons. By the time the book of Exodus begins, the *children* of Israel are *collectively* called 'God's firstborn' (Exod. 4:22). The closing scene of Genesis in which the brothers are reconciled and live peaceably together marks *the rejection of rejection*. Henceforth, all the children of the covenantal family will be chosen. Later, at the time of the Golden Calf, when God says to Moses, 'Now leave me alone . . . that I may destroy them; and I will make you into a great nation' (Exod. 32:10), Moses reminds him of his covenant with Abraham, Isaac and Jacob. From now on, none of the people of the covenant may be unchosen.

This precisely mirrors the end of the earlier cycle of stories that began with Adam and Eve and culminated in God's covenant with Noah. God had twice chosen: Abel rather than Cain, and Noah rather than humanity as a whole. After the Flood, however, there is a decisive change:

The Lord smelled the pleasing aroma and said in his heart: 'Never again will I curse the soil because of man, for the inclination of man's heart is evil from his youth. I will never again strike down all life as I have done. As long as the earth endures, seedtime and harvest, cold and heat, summer and winter, day and night will never cease.' (Gen. 8:21–22)

A new principle enters the relationship between God and humanity. Where earlier the wickedness of the human heart had been a reason to destroy the earth, it now becomes a reason *not* to destroy it. God forgives, pre-emptively. Divine justice has given way to divine mercy. In making his covenant with Noah, *God rejects rejection.*

Love, the very emotion that forms human bonds, bringing new life into the world, is neither simple nor universally benign in its effects. If we are human we cannot help but love X differently from the way we love Y, simply because X and Y are not the same. To be sure, we might love platonically, caring for all equally. But that would no longer be *human* love, the love of husband and wife, parent and child. A world in which we loved strangers as much as friends, non-kin as deeply as kin, someone else's children as much as our own, would not be recognisably human at all – and whatever else it is, the Hebrew Bible is about the 'crooked timber of humanity'. The question it poses is: how shall we live – we who are human, who have passions, delights, desires, loves, and therefore vulnerabilities? A love that made no distinctions, that was remote, distant, undifferentiating, would simply not be love for another human being in his or her particularity.

But this has profound consequences. To love X differently from the way we love Y is to create the possibility that Y – Ishmael, Esau, Leah, Joseph's brothers – will feel rejected. If one thing is clear from the narratives we have analysed, it is that God feels the plight of the rejected. The narrative genius of Genesis is precisely that it forces us to undergo role reversal. We don't just see the world through the eyes of the chosen. We identify with Ishmael,

Esau, Leah, the people on the other side of the equation, and we cannot *but* identify with them if we listen to the text with an open heart. We feel their sense of rejection. Genesis, otherwise sparing in its prose, goes out of its way to draw us into their world, their plight, their sense of abandonment.

That is why Genesis is the story of two covenants (why two, we will explore in chapter 11): between God and humanity on the one hand, God and Jacob's children on the other. God unconditionally affirms both, the former as his 'image', the latter as his 'children'. The conclusion to which the whole of Genesis has been leading is *the rejection of rejection*.

*

Genesis, the foundational book of Abrahamic monotheism, directly addresses many of the themes we explored in Part I as lying at the roots of pathological dualism. First, it is a stunning rejection of dehumanisation, demonisation and the division of humanity into the all-good and the all-bad, the children of light versus the children of darkness. None of the central figures in these dramas is either all good or all bad. The best have their faults. The worst have their virtues. As we noted in chapter 3, Abraham and Isaac pass their wives off as their sisters. Jacob deceives his blind father. At key points in the narrative our sympathies are drawn to Ishmael and Esau. Joseph, who initially appears as a young man of overweening ambition, eventually emerges as the man who saved a whole region from starvation. Judah, the person who proposed selling Joseph as a slave, becomes the moral hero who is prepared to spend the rest of his life as a slave so that his brother Benjamin can go free. There is nothing predictable or one-dimensional about any of these characters. They are studies in moral complexity. We now understand why. Dividing the world into saints and sinners, the saved and the damned, the children of God and the children of the devil, is the first step down the road to violence in the name of God.

Note also that Genesis contains a powerful argument against the second step: seeing yourself as a victim. That is precisely what the first humans do. Adam and Eve sin, but when challenged by God, both deny responsibility. Adam says, 'The woman you put here with me – *she* gave me some fruit from the tree, and I ate' (Gen. 3:12). The woman says, 'The serpent deceived me, and I ate' (3:13). Both define themselves as victims. By the end of Genesis, however, Joseph, who really was a victim, refuses to define himself as such. He says to his brothers, 'You may have intended to harm me, but God intended it for good so that it would come about as it is today, saving many people's lives. So then, don't be afraid. I will provide for you and your children' (Gen. 50:20–21). This is an immensely significant transformation. Instead of asking, 'Who did this to me?' Joseph asks about his suffering, 'What redemptive deed has this put me in a position to perform?' He looks forward, not back. Instead of blaming others, he exercises responsibility. Joseph represents the first great biblical rejection of the culture of victimhood, the reaction that caused the first humans to lose paradise.

Finally, Genesis tells us that sibling rivalry is not a given of the human condition. For what it tells are not just four narratives of conflict between brothers. The stories themselves tell a larger story. We can see this by one simple move: looking at *the last scene in each story.* At the end of the first, Cain and Abel, Abel is dead and Cain wears the mark of a murderer. At the end of the second, Isaac and Ishmael are standing together at their father's grave. At the end of the third, Jacob and Esau meet, embrace and go their separate ways. At the end of the fourth, Joseph and his brothers work through a process of forgiveness and reconciliation. This is a highly structured literary sequence whose unmistakable message is that *sibling rivalry may be natural, but it is not inevitable.* It can be conquered: by generosity of spirit, active efforts of reconciliation, and the realisation – dramatised in Jacob's struggle with the angel at night – that mimetic desire is misconceived. There is no need to want someone else's blessing. We each have our own.

All of this prepares the way for the fifth story of siblings in the Bible, one that will gloriously transcend all the others: Moses, Aaron and Miriam, between whom there is no rivalry. To the contrary, it is Miriam who watches over the young Moses and ensures he knows who his parents and his people are. It is Aaron who acts as Moses' spokesman in Egypt, and who becomes the first priest to stand beside the greatest of the prophets. The implication is that *only when a people has overcome its internal rivalries is it ready for the journey from slavery to freedom.*

So Cain and Abel are the first word about the human condition, not the last. 'How good and pleasant it is for brothers to dwell together,' says the psalmist (Ps. 133:1), to which we might add, in the light of Genesis, 'and how rare'. Yet it is possible, and until it has been *shown* to be possible, the human story cannot continue. Genesis, the story of human relationships, is the necessary prelude to Exodus, the story of nations and political systems. Each child of Jacob – like each of the seventy nations and languages of Genesis 10 – has his own character and contribution. Each will become a tribe, and only as a confederation of tribes can Israel exist. Only as a confederation of nations can the world exist.

*

Genesis is not simply a work of history, or a cosmology. It is a subtle, multilayered philosophical treatise constructed in the narrative mode. It represents truth-as-story rather than truth-as-system, and it does so for a profoundly philosophical reason: it is about *meanings*, and meanings cannot be conveyed except through narrative – by a plot that unfolds through time, allowing us to enter the several perspectives of its dramatis personae and sense the multiple interpretations (narrative and counter-narrative) to which stories give rise. Unlike philosophical systems, which we either understand or don't, biblical narrative functions at many different levels of comprehension. Our understanding of it deepens as we grow. Biblical consciousness is *chronological,* not *logical*. Its connections are not abstract and conceptual, but real encounters of challenge and response, during which wisdom matures and relationships are honed and refined.

God, in Genesis 1, creates a world of natural order, then, beginning in Genesis 2, invites us to create a world of social order, one in which every being has its integrity in the scheme of things. None is meant to supplant or displace others. This is a high ideal, but not an impossible one. Genesis shows us how it plays out in human terms, in a series of stories about love: real love, neither romanticised nor idealised. It is not only hate that creates conflict. So too does love. Hence the dramas of Isaac and Ishmael, Jacob and Esau, Leah and Rachel, Joseph and his brothers. Time and again Genesis forces us to engage in role reversal: to see not only from the perspective of the chosen but also from that of the unchosen – to hear the tears of Hagar and Ishmael, Esau and Leah. Joseph forces his brothers to experience what they inflicted on him, for only one who knows what it feels like to be a victim can experience the change of heart (*teshuvah, metanoia, tabwa*) that prevents him from being a victimiser.

In the end, Genesis affirms the incommensurability of the human person and of different civilisations. We are all different, but we each carry in our being the trace of the one God. God cares for all he creates. In chapter 5, I argued that sibling rivalry lies at the heart of the adversarial relationship between Judaism, Christianity and Islam, leading to a tragic history of religiously motivated hatred. In these past four chapters I have shown why the idea arises, and why it is wrong. On the surface, Genesis is a series of stories in which the elder is supplanted by the younger. Beneath the surface, in a series of counter-narratives, it tells the opposite story, subverting the whole frame of mind that says, 'Either you or me. If you win, I lose. If I win, you lose.' That may be true of scarce goods like wealth or power. It is not true of divine love, which is governed by the principle of plenitude.

A tendency to think in terms of sibling rivalry is deeply rooted, genetically encoded, in the human mind. It can exist among good and religious persons. That is why it cannot be refuted, merely subverted, in the form of narratives that only reveal their full meaning to those who have undergone a long process of moral growth. It is not surprising that the interpretations I have given are missed by most readers of the text. But they exist; they have not been artificially read into the text. If so, we have just encountered the Bible's own theological refutation of the mindset that says that human beings who stand outside our community of faith are somehow less than fully human. This is God's reply to those who commit violence in his name. God does not prove his love for some by hating others. Neither, if we follow him, may we.

PART THREE

The Open Heart

10

The Stranger

I am a stranger on earth;
do not hide your commands from me.
Psalm 119:19

Jobbik, otherwise known as the Movement for a Better Hungary, is an ultra-nationalist Hungarian political party that has been described as fascist, neo-Nazi, racist and antisemitic, though it resists these labels. It has accused Jews of being part of a 'cabal of western economic interests' attempting to control the world: the libel otherwise known as the *Protocols of the Elders of Zion*. In the Hungarian parliamentary elections in April 2014 it secured over 20 per cent of the votes, making it the third largest party.

Until 2012 one of its leading members was a politician in his late twenties, Csanad Szegedi. Szegedi was a rising star in the movement, widely spoken of as its future leader. Until one day in 2012. That was the day Szegedi discovered he was a Jew.

Some of the members of the party had wanted to stop his progress, so they spent time investigating his background to see whether they could find anything that would do him damage. What they found was that his maternal grandmother was a Jewish survivor of Auschwitz. So was his maternal grandfather. Half of Szegedi's family were killed during the Holocaust.

Szegedi's opponents started spreading rumours about his Jewish ancestry on the Internet. Soon Szegedi himself discovered what was being said and decided to check whether the claims were true. They were. After Auschwitz his grandparents, once Orthodox Jews, decided to hide their identity completely. When his mother was fourteen, her father told her the secret but ordered her not to reveal it to anyone. Szegedi now knew the truth about himself.

He decided to resign from the party and find out more about Judaism. He went to a local Chabad rabbi, Slomó Köves, who at first thought he was joking. Nonetheless he arranged for Szegedi to attend classes on Judaism and to come to the synagogue. At first, Szegedi says, people were shocked. He was treated by some as 'a leper'. But he persisted. Today he attends synagogue, keeps Shabbat, has learned Hebrew, calls himself Dovid, and in 2013 underwent circumcision.

When he first admitted the truth about his Jewish ancestry, one of his friends in the Jobbik party said, 'The best thing would be if we shoot you so you can be buried as a pure Hungarian.' Another urged him to make a public apology. It was this comment, he says, that made him leave the party. 'I thought, wait a minute, I am supposed to apologise for the fact that my family was killed at Auschwitz?'

As the realisation that he was a Jew began to change his life, it also transformed his understanding of the world. Today, he says, his focus as a politician is to defend human rights for everyone. 'I am aware of my responsibility and I know I will have to make it right in the future.'

Szegedi is the antisemite who discovered he was a Jew.

*

Szegedi's story is not just a curiosity. It takes us to the heart of darkness in the human condition, and to why the biblical narratives we have been studying are what they are.

We have, collectively, a propensity to violence. The historian Will Durant once estimated that there have only been twenty-nine years since history began in which there were no wars. In 1989, as the Berlin Wall fell, the Soviet Union collapsed and the Cold War came to an end, several serious analysts, most famously Francis Fukuyama, argued that we had reached the 'end of history' in the sense of serious national or ideological wars. The market economy and liberal democracy had triumphed and would eventually spread throughout the world. A quarter-century later the West finds itself facing a rising tide of terror. Several countries in the Middle East have descended into chaos. Religious extremism, profoundly hostile to the values of the West, is growing.

Our argument has been that what is best in us and what is worst both come from the same source: our tendency to form ourselves into groups, to think highly of our own and negatively of others. Morality, in Jonathan Haidt's phrase, binds and blinds.[1] It binds us to others in a bond of reciprocal altruism. But it also blinds us to the humanity of those who stand outside that bond. It turns the 'I' of self-interest into the 'We' of the common good. But the very act of creating an 'Us' simultaneously creates a 'Them', the people not like us. Even the most universalistic of religions, founded on principles of love and compassion, have been capable of seeing those outside the faith as Satan, the infidel, the antichrist, the children of darkness, the unredeemed. They have committed unspeakable acts of brutality in the name of God.

There are times when only one thing has the power to defeat dualism and the division of the world into two, namely role reversal. *To be cured of potential violence towards the Other, I must be able to imagine myself as the Other.* The Hutu in Rwanda has to experience what it is like to be a Tutsi. The Serb has to imagine himself a Croat or a Muslim. The antisemite has to discover he is a Jew.

This is something moral philosophy has failed adequately to confront. Since Plato, thinkers have explored the many factors that make us moral: knowledge, habit, virtue, empathy, sympathy, rationality, intuition. Yet we saw how all these things failed in Germany in the 1930s, and not only among the masses but even among some of the greatest minds of the day. That is the power of dualism to subvert and anaesthetise the moral sense. If we divide the world into the children of light and the children of darkness, we are capable of dehumanising and demonising the Other, seeing ourselves as a victim and committing altruistic evil. Dualism is alive and well in parts of the world today, it has a religious source, or at least speaks a religious language, and it is leading to terror, brutality, civil war and chaos on an ever-widening scale.

The Hebrew Bible, in the narratives we studied, was confronting this fact at its roots, forcing us to enter into the humanness of the Other: Ishmael, Hagar, Esau, Joseph and his brothers, Leah and her children. We know that Sarah and Isaac are part of the covenant. Hagar and Ishmael are not. But our sympathies are unmistakably drawn to them in some of the most powerful scenes of pathos in the Bible, Hagar cast out into the desert, the young Ishmael dying of heat and thirst.

We saw the same with Isaac and Esau in the great scene where Jacob takes the blessing, deceiving his blind father. We saw how Joseph and his brothers had to overcome their mutual estrangement, and we saw how Leah cried out for love and was heard by God. These are extraordinary stories because they force us to enter into the mindset of the characters who are not chosen, who seem to be left out – displaced. They do for us what discovering he was a Jew did for Szegedi. They force us into an imaginative act of role reversal. They show us that humanity, light and virtue are not confined to our side. They exist on the other side also. They humanise the Other.

And they defeat dualism. What readers of the Bible often find so disconcerting is that the heroes have faults and the villains have virtues. There are times when Esau seems to act more morally than Jacob. Joseph tells tales about his brothers and upsets the rest of the family by talking about his dreams. Judah, who emerges at the end as a hero, at the beginning was the man who proposed selling Joseph as a slave. Though it is a much larger subject and beyond the scope of this book, this is a general feature of biblical narrative. It is not confined to Genesis.

Some readers who are unsympathetic to Judaism take this as a sign that the Hebrew Bible is morally ambivalent. Precisely the reverse is the case. It is engaging with morality at its most fundamental level. It is forcing us to see that the Other, the outsider, the one who stands outside our circle of salvation, is also human – that to be human is to be a mix of good and bad – and to wrestle with that fact as Jacob wrestled with the angel. Only when we understand this do we become immune to dualism and religiously or ideologically motivated hate.

*

We saw that morality begins with kin, those who are genetically related to me. It extends to the group on the basis of reciprocal altruism, Tit-for-Tat, and the trust we have in others on the basis of repeated interaction. Eventually it extends to the city and the nation, originally on the basis of religion. From an evolutionary point of view, religion made possible the single greatest distinction between us and other social animals. It solved the problem of trust on a macro-scale by moving beyond Tit-for-Tat to the extended community of faith. The highest expression of this, central to the Judeo-Christian ethic, is the command, 'You shall love your neighbour as yourself.'

The Hebrew Bible, though, goes significantly further. It is not difficult to love your neighbour as yourself because in many respects your neighbour is like yourself. He or she belongs to the same nation, the same culture, the same economy, the same political dispensation, the same fate of peace or war. We are part of the same community of fate, and we participate in the same common good. What is difficult is *loving the stranger*.

We are genetically disposed to defensive-aggressive conduct when faced with someone not like us, outside the group, not bound by its code of mutual identity and reciprocity. The stranger is always potentially a threat. *What* he or she threatens depends on time and place: sometimes our lives, at others our territory or livelihoods, perhaps, in the case of immigrants and asylum seekers, no more than our sense of the familiar, the faces, voices and smells we recognise and that make us feel at home.

That is what makes classic theories of morality inadequate. They fail to distinguish between kin and non-kin, brother and other, neighbour and stranger. They account for altruistic behaviour *within* the group. They tell us: treat the alike, alike. What they do not fully confront is the problem of altruistic behaviour *beyond* the group. Why *should* I behave well to someone not like me? Because he or she is human, because we can empathise, because as a matter of principle we treat people as ends not means. All these things are true and sound and noble. But you will not feel them if you decide that the Other is less than human, significantly different, an evil force, a threat. That is why rational human beings who love their people can nonetheless commit crimes against humanity for the sake of their people. It is why people of God have sometimes conquered, converted and burned people at the stake, for the greater glory of God and the salvation of their victims' souls.

'Religion' comes from the Latin *ligare*, meaning to *join* or *bind*. Religion binds people within the group – Christian to Christian, Muslim to Muslim, Jew to Jew. More specifically, since some of the most bitter conflicts take place within a faith, it bonds members of the same sect, church or denomination. It invests group solidarity with sanctity. What it does *not* do is provide people with a reason to be gracious to, or even tolerant of, those outside the group.

To be sure, the great monotheisms believe in humanity as such, but often with one significant qualification: *you must share our faith to be fully human.* If not, we must at least subjugate you, treat you as *dhimmi*, regard you as pariahs. Now we see why. For a Jew, Christian or Muslim to make space for the Other, he or she would have to undergo the most profound and disorienting role reversal. A Christian would have to imagine what it would have been like to be a French or German Jew at the time of the Crusades. A Muslim would have to imagine what it would have been like to be a Jew in Baghdad in the eighth century, forced to bear a yellow badge of shame, walk the street with downcast eyes, and stand and be silent in the presence of a Muslim. A Jew would have to imagine what it would be like to be a Christian or Muslim facing the threat of death because of their faith in Syria or Iraq today.

A humanitarian as opposed to a group ethic requires the most difficult of all imaginative exercises: role reversal – putting yourself in the place of those you despise, or pity, or simply do not understand. Not only do most religions not do this. They make it almost impossible to do so.[2] For those who think in secular terms, there is more than one country, nation, language, culture or code of conduct. It is not impossible for an Englishman to imagine what it would be like to be French or Italian or African or Indian. But for those who are monotheistically religious, there is usually only one way to be holy, or true to God, or saved.

Empathy with the other *as the Other* is ruled out *ab initio*. It is hard to identify with one whom you believe to be fundamentally in error, except with a view to converting him or her. Empathy across boundaries can sometimes threaten religion at its roots, because one of the sacred tasks of religion is boundary maintenance. Monotheism is not relativism. That is why, historically, the great monotheisms have not been in the vanguard of tolerance. Even John Locke, father of the doctrine of toleration, would not extend citizenship to Catholics or atheists.

Only against this background can we appreciate the extreme radicalism of the Genesis narratives. They are telling us – not by way of abstract theory, but by using the full resources of narrative to engage our imaginative identification – that the one *outside* the covenant, Hagar, Ishmael, Esau, is also human, also loved, also blessed by God.

All this is a prelude to the great historical drama about to be enacted when the entire covenantal family experiences exile and enslavement in Egypt. It will be there that every member of the nation will undergo an act of moral education that, if remembered through time, will transform their view of humanity and morality.

> Do not wrong or oppress the stranger, for *you yourselves were once strangers* in the land of Egypt. (Exod. 22:21)

> Do not oppress a stranger, for *you know what it feels like* to be a stranger, for you yourselves were once strangers in the land of Egypt. (Exod. 23:9)

Note that these commands are given shortly after the Exodus. Implicit in them is the radical idea that care for the stranger is why the Israelites had to experience exile and slavery before they could enter the Promised Land and build their own society and state. You will not succeed in caring for the stranger, implies God, until you yourselves know in your very bones and sinews what it feels like to be a stranger. And lest you forget, I have already commanded you to remind yourselves and your children of the taste of affliction and bitterness every year on Pesach. Those who forget what it feels like to be a stranger eventually come to oppress strangers, and if the children of Abraham oppress strangers, why did I make them my covenantal partners?

Note also how the Hebrew Bible speaks not primarily of knowledge, reason or emotion, but of *memory*. 'Remember that you were slaves in Egypt.' The imperative of memory echoes like a leitmotif throughout biblical prose: the verb *zakhor*, 'remember', appears no less than 169 times.[3] Memory in this sense *is* role reversal: do not harm the stranger because you were once where he is now. See the world from his perspective because it is where your ancestors stood, and you have never ceased to recall and re-enact their story. Biblical ethics is a prolonged tutorial in role reversal.

*

There is a striking literary feature of the Hebrew Bible as a whole, namely its use of what Julia Kristeva called *intertextuality*, the way in which one text may be the 'absorption and transformation of another'. Intertextuality – what Michael Fishbane calls 'inner-biblical exegesis'[4] – is part of the compositional structure of the Bible. 'The words of the Torah are poor in one place, rich in another,'[5] said the sages, meaning that the full significance of a word or phrase is only grasped within the totality of the whole. The meaning of a word *here* may lie in that word *there*, far separated in topic and time.

The first time we encounter the phrase 'stranger and temporary resident' (*ger ve-toshav*) is in Genesis 23. Sarah has just died, and Abraham must bury her. It is an ironic situation. Many times he had been promised the land but now, when he needed only a burial plot for his wife, he had none, nor, as a nomad and outsider, did he have any presumptive right to acquire one. Abraham enters into negotiation with the Hittites in Hebron, beginning with these words:

I am a *stranger and a temporary resident* among you. (Gen. 23:4)

This is no mere formulaic utterance. Abraham is acknowledging his legal lack of standing. As a stranger and temporary resident, he has no entitlement to own land. He depends on the goodwill of the Hittites even to begin the conversation with the cave's owner, Ephron.

This sets up for us, the readers, a cognitive dissonance that can be resolved only one way: we assume that the text represents Israel's prehistory. Genesis is about the promise, not the fulfilment. One day, this will change. Israel will become a nation with its own land. Abraham's children will have a home. Time passes. Israel goes into exile. It is redeemed from slavery. Moses leads the people out of Egypt on their way to the land. There, we cannot but expect, the people will find a home. At last, they will own the land. They will no longer be as Abraham was. Then, in one of the great paradigm-shifting moments of the Bible, the twenty-fifth chapter of Leviticus turns this expectation on its head:

> The land shall not be sold in perpetuity, for the land is mine; you are *strangers and temporary residents* with me. (Lev. 25:23)

The fate of Abraham's family, we now discover, will be not temporary but permanent – permanently temporary. They will know no certainty, have no fixed and unconditional home, even in the land of promise. Abraham had been told, in a dark vision of exile, that his offspring would be 'a stranger in a land not theirs'. That, we thought, meant Egypt. It now turns out to mean Israel as well. This is the central, haunting irony of the Pentateuch.

Again, time passes. Israel enters the land. It begins as an amphictyony, a loose federation of tribes, led at times of emergency by charismatic figures known as judges. Then, in the days of Samuel, it becomes a kingdom. A generation later, during the reign of David, the monarchy becomes hereditary (an 'everlasting covenant') and Israel has a capital city, Jerusalem. The final building block is almost in place: the Temple. For this, David makes plans, but is told that the work will only be completed by his son. At this moment, the high point of Israel's history, David gathers the people and utters a prayer:

> Praise be to you, O Lord, God of our father Israel, from everlasting to everlasting . . .
>
> We are *strangers and temporary residents* in your sight, as were all our forefathers. Our days on earth are like a shadow, without hope. O Lord our God, as for all this abundance that we have provided for building you a Temple for your Holy Name, it comes from your hand, and all of it belongs to you. (1 Chr. 29:10–16)

Even at their greatest moment, the Israelites know that they are strangers in a land not their own. In this extraordinary intertextual arch, from Abraham through Moses to David, from Israel's earliest prehistory to its summit as a sovereign power, we hear the same unchanging message: the people of the covenant will be strangers at home, so that they are able to make strangers feel at home. Only thus can they defeat the most powerful of all drives to evil: the sense of being threatened by the Other, the one not like me.

*

Abraham and Moses, the key figures of the Pentateuch, know exactly what it is to be a stranger. Abraham's journey begins with the command to 'leave your land, your birthplace and your father's house' (Gen. 12:1) – everywhere he is *not* a stranger. Moses, leader of the Israelites, does not grow up with the Israelites. He is thus doubly a stranger, to the Egyptians because he is an Israelite, to the Israelites because he looks like an Egyptian. He flees to Midian – yet another estrangement, marries Zipporah, daughter of a Midianite priest, and has a child. He gives his son a poignant name, Gershom, meaning 'I was a stranger in a strange land' (Exod. 2:22).

The people charged with carrying this message, the Israelites, have a specific function to play in the divine economy. They are to be the embodiment of strangeness. How Israel behaves in relation to strangers, and how nations behave towards Israel, the strange nation, will be the ongoing litmus tests of the moral acceptability of a civilisation.

Empathy, sympathy, knowledge and rationality are usually enough to let us live at peace with others. But not in hard times. Serbs, Croats and Muslims lived peaceably together in Bosnia for years. So did Hutus and Tutsis in Rwanda. The problem arises at times of change and disruption when people are anxious and afraid. That is why exceptional defences are necessary, which is why the Bible speaks of memory and history – things that go to the very heart of our identity. We have to remember that we were once on the other side of the equation. We were once strangers: the oppressed, the victims. Remembering the Jewish past forces us to undergo role reversal. In the midst of freedom we have to remind ourselves of what it feels like to be a slave.

What happened to Csanad, now Dovid, Szegedi was exactly that: role reversal. He was a hater who discovered that he belonged among the hated. What cured him of antisemitism was his role-reversing discovery that he was a Jew. That, for him, was a life-changing revelation. The Hebrew Bible tells us that the experience of the Israelites in Egypt was meant to be life-changing as well. Having lived and suffered as strangers, they became the people commanded to care for strangers.

The best way of curing antisemitism is to get people to experience what it feels like to be a Jew. The best way of curing hostility to strangers is to remember that we too, from someone else's perspective, are strangers. Memory and role reversal are the most powerful resources we have to cure the darkness that can sometimes occlude the human soul.

I I

The Universality of Justice, the Particularity of Love

In the emerging world of ethnic conflict and civilizational clash, Western belief in the universality of Western culture suffers three problems: it is false; it is immoral; and it is dangerous . . . Imperialism is the necessary logical consequence of universalism.
Samuel Huntington, The Clash of Civilizations and the Remaking of World Order[1]

Behind this whole analysis is the obvious question. Why does God need to choose in the first place? Why this drama of chosen and unchosen sons? Why Isaac, not Ishmael? Why Jacob, not Esau? Why Abraham, not everyone? Why Israel and not all humankind?

This phenomenon has aroused more anger and vituperation, perplexity and misunderstanding than any other in the history of Western spirituality. *Why does God choose?* Judaism seems caught midway between the particularities of the pagan world – each nation with its own gods – and the universalities of Christianity and Islam: one God, one truth, one way, one path to salvation, one gateway to heaven.

These two other Abrahamic monotheisms borrowed much from Judaism – its belief in one God and its sacred scriptures in the case of Christianity, its stories and prophets in the case of Islam – yet they did not borrow Judaism's most singular feature: its *distinction between the universality of God as Creator and Sovereign of the universe, and the particularity of the covenant, first with Abraham, then with Moses and the Israelites.* It is easy to see why. If God is the God of all humanity, logic would seem to dictate that the way of serving him should be the same for all humanity.

What, though, if *a fundamental concern of the Hebrew Bible were precisely violence in the name of God?* What if the Bible is confronting this directly? What if this should guide our reading of the text? That the Bible is preoccupied by violence is evident at the outset. The first recorded act of worship, the offerings brought by Cain and Abel, led directly to the first murder. Thus the connection between religion and violence is struck at the start. The reason the Bible gives for the Flood is that 'the earth was corrupt before God, *the earth was filled with violence*' (Gen. 6:11). Violence is not a marginal theme in Genesis. It is central. It makes God 'regret that he made man on earth' (Gen. 6:6).

We saw in chapter 2 *why* humans are violent. It has to do with the fact that we are social animals. We form groups. We are tribal beings. We are divided into different nations, languages, cultures and codes, and these are the bases of identity. There is no such thing as humanity in the abstract, just as there is no such thing as language or literature or love in the abstract. Identity is inescapably plural. That is why it leads to violence. It divides the world into Us and Them. This is the source of war. At extreme times like now it leads to pathological dualism, turning human beings into barbarians, sometimes in the name of God.

We also saw in chapter 2 that there have been three major attempts in history to escape from identity but that none succeeded. Christianity and Islam both said, in effect: one God, therefore one ultimate identity. That is why they clashed in the Middle Ages, and it is why they clash today in the Middle East, Africa and parts of Asia. The principle of one God, one truth, one way does not make for peace in a world in which other people have other ways. Perhaps one day we will all see the world, ourselves and God the same way. That is the prophetic vision. But not now, not yet.

The second great attempt, as we saw, was the Enlightenment, the secular European substitute for Christianity, based on the universality not of God but of reason. Science and philosophy would, people thought, succeed where religion and revelation had failed. They would unite humankind in what Kant called 'perpetual peace'. The reaction to this, a century later, was the emergence of nationalism, racism and communism, two world wars, the Holocaust and the Gulag. It was the return of the repressed.

The third attempt – by the West today – has been to dethrone the group in favour of the individual. The result has been the atomisation of society, the collapse of the traditional family, the erosion of community and the loss of national identity, leading to the counter-reaction of religious extremism among those who still seek identity and community. Try as the West may, the tribes keep coming back, angrier each time.

The argument of this chapter is that the Bible addresses this issue directly and with great originality. It does so in Genesis 6–11, by way of two famous stories: the Flood and the Tower of Babel.

*

The Bible is explicit about the failings of the generation of the Flood. The people were wicked, violent, and 'every inclination of the thoughts of their heart was only evil all the time' (Gen. 6:5). This is the language of systemic moral failure.

The mood at the beginning of the story of Babel seems, by contrast, almost idyllic. 'The entire earth had one language and a common speech' (11:1). Unity seems to prevail. The builders are intent on construction, not destruction. It is far from clear what their sin was. Yet from the Bible's point of view Babel represents another serious wrong turn, because immediately thereafter God summons Abraham to begin an entirely new chapter in the religious story of humankind.

In fact, the stories of the Flood and Babel are precisely matched accounts of the two great alternatives: identity without universality and universality without identity. The best account of the Flood, though he does not refer to it explicitly, was given by the man who laid the foundations of modern politics, Thomas Hobbes, in his classic *Leviathan* (1651). Before there were political institutions, said Hobbes, human beings were in a 'state of nature'. They were individuals or small groups. Lacking a stable ruler, an effective government and enforceable laws, people were in a state of permanent and violent chaos – 'a war of every man against every man' – as they competed for scarce resources. There was 'continual fear, and danger of violent death'. That is precisely the Bible's description of life before the Flood. *When there is no overarching rule of law, the world is filled with violence.*

The story of Babel explores the opposite reality. It has usually been misunderstood. The conventional reading is that it is an etiological tale explaining how humankind, which originally had 'one language and a common speech', came to be divided into many languages. This reading is plausible but wrong. The reason is that the previous chapter, Genesis 10, has *already* described the division of humanity into seventy nations, 'each with its own language' (Gen. 10:5). The only way the conventional reading makes sense is if Genesis 10 and 11 are not in the correct chronological sequence.[2] There is, though, no reason to suppose this at all.

To the contrary, the unity of language at the beginning of chapter 11 was not natural but imposed. It is describing the practice of the world's first empires. We have historical evidence dating back to the neo-Assyrians that conquerors imposed their own language on the peoples they defeated. One inscription of the time records that Ashurbanipal II 'made the totality of all peoples *speak one speech*'. A cylinder inscription of Sargon II says, 'Populations of the four quarters of the world with strange tongues and incompatible speech . . . whom I had taken as booty at the command of Ashur my lord by the might of my sceptre, *I caused to accept a single voice*.'[3] The neo-Assyrians asserted their supremacy by insisting that their language was the only one to be used by the nations and populations they had defeated. Babel is a critique of imperialism.

There is even a subtle hint of this in the parallelism of language between the builders of Babel and the Pharaoh who enslaved the Israelites. In Babel they said, 'Come, [*hava*] let us build ourselves a city and a tower . . . lest [*pen*] we be scattered over the face of the earth' (Gen. 11:4). In Egypt Pharaoh said, 'Come, [*hava*] let us deal wisely with them, lest [*pen*] they increase . . .' (Exod. 1:10). These are the only places in the entire Hebrew Bible where the locution 'Come, let us . . . lest' occurs. The connection is too pronounced to be accidental. Babel, like Egypt, represents an empire that subjugates entire populations at the cost of their distinct identities and liberties. *If the Flood is about freedom without order, Babel and Egypt are about order without freedom.*

The story the Bible is telling is this: Genesis 10 describes the division of humanity into seventy nations and seventy languages. Genesis 11 tells of how one imperial power conquered smaller nations, imposing its language and culture on them, thus directly contravening God's wish that humans should respect the integrity of each nation and each individual. When at the end of the Babel story God 'confuses the language' of the builders, he is not creating a new state of affairs but restoring the old.

Interpreted thus, the stories of the Flood and the Tower of Babel are not just historical narratives. Together they constitute a philosophical statement about identity and violence. The Flood is what happens when there are Us and Them and no overarching law to keep the peace. The result is anarchy and violence. Babel is what happens when people attempt to impose a universal order, forcing Them to become Us. The result is imperialism and the loss of liberty. Recall Samuel Huntington's words at the heading of this chapter: 'Western belief in the universality of Western culture suffers three problems: it is false; it is immoral; and it is dangerous . . . Imperialism is the necessary logical consequence of universalism.' *When a single culture is imposed on all, suppressing the diversity of languages and traditions, this is an assault on our God-given differences.* As the Qur'an (49:13) puts it, 'O mankind! We created you from a single (pair) of a male and a female, and made you into nations and tribes, that ye may know each other (not that ye may despise each other).'

So the Flood and the Tower of Babel between them define the fundamental human dilemma. We are different. We are tribal. And tribes clash. The result is the violence that, in the Flood, almost destroyed humankind. But eliminate difference by imposing a single culture, religious or secular, on all, and the result is tyranny and oppression. The Hebrew Bible is a unique attempt to find a way out of the dilemma by showing how the unity of God can co-exist with the diversity of humankind.

*

Diversity is what gives colour and texture to our life on earth. Art, architecture, music, stories, celebrations, food, drink, dance: all of these are particular. None of them is an abstract universal. The late Sidney Morganbesser was a philosophy professor at Columbia University with a wonderful sense of humour. (Shortly before dying, he asked another philosopher, 'Why is God making me suffer so much? – Just because I don't believe in him?') He once took his students to a restaurant and ordered soup. 'Which soup,' asked the waiter, 'chicken, carrot or borsht?' 'None of those,' he replied, 'just soup.' The waiter, not being a philosopher, gave up. Morganbesser's point is that you can't drink soup in the abstract, you can't speak a language that is universal, and you can't have an identity that says, 'I'm just a human being.' Some ancient Greeks thought that, but that was because they did not regard non-Greeks as fully human. Identity is plural. That constitutes the inescapable diversity of humankind.

How then do we avoid the violence that comes when different groups meet and clash? The answer proposed by the Bible is that something transcends our differences. That something is God, and he has set his image on each of us. That is why every life is sacred and each life is like a universe. The unity of God asks us to respect the stranger, the outsider, the alien, because even though he or she is not in our image – their ethnicity, faith or culture is not ours – nonetheless they are in God's image.

So God is universal. But our relationship with him is particular. The Hebrew Bible expresses this in the two primary words by which it refers to God: *Elokim* (E) and *Hashem* (called by Bible scholars J). *Elokim* is God in his universality. In Genesis, *Elokim* speaks to Abimelech, king of Gerar (Gen. 20:3). Joseph, declining the advances of Potiphar's wife, says, 'Should I sin against *Elokim*?' (39:9). Pharaoh, appointing Joseph, says, 'Can we find anyone like this man, one in whom is the spirit of *Elokim*?' (41:38). Morality in general is described as 'fear of *Elokim*' (20:11). *Elokim* is a purely universal term that applies to people's relationship with God, whether they are inside or outside the covenant with Abraham.

Hashem, by contrast, is particular. It is what God is called in the context of the Abrahamic and later Mosaic covenant. It is a proper name, not a generic noun. It is the language of intimacy and relationship. When the Bible wants to describe what Martin Buber called an I–Thou relationship, it uses the word *Hashem*.

That is why Genesis describes *two* covenants, the first with Noah and all humankind, the second with Abraham and his children, who are not all humankind, just one particular people within it. The covenant with Noah (Gen. 9) uses the word *Elokim* throughout, while the covenant with Abraham uses the word *Hashem* (15:18; 17:1–2). The Noah covenant expresses the unity of God and the shared dignity and responsibility of humankind. The Abrahamic covenant expresses the particularity of our relationship with God, which has to do with our specific identity, history, language and literature. The result is that in the Bible there is both a *morality* that applies to everyone, insider and outsider alike, and an *ethic*, that is, a specific code of conduct that frames relationships within the group. To use the language of contemporary philosophy, morality is thin (abstract, general) while ethics is thick (full of local texture and specificity).

The morality that applies to everyone, according to the

Hebrew Bible, is justice, fairness and the avoidance of causing harm. That was the first thing Abraham was to teach his children: 'to keep the way of the Lord by doing what is right and just'. Justice, fairness and the avoidance of harm are what we owe everyone, Jew and Gentile, believer and atheist, friend and stranger, fellow countryman and foreigner.

The ethic that applies *within* the covenantal community involves thicker concepts such as sanctity, reverence, loyalty and respect. It is an ethic of the holy, not just the good. It is also an ethic of what the French revolutionaries called fraternity. The Bible often says things like, 'If your brother is destitute . . .' It applies the language of kin to the group. The Abrahamic covenant is not just a kinship group. It is not a matter of biological descent only. There is conversion. Ruth, heroine of the book that bears her name, was not ethnically Jewish. She was a Moabite. But she became part of the covenant community and great-grandmother of David, Israel's greatest king. So when the Bible uses the language of family it does so metaphorically. But it is a strong metaphor. Jews feel responsible for one another as if they were a single extended family.

So the Hebrew Bible combines the two fundamentally different elements of the moral/ethical life. There is justice, and there is love. Justice is universal. Love is particular. Justice must be detached, impartial, applied equally to all. Love plays no part in it. If I decide in favour of the plaintiff because he is a family member or a friend, that is not justice but the perversion of justice. Love, on the other hand, is utterly particular. Read the wonderful biblical duet The Song of Songs, and you will hear how lover and beloved talk endlessly about what they find beautiful in the other: hair, neck, forehead, feet. There is nothing universal here at all. It is about what Wallace Stevens called 'the particulars of rapture'. It follows that *Elokim*, God as universal, is God-as-justice. *Hashem*, God as particular, is God-as-love.

*

We can now understand why, after Babel and the attempt to impose by force a single language on a diverse population, God chooses Abraham and tells him to leave home and travel to a place where he will be a stranger and outsider: different. Noah and his covenant represent universality and justice. Abraham and his descendants represent particularity and love.

The Noah covenant is the Bible's universal code, the basic infrastructure of a just social order. The Noahide laws, as understood by Judaism's sages, set out the broad parameters of a decent society: respect for God, human life, the family, property, animal welfare and the rule of law.[4] These principles are general, not specific: thin, not thick. They apply to everyone in virtue of the fact that they are in the image of God, therefore worthy of dignity and respect. They are universal rules of what today we would call responsibilities and rights.

But they apply to what we have in common, not what makes us different. So the Bible moves on from the universal to the particular – the narrative of Abraham and Sarah and the children of Israel as they journey through time and space to the Promised Land. This is a story of what it is to live closely and continuously under the sovereignty and tutelage of God. It is a story not of justice only, but also and essentially of love.

There is no implication that Abraham's or the Israelites' is the only story. To the contrary, as Amos 9:7 says: 'Are not you Israelites the same to me as the Cushites? – declares the Lord – Did I not bring Israel up from Egypt, the Philistines from Caphtor, and the Arameans from Kir?' God is active in the history of other nations. He sends a prophet, Jonah, to Israel's enemy, Assyria, to persuade them to repent and be saved from catastrophe. Isaiah even foresees a day when God will do for Israel's other great enemy, Egypt, what he did for the Israelites against Egypt itself – rescue them from oppression:

In that day there will be an altar to the Lord in the heart of Egypt . . . When they cry out to the Lord because of their oppressors, he will send them a savior and mighty one, and he will rescue them. So the Lord will make Himself known to the Egyptians . . . In that day there will be an altar in the midst of the land of Egypt to Assyria. The Assyrians will go to Egypt and the Egyptians to Assyria. The Egyptians and Assyrians will worship together. In that day Israel will be the third, along with Egypt and Assyria, a blessing on the earth. The Lord of hosts will bless them, saying, 'Blessed be Egypt my people, Assyria the work of my hands, and Israel my inheritance.' (Isa. 19:19–25)

Nor is there any intimation in the Bible that Abraham's family have a monopoly of virtue. One of the heroines of the Exodus, without whom there would have been no Moses, was Pharaoh's daughter. Rahab, who shelters Joshua's spies, is a prostitute from Jericho (Josh. 2). Jael, the heroine who saves Israel from Sisera, is a Kenite (Judg. 4). Uriah, whose faithfulness to David contrasts so sharply with David's faithlessness to him, is a Hittite (2 Sam. 11). Job, the Bible's most conspicuous example of a wholly righteous man, is not an Israelite.

Moses repeatedly criticises the Israelites, telling them, 'It is not because of your righteousness or the uprightness of your heart that you are going to take possession of the land' (Deut. 9:5). This note is sustained to the end of the prophetic age. Malachi, last of the prophets, says, 'From the rising of the sun to its setting, my name is great among the nations . . . but you profane it' (Mal. 1:11–12).

This is a point of immense consequence. *A chosen people is the opposite of a master race*, first, because it is not a race but a covenant; second, because it exists to serve God, not to master others.[5] A master race worships itself; a chosen people worships something beyond itself. A master race values power; a chosen people cares for the powerless. A master race believes it has rights; a chosen people knows only that it has responsibilities. The key virtues of a master race are pride, honour and fame. The key virtue of a chosen people is humility. A master race produces monumental buildings, triumphal inscriptions and a literature of self-congratulation. Israel, to a degree unique in history, produced a literature of almost uninterrupted self-criticism.

Why then Isaac, not Ishmael? Why Jacob, not Esau? Because Ishmael and Esau are strong, resourceful people who survive by their own skill and dexterity. The people of the covenant are to be witnesses *in* themselves to something *beyond* themselves. Isaac and Jacob are not strong. They are favoured by their mothers, not their fathers. They are the younger, not the elder. The patriarchs are given two blessings by God: they will have many children and a land. Yet Sarah, Rebekah and Rachel are all infertile. The patriarchs never acquire the land. Abraham has to beg for permission to buy a cave in which to bury his wife. Isaac is threatened by the local population when he reopens his father's wells. Jacob has to pay a hundred pieces of silver to buy land on which to pitch his tent.

Moses, the man of God's word, is the one who says, 'I am not a man of words . . . I am slow of speech and tongue' (Exod. 4:10). Israel was to be the people whose strength is not its own, as Moses was the man whose words were not his own. It was to become the people whose existence ran contrary to nature. It was small. Its land, a strategic location between empires, would always be vulnerable to conquest. Unlike the Nile delta or the Tigris-Euphrates valley, it had no natural water supply and would be constantly dependent on rain. Its people would find themselves looking up to the sky rather than down to the earth. It preserved in its collective memory no sense of being at home as of right ('You are merely strangers and temporary residents with me', Lev. 25:23). The children of Israel would always be dependent on forces beyond themselves. A chosen people is not a master race but its opposite: a servant community. That is why Jewry has always been attacked by – because its existence is an affront to – those who see themselves as a master race, an imperial power, or sole guardians of God's truth.

*

199

We now understand the powerful idea implicit in the structuring of the Genesis narrative. It begins with universal archetypes – Adam, Eve, Cain, Abel, the Flood, the covenant with Noah and the critique of Babel – and only then turns to the particularity of the Abrahamic covenant to tell us that *our common humanity precedes our religious differences*. Any religion that dehumanises others merely because their faith is different has misunderstood the God of Abraham.

Jews became the test-case of this truth. They were different: monotheists in a pagan age, then non-Christians in a Christian Europe. Today they are the most conspicuous non-Muslims in an Islamic Middle East. The fate of Jewry through the ages has been the clearest indicator of whether a culture, faith or empire has been willing to accord dignity or rights to the one-who-is-not-like-them. The story that tells of how God bestowed his love on the weak, the few, the vulnerable and the different is what makes the Hebrew Bible the great narrative of hope in Western civilisation.

The love of which the prophets spoke, of God for Israel, that fractious, sometimes disobedient people, is love for those who are different because of their difference, not for those who are the same because of their sameness. *Love is particular*. That is why, having given humankind, in the Noahide covenant, the general rules of a moral society, God turns to Abraham and commands him and his descendants to be a living example of what it is to love and be loved by God.

There is no single, simple system that will honour both our commonalities and our differences. Tribalism – identity without universality – leads to violence. Imperialism – universality without identity – leads to the loss of freedom and the suppression of the very diversity that makes us human. That is why the Bible sets out two covenants, not one: one that honours our common humanity, the other that sanctifies diversity and the particularity of love. *And the universal comes first.* You cannot love God without first honouring the universal dignity of humanity as the image and likeness of the universal God.

Note also that the phrase 'image of God', as it appears in the Bible, constitutes a paradox, almost a contradiction. It is axiomatic to the Bible that God *has no image*. To suggest otherwise – to make or worship an image of God – is the paradigm case of idolatry. When Moses asks God who he is, his reply is: 'I will be what I will be' (Exod. 3:14). God transcends categorisation. Were he to have an image, he would be like this, not that; here, not there; in this colour, creed or code, not that. Judaism's sages fully understood the implication:

> For this reason man was created alone, to teach that whoever destroys a single life is as if he destroyed a complete universe . . . and for the sake of peace among humanity, so that no one could say to another, 'My father is greater than yours' . . . and to proclaim the greatness of the Holy One, blessed be He, for when a human being makes many coins from one mould, they are all the same, but the supreme King of kings makes every human being in the same image, yet all are different.[6]

As God resists categorisation, so does humankind.

The Bible has a second surprise for us. The same phrase reappears, eight chapters later, after the Flood as part of God's covenant with Noah:

> Whoever sheds the blood of man,
> by man shall his blood be shed;
> for in the image of God
> has God made man. (Gen. 9:6)

This sounds like a restatement of Genesis 1. In fact, though, it is the opposite. Genesis 1 tells us that *we* are in God's image. Genesis 9 tells us that the *other person* is in God's image. Genesis 1 speaks of the pre-eminence of humankind ('Fill the earth and master it'). Genesis 9 declares the prohibition against murder. Between the two lies tragedy. Granted mastery over nature, human beings used that power to attempt mastery over other human beings, and the result – from Cain to the Flood – was violence and murder. It still is. That is why Genesis 9 is *not a repetition but a reversal* of Genesis 1.

Genesis 1 is about the self, Genesis 9 about the human Other. *One who is not in my image is nonetheless in God's image* – that is the basis of God's covenant with Noah, a universal requirement of all cultures if they are to honour God who gave us life. Terror, the killing of the innocent and the sacrifice of human life in pursuit of political ends are not mere crimes. They are sacrilege. Those who murder God's image in God's name commit a double sacrilege.

*

The unique structure of biblical spirituality – its calibrated tension between the universality of justice and the particularity of love – is the most compelling way I know of giving religious expression to *both* our common humanity *and* our religious differences. How does this work out in practice?

Consider the life of Abraham. Readers of the Bible are so familiar with his story that they often fail to notice how strange it is. Here is the father of monotheism, yet in the biblical text itself Abraham breaks no idol, challenges no polytheist, seeks no disciples,[7] and establishes no new religious movement. He lives among people whose beliefs and practices were alien to his own, yet he does not reprimand them, except when the servants of Abimelek, a king with whom he had made a treaty, seize one of the wells he had dug (Gen. 21:25). He holds them to the standards of morality, not those of ethics or holiness.

When his nephew Lot chooses to live among the people of Sodom, about whom the Bible says that they 'were wicked and were sinning greatly against the Lord' (13:13), Abraham does not criticise him. Nor does he condemn them. To the contrary, he fights a battle on their behalf (Gen. 14) and when he hears that

God is planning to punish them, he pleads for them in one of the most audacious prayers in the Bible: 'Shall the Judge of all the earth not do justice?' (18:25).

Abraham does not seek to impose his views on others. Yet his contemporaries sense that there is something special, Godly, about him. Melchizedek, king of Salem, salutes him with the words, 'Blessed be Abram by God Most High, Creator of heaven and earth' (14:19). The Hittites say to him, 'You are a prince of God among us' (23:6). Abraham impresses his contemporaries by the way he lives, not the way he forces, or even urges, others to live. He seeks to be *true to his faith while being a blessing to others regardless of their faith*. That seems to me a truth for the twenty-first century.

There was clearly a profound love between Abraham and God, and it is this that eventually inspired not only Jews but Christians and Muslims also, in their different ways, to see themselves as his heirs. But all who embrace Abraham must aspire to live like Abraham. Nothing could be more alien to the spirit of Abrahamic monotheism than what is happening today in the name of jihad. Barbarism and brutality, the embrace of terror and the murder of the innocent, the cold, cruel killing of those with whom you disagree, the pursuit of power in the name of empire, and the idea that you can impose truth by force: these are pagan ideas that have no place in the universe of Abraham or Abraham's God. They constitute neither justice nor love. They are a desecration.

To be a child of Abraham is to be open to the divine presence wherever it reveals itself. The faith of Abraham's children is told in a series of stories about how strangers turned out to be not what they seemed. Tamar is not a prostitute. Ruth is not an alien. Moses is not an Egyptian. Abraham's three visitors are not mere men. Strangers can turn out to be angels. Pharaoh's daughter may be a heroine. David, the inconsequential child, becomes the greatest of Israel's kings. The ethical imperative to emerge from such a faith is: search for the trace of God in the face of the Other. Never believe that God is defined by and confined to the people like you.

God is larger than any nation, language, culture or creed. He lives within our group, but he also lives beyond.

*

'Because that which connects human thought and feeling with the infinite and all-surpassing Divine light must [be refracted into] a multiplicity of colours, therefore every people and society must have a different spiritual way of life.' So said Rabbi Abraham Kook, first chief rabbi of pre-state Israel.[8] 'The righteous of all nations have a share in the world to come,' said the rabbis in the second century.[9] Rabbi Akiva, the sage of the late first century, said, 'Beloved is every human person for he or she is in the image of God. Beloved is Israel (i.e. each Jew), for each of us is one of the children of God.'[10] That is how Jews defined themselves in the past and do today. We feel ourselves close to God but we equally believe that God has a relationship with all humanity as defined in the Noahide code.

There are times when the Bible portrays Gentiles as conspicuously more religious than Jews. On the holiest day of the Jewish year, Yom Kippur, we read the book of Jonah, in which the prophet is sent to Israel's enemies, the Assyrians at Nineveh, to preach repentance. Jonah tries to run away. Who wants to see their enemies forgiven? Yet God refuses to let him escape. Jonah delivers his message, a mere five words in Hebrew, and the entire people repent. There is no instance in the entire Hebrew Bible of the Israelites responding with such alacrity to a prophetic call. The effect of reading this story at this most sacred of times forces one into a sense of humility. For all the natural pride we feel in being part of our group – the people of the covenant, a holy nation – we are brought face to face with the fact that others may sometimes respond to the word of God better than we do.

That is what the dual structure of Hebrew spirituality does. It accepts the inevitability of identity in the here-and-now. We are not all the same. There is an Us and Them. But God is universal as well as particular, which means that he can be found among Them as well as among Us. God transcends our particularities. That is why he often appears where we least expect him. Sometimes he speaks in the voice of a stranger, the man who wrestled with Jacob at night, or the one who found Joseph wandering in a field, or even the pagan prophet Balaam. The unique dialectic in the Hebrew Bible – so rarely understood, so often reviled – between universality and particularity is precisely what is necessary if we are to have identity without violence.

For though God is our God, he is also the God of all, accessible to all: the God who blesses Ishmael, who tells the children of Jacob not to hate the descendants of Esau, who listens to the prayers of strangers and whose messengers appear as strangers. Only a faith that recognises both types of covenant – the universal and the particular – is capable of understanding that God's image may be present in the one whose faith is not mine and whose relationship with God is different from mine.

Humanity lives suspended between the twin facts of commonality and difference. *If we were completely unalike, we would be unable to communicate. If we were completely alike, we would have nothing to say.* The Noah covenant speaks to our commonality, the Abraham and Sinai covenants to our differences. That is what makes Abrahamic monotheism different from tribalism on the one hand (each nation with its own God) and universalism on the other (one God, therefore one way). Neither tribalism nor universalism is adequate to the human situation. Tribalism envisages a world permanently at war (my god is stronger than yours). Universalism risks a dualistic world divided between the saved and the damned (I have the truth, you have only error[11]), and hence to holy wars, crusades and jihads.

What if the God of the crusaders, the terrorists, the inquisitors, the witch-burners and the jihadists were also the God of their victims? What if one could not, with absolute certainty, rule out that possibility? Humanity lives in that 'what if' and cannot survive without it. For we are finite, but God is infinite. We are limited, but God is unlimited. However perfect our faith, there is something of God that lies beyond, which is known to God but cannot be known to the frail, fallible humanity that is all we are and ever will be, this side of heaven.

12

Hard Texts

Both read the Bible day and night,
But thou read'st black where I read white.
                              William Blake[1]

Never say, I hate, I kill, because my religion says so. Every text
needs interpretation. Every interpretation needs wisdom. Every
wisdom needs careful negotiation between the timeless and time.
Fundamentalism reads texts as if God were as simple as we are.
That is unlikely to be true.

Religions, especially religions of the Book, have hard texts: verses,
commands, episodes, narratives, that if understood literally and
applied directly would not merely offend our moral sense. They
would also go against our best understanding of the religion itself.
There are many examples in the Hebrew Bible. There is the war of
revenge against the Midianites. There is the war mandated against
the seven nations in the land of Canaan. There is the book of Joshua
with its wars of conquest, and the bloody revenge against the Amalekites in the book of Samuel. These strike us as barbaric and at odds
with an ethic of compassion, or even with a just war doctrine of the
kind that emerged in both the Jewish and Christian traditions.

There were other internal laws that the rabbis found puzzling
and morally problematic. There is, for instance, in Deuteronomy,
a law about a stubborn and rebellious son who is to be put to
death for what appears to us to be no worse than a serious case
of juvenile delinquency. So incompatible did this seem with the
principles of justice that the Talmud records the view that the law
was never put into effect and exists only for didactic purposes and
not to be implemented in practice.[2]

These texts – and there are notorious examples in the New Testament, the Qur'an and Hadith also – require the most careful interpretation if they are not to do great harm. That is why every text-based religion develops its own traditions of interpretation. Rabbinic Judaism declared Biblicism – accepting the authority of the written word while rejecting oral tradition, the position of the Sadducees and Karaites – as heresy. The rabbis said: 'One who translates a verse literally is a liar.'³ The point is clear: no text without interpretation; no interpretation without tradition; or, as 2 Corinthians puts it, 'The letter kills, but the spirit gives life' (NIV, 2 Cor. 3:6).

For almost the whole of their histories, Jews, Christians and Muslims have wrestled with the meanings of their scriptures, developing in the process elaborate hermeneutic and jurisprudential systems. Medieval Christianity had its four levels of interpretation: literal, allegorical, moral and eschatological. Islam has its *fiqh*; its four schools of Sunni jurisprudence and their Shia counterparts; its principles of *taqleed*, *itjihad* and *qiyas*. Hard texts need interpreting; without it, they lead to violence. God has given us both the mandate and the responsibility to do just that. We are guardians of his word for the sake of his world.

That is why fundamentalism is so dangerous and so untraditional. It refers to many things in different contexts, but one of them is the tendency to read texts literally and apply them directly: to go straight from revelation to application without interpretation. In many religions, including Judaism, this is heretical. In most, it is schismatic. Internal battles have been fought over these issues in many faiths. But the general conclusion at which most have arrived is that it needs great wisdom together with a deep grounding in tradition to know how to apply the word to the world.

One reason is, of course, that these are often very ancient texts, originally directed to times and conditions quite unlike ours. The war commands of Deuteronomy and the book of Joshua, for example, belong to a time when warfare was systemic, endemic and brutal. The massacre of populations was commonplace. Another reason is that we are dealing with sacred scripture, texts invested with the ultimate authority of God himself. How do you take the word of eternity and apply it to the here-and-now? That is never simple and self-understood. That is why, for much of the biblical era, ancient Israel had its prophets who delivered, not the word of the Lord for all time – that had been done by Moses – but the word of the Lord for *this* time. There are things that may be justified in an age of prophecy that are wholly unjustifiable at other times.

As a general rule, though, the application of every ancient text to another age involves an act of interpretation, and there is nothing inherently religious about this. It is a central problem in secular law and jurisprudence, deliberated over in every Supreme Court. How is a law enacted then to be understood now? It is a problem every theatrical director faces in deciding how, for example, to stage *The Merchant of Venice* for a contemporary audience. In each case, the issue is how to apply the-word-then to the-world-now, bridging the hermeneutical abyss of time and change. Religions develop rules of interpretation and structures of authority. Without these, as we see today, any group can do almost anything in the name of religion, selecting texts, taking them out of context, reading them literally and ignoring the rest. Without rules, principles and authority, sacred texts provide the charisma of seemingly divine authority for purposes that are all too human. As Shakespeare said, 'The devil can cite Scripture for his purpose.'[4]

What happens in the case of fundamentalism is a kind of principled impatience with this whole process. A radical thinker decides that the religious establishment is corrupt. In his eyes it has made its peace with the world, compromised its ideals and failed to live up to the pristine demands of the faith. Therefore let us live by the holy word as it was before it was interpreted and rendered pliable and easy-going. Recall that even the founder of Christianity told his disciples, 'Do not suppose that I have come to bring peace to the earth. I did not come to bring peace, but a sword' (NIV, Matt. 10:34). There is always a confrontational as well as an accommodationist reading of any tradition.

Usually, of course, radical religious movements within an established faith tend to be sectarian and small-scale. What makes the present moment different is precisely what made the Reformation different in Christianity: the emergence, at roughly the same time, of a back-to-the-text-as-it-was-in-the-beginning religiosity, together with a revolution in information technology that allows the radicals to bypass conventional means of communication: church sermons in the age of printing, local imams and community elders in the age of the Internet. Suddenly the radicals command the heights and address the masses, while the religious establishment is left flat-footed and outpaced and looking old.

There is another factor also, that has been present in the background of all three Abrahamic monotheisms, namely the sheer dissonance between the world of tradition and the secular domain. It begins to seem impossible to hold religion and society together. There comes a tipping point at which faith can no longer be seen as supporting the social or cultural order and becomes instead radically antagonistic towards it. The term 'fundamentalism', for example, was originally coined in the early twentieth century to describe a reaction within the Protestant church in America against what seemed to traditionalists to be a steady erosion of faith in the light of modern science and biblical criticism. There was a similar movement in Orthodox Judaism against any accommodation with the intellectual doctrines of the Enlightenment or the social pressures involved in Emancipation.

In Islam much of the energy that produced the new radicalism came out of a deep disillusionment with the secularisation and Westernisation of traditional societies after the First World War and the fall of the Ottoman Empire. In each case, the radical neo-traditionalists felt the force of the echoing question: 'What shall it profit a man, if he shall gain the whole world, and lose his own soul?' (KJV, Mark 8:36) Fundamentalism emerges when people feel that the world has been allowed to defeat the word. They, by contrast, are determined to defeat the world by means of the word.

*

To see how tradition has traditionally worked, let us take the single example of the war traditions in Judaism, those that most directly concern the relationship between religion and violence.

The first thing to note is that despite the apparent militarism of the early texts of Judaism, their underlying value was always peace. Already in Leviticus (26:6) we find the blessing, 'I will grant peace in the land . . . and the sword will not pass through your country.' The priestly benedictions end with a prayer for peace (Num. 6:26). By the eighth century BCE the prophets of Israel had become the first people in history to envisage a world at peace. The classic instance is Isaiah, who foresaw a time when the nations 'will beat their swords into ploughshares and their spears into pruning hooks. Nation will not take up sword against nation, nor will they train for war any more' (Isa. 2:4). His vision of a world in which 'they will neither harm nor destroy on all my holy mountain, for the earth will be full of the knowledge of the Lord as the waters cover the sea' (Isa. 11:9) is part of the Hebrew Bible's decisive break with the ethic of militarism that dominated the ancient world. It would not be revived, outside the Judeo-Christian tradition, until Kant's secular essay on 'perpetual peace' in 1795.

One way of seeing the change that had come over the nation is by comparing two biblical texts, both of which describe the same moment: when God told King David not to build the Temple, assuring him that the work would be done by his son, Solomon. In 2 Samuel 7:6–7, God explains:

> I have not dwelt in a house from the day I brought the Israelites up out of Egypt to this day. I have been moving about in a tent and a tabernacle. Wherever I have moved about among all the

people of Israel, did I ever speak a word to any of the tribal leaders of Israel whom I commanded to shepherd my people Israel, 'Why have you not built me a house of cedar?'

The implication is that God does not need a monumental home of the kind built to ancient deities. He lives not in a building of cedar but in the human heart. In 1 Chronicles 22:8, written later, however, a further explanation is attributed to David:

> The word of God came to me: 'You have shed much blood. You have fought many wars. You shall not build a house for my Name, because you have shed much blood on the earth in my sight.'

The two passages are not incompatible: the commentators found no difficulty in reconciling them. But the new emphasis is palpable. War may sometimes be necessary, but it has no place in the domain of the holy. One who has 'shed much blood' may not build a house of God.

Centuries later the rabbis went much further still, and we can identify the moment at which they did so. It took place at the time – the late first or early second century CE – when Rabban Gamliel II was deposed as spiritual head of the Jewish community in Israel for his autocratic behaviour towards one of his colleagues, and R. Elazar ben Azariah was appointed in his place. At that time many disputed issues were resolved. This is how the Talmud describes one of them:

> On that day, Judah, an Ammonite proselyte, came before them in the House of Study and asked: 'Am I permitted to enter the assembly?' R. Joshua said, 'You are permitted to enter the congregation.' Rabban Gamliel said, 'Is it not a law that *An Ammonite or a Moabite may not enter the assembly of the Lord* (Deut. 23:4)?' R. Joshua replied, 'Do Ammon and Moab still live in their original homes? Long ago Sennacherib king of Assyria came and mixed up all the nations, as it says, *I removed*

the boundaries of nations, I plundered their treasures; like a mighty one I subdued their kings (Isaiah 10:13), and whatever is detached [from a group] is assumed to belong to the majority of the group . . . They then permitted [Judah the Ammonite] to enter the congregation.[5]

At a stroke the entire biblical legislation relating to Israel's neighbours and enemies was declared inoperative, on the grounds that after Sennacherib's conquests and population transfers (722–705 BCE), the 'nations' could no longer be identified. As Maimonides writes about the seven nations against which Israel was commanded to wage war, 'their memory has already perished'.[6] We no longer know who is who. That chapter in Jewish history is closed.

What of Joshua's campaign to conquer the land? Again the Talmud offers a radical interpretation, summarised by Maimonides in these words:

No war, either permitted or obligatory [such as a war of self-defence] may be initiated without first offering terms of peace . . . Joshua sent three messages before entering the land: the first, 'Whoever wishes to flee, let him flee,' the second, 'Whoever wishes to make peace, let him make peace,' the third, 'Whoever wishes to make war, let him make war.'[7]

War, for Maimonides, is *never* mandated except when the effort to make peace has been tried, and failed.

What of the Amalekites, about whom the Bible commands the Israelites to 'blot out their memory from under heaven'? Maimonides ruled that even at the outset the command only applied if the Amalekites refused to make peace and accept the seven Noahide laws. There was no categorical imperative to destroy them. To the contrary, even here peace was preferable. Maimonides added that in any case it was no longer applicable since what applied to the seven nations applied to the Amalekites also. Sennacherib had transported and resettled the nations so that it was no longer possible to identify the ethnicity of any of the original people against whom the Israelites were commanded to fight. He also said, in *The Guide for the Perplexed*, that the command only applied to people of specific biological descent. It is not to be applied in general to enemies or haters of the Jewish people. So the command to wage war against the Amalekites no longer applies.[8]

Thereafter in Judaism Amalek became a mere symbol of gratuitous evil, a metaphor, not an actual people. R. Levi Yitzhak of Berditchev, for example, speaks of Amalek as the evil inclination within each of us, whom we must defeat.[9] War, except in self-defence, no longer takes place on the battlefield; it becomes a struggle within the soul (Islam has a similar reinterpretation of the word *jihad*[10]). At a stroke, the biblical texts relating to Israel's enemies were rendered inoperative. They speak of then, not now; of ancient nations, not contemporary ones.

*

If we seek, though, to understand the real transformation that took place in Judaism between the biblical era and the age of the rabbis, we need to listen to an extraordinary conversation, reported in the Talmud, between the Jewish sages in the late first century CE. The subject under discussion is not war as such, but rather a detail in the laws of the Sabbath. In Jewish law one may not carry a burden on the seventh day, whether from a private domain into the street or in the street itself. That is one of the categories of forbidden 'work'. The question was: what is a burden and what, precisely, counts as carrying? Wearing clothes is clearly not carrying. Taking an object from home into the street clearly is. What the sages are debating here is a borderline case: wearing a sword or other weapon. Is this *wearing*, in which case it is permitted, or is it *carrying*, in which case it is forbidden?

What is at stake is not a narrow issue. It goes to the heart of the value system of Jews at a critical point in their history, between the two great rebellions against Rome in the first and second centuries. Are weapons an ornament, and thus an item of clothing, or are they negative testimony to the existence of armed conflict and lack of peace, and thus a burden? At stake is how the sages saw the war against the Romans, and something deeper: how they viewed the very culture of military valour. The Mishnah records the following disagreement:

> A man must not go out with a sword, bow, shield, lance or spear, and if he does go out, he incurs a sin offering. R. Eliezer, however, said: They are ornaments for him. But the sages maintain that they are merely shameful, for it is said, 'And they shall beat their swords into ploughshares and their spears into pruning hooks. Nation shall not lift up sword against nation, neither shall they learn war any more' (Isaiah 2:4).[11]

The difference of opinion is clear. For R. Eliezer, weapons are 'ornaments'. There is honour in fighting for your freedom and resisting an imperial power. The sages – the majority – disagree. Their proof-text is the famous verse from Isaiah in which the prophet envisions a world without war. They took this to mean that military confrontation may sometimes be necessary in self-defence but it is not, in Judaism, a positive value. In the messianic age there will be no more weapons. Those that exist will be turned to peaceful uses. Even now, therefore, they are 'merely shameful' and may not be worn on the seventh day. They are not a badge of honour but a burden.

That is the argument as it took place in the first century. But there is an obvious lacuna in the Mishnah text. The sages cite a biblical verse in support of their view. R. Eliezer does not. Clearly, though, he must have had another biblical verse in mind. He knew the verse from Isaiah – the rabbis knew their Bible – and must have had some other textual warrant for his dissenting opinion. The Talmud[12] fills in the gap:

Abaye asked R. Dimi . . . 'What is R. Eliezer's reason for maintaining that [weapons] are ornaments?'

[He replied]: 'Because it is written, "Gird thy sword upon thy
thigh, O mighty one, it is thy glory and thy majesty" (Psalm
45:4).'

R. Kahana raised an objection to Mar, son of R. Huna: 'But
this refers to the words of the Torah!'

He replied: 'A verse cannot depart from its plain meaning.'

R. Kahana said: 'When I was eighteen I knew the whole six
orders [of the Mishnah] yet I did not know until today that a
verse cannot depart from its plain meaning.'

Some two centuries had passed between this exchange and the
original Mishnah teaching, but more than time has changed.
R. Kahana can *no longer understand* that when a psalm refers to
a sword it actually means a sword. For him it was self-evident that
it means 'words', teachings, texts. With what else does the Jewish
people defend itself, if not its sacred merits achieved by devotion
to religious learning?

The idea that Jews might fight battles, wage wars and glory in
their victories is absurd, unthinkable. Jews do not seek honour
on the battlefield. They spend their time in the house of study. By
R. Kahana's day, the nation of the sword had become the people
of the book. To understand R. Eliezer's view a mere two or three
centuries earlier, R. Kahana has to be exposed to a principle he
had never considered before, namely that one cannot ignore the
literal meaning of a biblical text. Whatever else a verse means, it
also means what it says.

In this conversation extended across several centuries we
witness one of the most profound metamorphoses in religious
history. After the disastrous rebellions against Rome, the entire
framework of existence of the Jewish people underwent a change.
The world of kings and high priests, the Maccabees and the
Hasmoneans, of military victories and all that went with them,
was over. The world of the rabbis had taken its place, a culture of

study and scholarship, in which words had replaced swords and the most important battles were intellectual ones.

Here is one delightful example. The book of Numbers contains a cryptic verse: 'Therefore the Book of the Wars of the Lord speaks of Waheb in Suphah.' By a verbal play, the sages read the last phrase as 'love in the end' (*ahavah ba-sof*) and explained it thus:

> Even father and son, or master and disciple, who study Torah at the same gate [=academy], become enemies of each other, yet they do not stir from there until they come to love each other, as it is written *Waheb in Suphah*, which is to be read as 'love in the end'.[13]

As in R. Kahana's reading of 'sword' as 'words', so here: the 'wars of the Lord' have become not physical battles but the cut and thrust of Talmudic debate. Study and what the sages called 'argument for the sake of heaven' have become a surrogate for war. No longer is violence an acceptable form of conflict resolution. In its place have come reasoned argument and the search for peace.

Even more significant is the way in which post-biblical Judaism encouraged Jews to *identify with and enter into the feelings of the victims of Israel's own victories*. The Talmud records a striking passage in which the angels are portrayed as wishing to sing a song of triumph at the division of the Red Sea. God silences them with the words, 'My creatures are drowning – and you wish to sing a song?'[14] Even Israel's enemies have become 'my creatures' (this, after all, is the point made at the end of the book of Jonah).

The fourteenth-century exegete David ben Joseph Abudarham explains that the reason for our custom of spilling drops of wine when reciting the Ten Plagues on the night of Passover is to shed symbolic tears for the Egyptians who suffered because of Pharaoh's hardness of heart.

These reinterpretations, long before modernity, show that by the second or third century rabbinic Judaism had internalised the full destructive force of religiously motivated violence, even when undertaken to preserve religious freedom against a capricious and sometimes overbearing Roman imperial power.

We often think, in the context of Judaism, of religious heroes – Moses, Joshua, Gideon, David – as men of war, and so in some respects they were. But at a later age, the real visionaries were those who realised that spiritual-cultural battles are often far more significant than military ones. In the sixth century BCE, Jeremiah argued tirelessly for some form of accommodation with the Babylonians. An attempt to wage war against them would result, he said, in national catastrophe. He was right, but unheeded and unpopular, and the result was the loss of the First Temple and the Babylonian exile.

In the first century, tradition attributes the same role to Rabban Yohanan ben Zakkai, who sought terms of peace with the Romans and was also disregarded. Thus was the Second Temple destroyed. All that was salvaged was the rabbinic academy at Yavneh, and Judaism survived through its scholars, not its soldiers. More than six centuries separate the prophet and the rabbi, but what they held in common was *spiritual maximalism and military minimalism*. They were not pacifists but they were realists. They knew that the real battles are the ones that take place in the mind and the soul. They change the world because they change us. That is the wisdom the zealots do not understand: not then, not now.

It takes wisdom to know how to translate the word of God into the world of human beings. In this book, I have offered a series of readings of biblical narrative, arguing that their consistent theme is not sibling rivalry – competition for God's love – but rather, understanding that we each have a place in God's universe of justice and love. Is there only one correct reading of these or other religious texts? Clearly not. The rabbis said that there are 'seventy faces' of scripture.[15] R. Samuel Edels said that the revelation at Sinai took place in the presence of 600,000 Israelites because the Torah can be interpreted in 600,000 different ways.[16] Each person carries part of the potential meaning of the text.

Living traditions constantly reinterpret their canonical texts.

That is what makes fundamentalism – text *without* interpretation – an act of violence against tradition. In fact, fundamentalists and today's atheists share the same approach to texts. They read them directly and literally, ignoring the single most important fact about a sacred text, namely that its meaning is not self-evident. It has a history and an authority of its own. Every religion must guard against a literal reading of its hard texts if it is not to show that it has learned nothing from history.

The sacred literatures of Judaism, Christianity and Islam all contain passages that, read literally, are capable of leading to violence and hate. We may and must reinterpret them. The great work of Jewish mysticism, the Zohar, says those who love the divine word penetrate beneath its outer garments to its soul. That is how, many centuries ago, the sages heard in biblical texts that on the surface spoke of a war, another meaning altogether. The 'wars of the Lord' became the debates in the house of study. They understood the deep spiritual truth that the idea of power is primitive: what makes us human is the power of ideas. The result was that they were able to shape a pacific faith capable of sustaining itself through centuries of exile and persecution. Hard texts are a challenge to the religious imagination and to our capacity to engage in *covenantal listening* to God's word as we seek to build a future that will honour the sacred legacy of the past.

The word, given in love, invites its interpretation in love.

13

Relinquishing Power

Power buries those who wield it.

Talmud[1]

To one who has a hammer, said Abraham Maslow, every problem looks like a nail. Politics is about power, but not every political problem has a solution that involves power. Failure to see this can cost a civilisation dear. It almost cost Judaism its life.

Jews in Israel in the first century had been restless under Roman rule for years, angered by its ineptitude, its heavy tax impositions and the indifference it showed to Jewish religious sensitivities. Finally, in 66 CE when procurator Gessius Florus failed to defend the Jews of Caesarea from a murderous onslaught by their Greek neighbours, fury became open revolt.

Hoping to repeat the victory of the Maccabees against the Greeks two centuries earlier, Jews fought to restore their independence and win back religious freedom. At first the rebellion went well. The Roman garrison in Jerusalem was overcome. The Roman army, massing its troops in Acre, was forced to retreat. Realising that it faced a major struggle, Rome sent its most distinguished general Vespasian, together with his son Titus, to quash the uprising.

We owe our most vivid description of the conflict to an eyewitness, Josephus. Sent to organise the Jewish population in Galilee, he soon realised that the task was hopeless. The population was divided, some in favour of armed resistance, others against. He was in Jotopata in 67 CE when the Romans laid siege to the town. Its inhabitants held out for two months, finally committing suicide rather than be taken captive, as did those in the last outpost of resistance at Masada six years later. Josephus, the sole survivor,[2] surrendered to Vespasian and thereafter observed the war from the Roman side.

The picture he paints is of hopeless factionalism.[3] The Jews of the late Second Temple period were deeply divided. There were three primary groups: the Sadducees, the upper echelons associated with the Temple and political power; the Essenes, a pietist group to which the Qumran sectarians may have been affiliated; and the Pharisees, attached to the oral tradition and rigorous observance of the Law. The Pharisees themselves were split, the Talmud going so far as to say that there was a risk that divisions between the disciples of Hillel and Shammai were so deep that Judaism was at risk of becoming 'two Torahs', that is, two religions, not one.[4] Cutting across these rifts were political disagreements between moderates and extremists, those who favoured war and those who were convinced that an accommodation had to be reached with Rome.

Particularly chilling is the scene Josephus describes of Jerusalem under siege. The Jews were heavily outnumbered. There were 25,000 within the city, facing Titus' well-equipped and disciplined army of 60,000 soldiers. They might have held out were it not that they too were split: the Zealots under Elazar ben Simon, an extremist faction led by Simon ben Giora, and a third force of Idumeans and others under John of Giscala. Josephus tells us that for much of the time these groups were more intent on attacking one another than the enemy outside the walls. They killed each other's men, destroyed one another's food supplies, and engaged in what Josephus calls 'incessant, suicidal strife'. At one point in his narrative he breaks off to lament: 'Unhappy city! What have you suffered from the Romans to compare with this?'[5]

What makes the fall of Jerusalem relevant to the politics of the twenty-first century is that it saw the first appearance in history of religiously motivated terror. The terrorists were known as the *Sicarii*, named after their favourite weapon, the short-bladed dagger. This is how Josephus describes them:

These in broad daylight in the middle of the city committed numerous murders. Their favourite trick was to mingle with festival crowds, concealing under their garments small daggers with which they stabbed their opponents . . . First to have his throat cut by them was Jonathan the High Priest, and after him many were murdered every day. More terrible than the crimes themselves was the fear they aroused, every man as in war hourly expecting death.[6]

Their aim, as with their successors today, was to inflame relations between the local population and the occupying power, to generate an atmosphere of fear, and to incite reprisals on both sides, adding fuel to the flames of conflict.

The failed rebellion, together with its disastrous sequel, the Bar Kochba rebellion (132–5 CE), left Jewish life in ruins. The Temple was destroyed. Jerusalem was levelled to the ground and rebuilt as a Roman polis, Aelia Capitolina. The Jewish population began to drift elsewhere, to Babylon, Egypt and the Mediterranean basin. Thus began an exile that was to last almost two thousand years. The tragedy was all the greater because it was self-inflicted. The institutions around which Israelite and Jewish life were organised in the days of the Bible had gone. There was now no compact nation, no sovereignty, no collective home. The age of priests, prophets and kings had gone. The Temple and its sacrifices were no more. Not until the rise of antisemitism throughout Europe towards the end of the nineteenth century were Jews to organise themselves politically again.[7]

Out of darkness, though, sometimes comes light. What Jews discovered when they had lost almost everything else was that *religion can survive without power*. Instead of the Temple they had the synagogue. Instead of sacrifices they had prayer and charity. Repentance, the direct turning of the heart to God, took the place of the high priest's service on the Day of Atonement. In place of the nation state, they had communities scattered across the world yet united by a covenantal bond of mutual responsibility. Jews became the world's first global people.

The rabbis achieved what kings, priests and prophets failed to achieve in the course of a thousand years of biblical history. Jews, who as the Israelites had often been seduced into the idolatrous cultures of their neighbours and who are portrayed in the Hebrew Bible as a fractious, wayward people, became a God-intoxicated nation often willing to die rather than renounce their faith. A minority everywhere, they kept their identity intact, becoming the only significant minority in history to survive without assimilating to the dominant culture or convert to the majority faith.

This is not an argument for powerlessness. A thousand years of persecution culminating in the Holocaust are sufficient to refute the notion that Jews, or any other nation, can survive without the ability to defend themselves. But to reach, as they did, the spiritual heights without any of the conventional accoutrements of nationhood and political self-determination is enough to tell us that religion and power are two different things altogether, even if both in their distinct ways and different senses are political.

*

Sixteen centuries later, Christians made the same discovery. In 1517 the young priest Martin Luther nailed his ninety-five theses to the door of All Saints' Church in Wittenberg, setting in motion one of the great upheavals of European history. Like the zealots of the Second Temple in their opposition to Hellenised Jews, Luther was incensed by what he saw as the corruption and decadence of the Renaissance papacy, its worldliness and abuses of power. Like the Maccabees of the second century BCE, and their successors in the first century CE, Luther sought a return to the original message of faith, its simplicity and fervour, and like them he found a wide receptivity to his message.

The Reformation set in motion far-reaching changes in the political map of Europe, challenging the authority and power of Rome. For more than a century, Europe became a battleground, an epidemic of wars brought to an end only by the Treaty of Westphalia in 1648. The aftermath in the seventeenth century was, for Europe, the birth of the modern. It witnessed the rise of science (Bacon, Galileo, Newton), a new mode of philosophy (Descartes) and a new way of thinking about politics spearheaded by Hobbes and Locke. What all these movements had in common was a quest for basic principles that did not rest on dogmatic religious foundations.

Christianity, which had hitherto been spacious enough to encompass the Renaissance, could no longer be relied on, for how could it resolve disputes when it itself was the greatest single source of dispute? As Abraham Lincoln put it later, during the American Civil War, 'Both read the same Bible and pray to the same God, and each invokes His aid against the other.'[8] If two professing Christians, one Protestant, the other Catholic, could not resolve their disagreements without anathemas, excommunications and violence, then religion could not become the basis of a sustainable social order.

Stephen Toulmin offered the best explanation of what motivated those who sought a new way: 'Failing any effective political way of getting the sectarians to stop killing each other, was there no other possible way ahead? Might not philosophers discover, for instance, a new and more rational basis for establishing a framework of concepts and beliefs capable of achieving the agreed certainty that the sceptics had said was impossible?'[9]

More gradually, but also more extensively, Western Christianity had to learn what Jews had been forced to discover in antiquity: how to survive without power. The similarity of these two processes, so far apart in time, suggests two hypotheses. First, no religion relinquishes power voluntarily. Second, it does so only when the adherents of a faith find themselves fighting, not the adherents of another religion, but their own fellow believers. The

Crusades – Christians against Muslims – did not provoke the same reaction, nor did the loss of the First Temple – Jews against Babylonians. It took the spectacle of Jew against Jew, Christian against Christian, to bring about the change. You do not learn to disbelieve in power when you are fighting an enemy, even when you lose. You do when, with a shock of recognition, you find yourself using it against the members of your own people, your own broadly defined creed.

That is happening within Islam today. The primary victims of Islamist violence are Muslims themselves, across the dividing lines of Sunni and Shia, modernist and neo-traditionalist, moderate against radical, and sometimes simply sect against rival sect.

Violence is what happens when you try to resolve a religious dispute by means of power. It cannot be done. Trying to resolve ultimate issues of faith, truth and interpretation by the use of force is a conceptual error of the most fundamental kind. Just as might does not establish right, so victory does not establish truth. Both sides may fight with equal passion and conviction, but at the end of the day, after thousands or millions have died, whole countries reduced to disaster zones, populations condemned to poverty and generations to hopelessness, after the very enterprise of faith has been degraded and disgraced, no one is a millimetre closer to God or salvation or illumination. *You cannot impose truth by force.* That is why religion and power are two separate enterprises that must never be confused.

*

What rescued Judaism in the first century and Christianity in the seventeenth was not success but failure, not victory but defeat. Out of the disaster of the rebellions against Rome came the rich heritage of early rabbinic Judaism – Midrash, Mishnah and Talmud – one of the most subtle and intricate of all religious literatures. The 'wars of the Lord' were now fought, not on the battlefield but in the house of study. Judaism became a culture of argument and debate, of words rather than weapons. The nation of the sword became the people of the book. Catastrophe honed and refined the Jewish message. Losing power, Judaism rediscovered itself.

The Christian corollary was best described by Alexis de Tocqueville after his visits to America in the early 1830s. He was struck by a phenomenon that seemed to defy something he had hitherto taken for granted:

> In France I had almost always seen the spirit of religion and the spirit of freedom marching in opposite directions. But in America I found they were intimately united and that they reigned in common over the same country.[10]

The explanation, he found, lay in the separation of church and state. Talking to clerical leaders, he found 'that most of its members seemed to retire of their own accord from the exercise of power, and that they made it the pride of their profession to abstain from politics'. The result was that although religion took no part in government, it was 'the first of their political institutions', providing the moral base of civic society, what he called its 'habits of the heart'. It created communities, strengthened families and motivated philanthropic endeavours. It lifted people beyond what he saw as the great danger of democracy – individualism, the retreat of people from public life into private satisfaction. Religion strengthened the 'art of association', the underlying strength of American society. Relinquishing power, religion was able to avoid the inescapable danger of those who wear the mantle of politics:

> The church cannot share the temporal power of the state without being the object of a portion of that animosity which the latter excites. In proportion as a nation assumes a democratic condition of society and those communities display democratic

propensities, it becomes more and more dangerous to connect religion with political institutions . . . The American clergy were the first to perceive this truth and to act in conformity with it. They saw that they must renounce their religious influence if they were to strive for political power, and they chose to give up the support of the state rather than share in its vicissitudes.[11]

*

Monotheism allied to power fails. Rabbi Naftali Zvi Yehudah Berlin (1817–93), head of the rabbinical seminary in Volozhin, made a fascinating comment on the biblical story of the Tower of Babel. It begins with the statement that 'The whole world had one language and shared words.' This, he says, was precisely what was wrong with it:

> Since the views of human beings are not the same, [the builders of Babel] were concerned that no one should have a contrary opinion. They therefore took care that no one be allowed to leave their city, and those who expressed contrary views were condemned to death by fire, as they sought to do to Abraham. Their 'shared words' became a stumbling-block because they resolved to kill anyone who did not think as they did.[12]

Berlin sees Babel as the first totalitarian state. The 'shared words' of its builders were a denial of the diversity of human opinion. Dissent was forbidden. Those who expressed it were threatened by death. Utopian-sectarian communities pride themselves on their unity, but it is secured at too high a price: hostility to those who do not share their views.

Berlin died before the Russian Revolution, but he anticipated its failure. His critique precisely echoes Aristotle's – and more recently Karl Popper's[13] – of Plato's *Republic*. Plato had argued that 'It is best for the whole state to be as unified as possible.' Aristotle disagreed: 'We ought not to attain this greatest unity even if we could, for it would be the destruction of the state.'[14] The degree of unity aspired to in the total society is incompatible with human freedom and the right to disagree. Politics should be the mediation, not the suppression, of conflict.

To be sure, there is a profound difference between the Greek and Judaic views of politics. The Athenians and Spartans had a civic ethic.[15] For them, the highest good was to serve the polis, respecting its laws, participating in its debates, being willing to fight and if need be die for its sake. *Dulce et decorum est pro patria mori*, 'It is pleasant and proper to die for one's country.'

The Hebrew Bible, by contrast, is a sustained critique of politics. The prophets denounced the corruption of rulers. God told Samuel that in their desire for a king, the people were rejecting God himself.[16] In one of the key sentences of the Bible, Gideon, invited by the people to become their king, says, 'I will not rule over you, nor will my son rule over you. The Lord will rule over you' (Judg. 8:23).

It is not accidental that the book of Exodus with its political themes – slavery, liberation, tyranny, freedom – is preceded by Genesis with its tales of family life, nor that the book of Ruth with its non-political message of love and loyalty is the historical prelude to the political books of Samuel and Kings. The function of these works is to emphasise *the primacy of the personal over the political*. The polis is not the *summum bonum*, the highest good. In Judaism the state exists to serve the individual; the individual does not exist to serve the state. This is anything but a cliché: it is a rejection at the most fundamental level of Hellenistic ethics. The state is a necessary evil. As Tom Paine put it in *Common Sense* (1776), 'Government, like dress, is the badge of lost innocence; the palaces of kings are built on the ruins of the bowers of paradise.'[17] The Hebrew Bible is an intensely political document, but it never loses sight of the limits of politics and the risk that those limits may be transgressed.

That, paradoxically, is *the religious significance of liberal democracy*. Western democracy is not Athenian democracy. It is a rare phenomenon in political history because of its modesty, its sense of limits, its self-restraint. The liberal democratic state does not aspire to be the embodiment of the good, the beautiful and the true. It merely seeks to keep the peace between contending factions. It is procedural rather than substantive. It makes no claim to represent the totality of life. It knows, with Oliver Goldsmith, 'How small, of all that human hearts endure / That part which laws or kings can cause or cure.'[18] In the eloquent words of Michael Novak:

> In a genuine pluralistic society, there is no one sacred canopy. *By intention* there is not. At its spiritual core, there is an empty shrine. That shrine is left empty in the knowledge that no one word, image, or symbol is worthy of what all seek there. Its emptiness, therefore, represents the transcendence which is approached by free consciences from a virtually infinite number of directions.[19]

That is what makes liberal democracy, however odd this sounds, the best way of instantiating the values of Abrahamic monotheism. It does not invite citizens to worship the polis, nor does it see civic virtue as the only virtue. It recognises (unlike Jean-Jacques Rousseau[20]) that politics is not a religion nor a substitute for one. The two are inherently different activities. Religion seeks truth, politics deals in power. Religion aims at unity, liberal democracy is about the mediation of conflict and respect for diversity. Religion refuses to compromise, politics is the art of compromise. Religion aspires to the ideal, politics lives in the real, the less-than-ideal. Religion is about the truths that do not change, politics is about the challenges that constantly change. Harold Wilson said, 'A week is a long time in politics.' The book of Psalms says, 'A thousand years are in your sight as yesterday when it is gone' (Ps. 90:4). Religion inhabits the pure mountain air of eternity, politics the bustle of the here-and-now.

More important still is what liberal democratic politics

achieves. It *makes space for difference*. It recognises that within a complex society there are many divergent views, traditions and moral systems. It makes no claim to know which is true. All it seeks to do is ensure that those who have differing views are able to live peaceably and graciously together, recognising that none of us has the right to impose our views on others. Coerced agreement is not consent, said the Jewish sages.[21] Give to Caesar what is Caesar's, and to God what is God's, said Jesus (Matt. 22:21). There is no compulsion in religion, says the Qur'an (2:256). Democratic politics has no higher aspiration than to allow individuals freedom to pursue the right as they see the right, with this proviso only, that they extend the same right to others. It seeks the maximum possible liberty compatible with an equal liberty for all.

That is what makes Abrahamic monotheism different from the religions that preceded it. In the ancient world, the pharaohs of Egypt, like the kings of Mesopotamian city states, combined temporal and ecclesiastical power. They were both head of state and head of the religion of the state. They claimed to be, and were seen as being, god made manifest or the child of the gods or the chief intercessor with the gods. They presided over religious rites. But the religion of Abraham was born in a *protest against* this very phenomenon. Eric Voegelin put it precisely:

> The world of politics is essentially polytheistic in the sense that every centre of power, however small and insignificant it may be, has a tendency to posit itself as an absolute entity in the world, regardless of the simultaneous existence of other centres which deem themselves equally absolute.[22]

Polytheism, with its vision of multiple forces and perennial conflict, is compatible with the sacralisation of politics. Monotheism is not.

Of course, religious history was rarely that simple. Judaism, Christianity and Islam all acquired political power in one form or another. In the biblical age Israel became a kingdom, soon splitting in two. Christianity and Islam both became imperial powers. Eventually, though, there comes a point of crisis when the religion encounters massive change, and an argument develops within the faith itself. Do we respond to change by change? Do we preserve institutions as they are? Do we return to the core message of the faith?

The argument itself is not the problem. Its resolution is. Having grown accustomed to power, religious leaders become used to getting their way by force. This time, however, there is more than one group claiming to act in the name of religion: the *same* religion. Force meets force, and the result is the religious equivalent of civil war, with all the bitterness of war and all the uncompromising passion of religion. That is what happened to Judaism in the first century, Christianity in the seventeenth, and Islam today. That is when religion discovers that power has different rules from those that apply in the life of the spirit. Either that, or it destroys itself.

*

The most disastrous form of politics associated with the Abrahamic faiths is *apocalyptic* politics, the politics of the end of days. Apocalypse comes late to the religion of Abraham, possibly from the same source – Zoroastrianism – as did the dualism we explored in chapter 3. It differs fundamentally from classical prophecy. The prophet thought in terms of normal history. Though there may be setbacks and defeats, the people of God, living by the law and love of God, will eventually find that righteousness is rewarded and evil brings about its own defeat. The prophet is the voice of hope.

Apocalypse, by contrast, is the voice of despair. Normal history has failed to bring about the long-awaited redemption. Evil, far from being an instinct within us that we can conquer, is an independent force, the work of Satan. The universe is framed by the conflict between God and his enemies, and is moving towards a final confrontation that will shake the world to its foundations. The reign of God will be restored, evil will be vanquished, and history with all its vicissitudes and disappointments will come to an end.

This is the vision that appears in the Hebrew Bible in the book of Daniel. It reappears in several intertestamental works (1 Enoch, 2 Esdras and others) excluded from the biblical canon. As we saw in chapter 3, it was a feature of the Qumran sect, and its classic expression in the New Testament is the book of Revelation. Today it figures centrally in the worldview of ISIS, which views itself as the prime mover of a process that will end in a cosmic battle between the armies of Islam and those of the Crusaders ('Rome'). The first significant battle will be in Dabiq, Northern Syria – so important is this to the thinking of ISIS that it chose *Dabiq* as the title of its official online journal. The Caliphate will then expand, conquering vast territories including Istanbul. A false messiah known as Dajjal will appear, inflicting heavy casualties on the Caliphate's army, until the final battle, and with it the global triumph of Islam, in Jerusalem.[23]

Apocalypse is what happens to prophecy when it loses hope, and to politics when it loses patience. Apocalyptic politics is the strange phenomenon of a revolutionary movement whose gaze is firmly fixed on the past. It arises at times of destabilising change, and speaks to those who feel unjustly left behind. Millenarian sects flourished within Judaism in the late Second Temple period, as they did in Christian Europe in the late Middle Ages: the Ranters, Flagellants, Hussites, Anabaptists and others.[24] At times of social and religious ferment, they spread like contagion. They hold particular attraction for those who feel alienated, estranged,

> Wandering between two worlds, one dead
> The other powerless to be born.[25]

The phenomenon takes secular forms as well. The thinkers of the French and Russian revolutions thought in terms of what the late J.L. Talmon called 'political messianism' or 'totalitarian democracy'.[26] There are two ways of applying the Exodus narrative to politics. One ('exodus politics') understands that the journey is long and fraught with setbacks. Change in the human heart takes time and is the work of many generations. The other ('messianic politics') believes that the destination is close and God is beckoning. 'Hence the readiness of messianic militants to welcome, even to initiate, the terrors that proceed the last days,' writes Michael Walzer; 'hence the strange politics of *the worse, the better*; and hence the will to sin, to risk any crime for the sake of the end.'[27]

Apocalyptic politics is the search for revolution without transformation, change without the slow process of education. It uses power in place of persuasion, daggers instead of debate. It simplifies the issue of truth to the most elemental choice: agree or die. It is the longing for the end of time in the midst of time, the search for redemption now. That is why it suspends the normal rules that restrain people from murdering the innocent. Talmon's conclusion (and remember that he is speaking about secular creeds) is so powerful that it deserves quotation at length:

> The most important lesson to be drawn from this enquiry is the incompatibility of the idea of an all-embracing and all-solving creed with liberty. The two ideals correspond to the two instincts most deeply embedded in human nature, the yearning for salvation and the love of freedom. To attempt to satisfy both at the same time is bound to result, if not in unmitigated tyranny and serfdom, at least in the monumental hypocrisy and self-deception which are the concomitants of totalitarian democracy. This is the curse on Salvationist creeds: to be born out of the noblest impulses of man, and to degenerate into weapons of tyranny. An exclusive creed cannot admit opposition. It is bound

to feel itself surrounded by innumerable enemies. Its believers can never settle down to a normal existence. From this sense of peril arise their continual demands for the protection of orthodoxy by recourse to terror.[28]

Apocalyptic politics always fails, because you cannot create eternity in the midst of time, or unity without dissent. It is like Samson in the temple of the Philistines, bringing down the building on his enemies but destroying himself in the process.

*

Religion is at its best when it relies on strength of argument and example. It is at its worst when it seeks to impose truth by force. We can trace how this idea was taken up by four different traditions. The first was the great Islamic thinker Ibn Roshd, otherwise known as Averroës (1126–98), who wrote distinguished commentaries on the works of Aristotle. One of the distinguished rabbis of the sixteenth century, Rabbi Judah Loewe of Prague (Maharal, 1525–1609), cites him in one of his own works. Averroës had argued that you should always, when presenting a philosophical argument, cite the views of your opponents. Failure to do so is an implicit acknowledgement of the weakness of your own case. R. Loewe adds:

> [Averroës'] words hold true for religion as well . . . It is not proper that we despise the words [of our adversaries], but rather we must draw them as close as we can . . . Therefore it is proper, out of love of reason and knowledge, that you should not summarily reject anything that opposes your own ideas, especially so if your adversary does not intend merely to provoke you, but rather to declare his beliefs. Even if such beliefs are opposed to your own faith and religion, do not say [to your opponent], 'Speak not, close your mouth.' If that happens, there will take place no purification of religion.

On the contrary, you should, at such times, say, 'Speak up as much as you want, say whatever you wish, and do not say later that had you been able to speak you would have replied further' . . . This is the opposite of what some people think, namely, that when you prevent someone from speaking against religion, that strengthens religion. That is not so, because curbing the words of an opponent in religious matters is nothing but the curbing and enfeebling of religion itself . . .

When a powerful man seeks out an opponent in order to demonstrate his own strength, he very much wants his opponent to exercise as much power as he can, so that if he defeats him his own victory will be more pronounced. What strength is manifested when the opponent is not permitted to fight? . . . Hence, one should not silence those who speak against religion . . . for to do so is an admission of weakness.[29]

Several decades later, John Milton made the same point in his defence of free speech, *Areopagitica* (1644): 'And though all the winds of doctrine were let loose to play upon the earth, so Truth be in the field, we do injuriously by licensing and prohibiting, to misdoubt her strength. Let her and Falsehood grapple; who ever knew Truth put to the worse, in a free and open encounter?'

Two centuries on, John Stuart Mill reiterated the argument in *On Liberty* (1859):

But the peculiar evil of silencing the expression of an opinion is, that it is robbing the human race; posterity as well as the existing generation; those who dissent from the opinion, still more than those who hold it. If the opinion is right, they are deprived of the opportunity of exchanging error for truth: if wrong, they lose, what is almost as great a benefit, the clearer perception and livelier impression of truth, produced by its collision with error.[30]

It is fascinating to see how in this conversation across seven centuries, first a Muslim, then a Jew, then a Christian, then a secular humanist come together to agree on the importance of free speech and *making space for dissent*. Greater is the pursuit of truth than the exercise of force.

Religion acquires influence when it relinquishes power. It is then that it takes its place, not among the rulers but among the ruled, not in the palaces of power but in the real lives of ordinary men and women who become extraordinary when brushed by the wings of eternity. It becomes the voice of the voiceless, the conscience of the community, the perennial reminder that there are moral limits of power and that the task of the state is to serve the people, not the people the state. That is why we remember prophets and continue to be inspired by them, while the names of emperors and tyrants are lost to collective memory. To paraphrase Kierkegaard: 'When a king dies, his power ends. When a prophet dies, his influence begins.'[31] When religion divests itself of power, it is freed from the burden of rearranging the deckchairs on the ship of state and returns to its real task: changing lives.

Religion – as understood by Abraham and those who followed him – is at its best when it resists the temptation of politics and opts instead for influence. For what it tells us is that civilisations are judged not by power but by their concern for the powerless; not by wealth but by how they treat the poor; not when they seek to become invulnerable but when they care for the vulnerable. Religion is not the voice of those who sit on earthly thrones but of those who, not seeking to wield power, are unafraid to criticise it when it corrupts those who hold it and diminishes those it is held against.

Elijah was a great prophet. He was 'zealous' for God's honour and bitterly opposed to the false prophets of Baal. He challenged them to a test on Mount Carmel. He won; they lost; the people were persuaded; the false prophets were killed – as convincing a demonstration of religious truth as any in the Bible. But the story

(1 Kgs 18–19) does not end there. Summoned by an angel to Mount Horeb, he witnesses an earthquake, a whirlwind and a raging fire. But 'God was not in' the earthquake or the wind or the fire. He came to Elijah in a 'still, small voice'. When religion becomes an earthquake, a whirlwind, a fire, it can no longer hear the still, small voice of God summoning us to freedom.

14

Letting Go of Hate

Darkness cannot drive out darkness: only light can do that. Hate cannot drive out hate: only love can do that. Hate multiplies hate, violence multiplies violence, and toughness multiplies toughness.

Martin Luther King[1]

I imagine one of the reasons people cling to their hates so stubbornly is because they sense, once hate is gone, they will be forced to deal with pain.

James Arthur Baldwin

To be free, you have to let go of hate.

There is an extraordinary moment in the Hebrew Bible, a passage so brief that you hardly notice it, but it may contain the truth most important for the twenty-first century. Here is the scene. Moses has spent forty years leading the Israelites. He has taken them out of slavery in Egypt, through the sea, across the desert and to the brink of the Promised Land. He has been told by God that he will not be allowed to cross the Jordan and enter the land himself. He will die outside, within sight of his destination but not yet there.

He understands this. It became a principle in Judaism: it is not for you to complete the work but neither are you free to desist from it. When it comes to social transformation, even the greatest cannot live to see the fulfilment of their dreams. For each of us there is a Jordan we will not cross. Once we know this, one thing becomes important above all others. Leave guidance to those who will follow you, for it is they who will continue the work. Be clear. Be focused. Be visionary.

That is what Moses did. The way the Hebrew Bible tells it, he spent the last month of his life addressing the nation in some of the most visionary speeches ever delivered. They exist today as the book of Deuteronomy. This is the book that contains the great command that defines Judaism as a religion of love: 'You shall love the Lord your God with all your heart, all your soul and all your might' (Deut. 6:5). It contains the most important inter-human command: 'Love the stranger for you yourselves were strangers in Egypt' (Deut. 10:19). Deuteronomy contains the word 'love' more than any other of the Mosaic books.

That is not surprising. Moses had spoken about love before, most famously in the command, 'Love your neighbour as yourself' (Lev. 19:18). Abrahamic monotheism was the first moral system to be based not just on justice and reciprocity – do for others what you would like them to do for you – but on love. What is really unexpected is what he says about hate:

Do not hate an Egyptian, because you were a stranger in his land. (Deut. 23:7)

This is a very counter-intuitive command. Recall what had happened. The Egyptians had enslaved the Israelites. They had initiated a policy of slow genocide, killing every male Israelite at birth. Moses had begged Pharaoh repeatedly to let the people go and he had refused. Moses also knew that this entire chapter of Israelite history was not accidental or incidental. It was their matrix as a nation, their formative experience. They were commanded to remember it for ever, enacting it once a year on Passover, eating the unleavened bread of affliction and the bitter herbs of slavery. All these, on the face of it, were reasons to hate the Egyptians or at the very least to look back with a sense of grievance, resentment, animosity and pain. Why then did Moses say the opposite? Do *not* hate them, because you were strangers in their land.

Because to be free, you have to let go of hate. That is what

Moses was saying. If the Israelites continued to hate their erstwhile enemies, Moses would have succeeded in taking the Israelites out of Egypt, but he would have failed to take Egypt out of the Israelites. Mentally, they would still be there, slaves to the past, prisoners of their memories. They would still be in chains, not of metal but of the mind. And chains of the mind are sometimes the worst of all.

*

On 7 May 2002, Iqraa, a Saudi Arabian–owned television channel, broadcast an interview that goes to the heart of the subject of this chapter. The programme was called *Muslim Woman Magazine*, its host was Doaa 'Amer, and she was interviewing a young child:

> 'Amer: What's your name?
> Child: Basmallah.
> 'Amer: Basmallah, how old are you?
> Child: Three and a half.
> 'Amer: Are you a Muslim?
> Child: Yes.
> 'Amer: Basmallah, are you familiar with the Jews?
> Child: Yes.
> 'Amer: Do you like them?
> Child: No.
> 'Amer: Why don't you like them?
> Child: Because . . .
> 'Amer: Because they are what?
> Child: They're apes and pigs.
> 'Amer: Because they are apes and pigs. Who said they are so?
> Child: Our God.
> 'Amer: Where did he say this?
> Child: In the Qur'an.

The interviewer concludes: 'Basmallah, Allah be praised. May our God bless her. No one could wish Allah could give him a more believing girl than she. May Allah bless her and her father and mother. The next generation of children must be true Muslims. We must educate them now while they are still children so that they will be true Muslims.'

There was a storm after the interview was shown. Yet, as we saw in chapter 4, the world of radical political Islam is awash with hate, above all with antisemitism. Indeed, the people who write most eloquently and critically about this are themselves Muslims, often women. They know that there is something fundamentally wrong about this, that it is not merely destructive but also self-destructive. They also know that this is not the traditional voice of Islam. As chapter 4 made clear, though there are negative verses about Jews in the Qur'an, antisemitism as such has its roots only in the nineteenth and twentieth centuries, when the Blood Libel and *The Protocols of the Elders of Zion* were transplanted from Europe to the Middle East.

Religion leads to violence when it consecrates hate. That was the tragedy that befell the Church in the fourth century. It took six centuries for the violence to follow, but it was inevitable. Enshrine hate within a culture, and it will remain dormant but still alive and potentially deadly. Christians did not kill only Jews. They killed Muslims, heretics, witches and sectarians, for the greater glory of God and in the name of the religion of love. Yet Christianity changed, not least because Pope John XXIII and his successors knew it had to change. Today the epicentre of hate is radical and neo-traditionalist Islam, sadly because Islam was immune to the virus for so long.

You cannot create a free society on the basis of hate. Resentment, rage, humiliation, a sense of victimhood and injustice, the desire to restore honour by inflicting injury on your former persecutors – sentiments communicated in our time by an endless stream of videos of beheadings and mass murders – are conditions of a profound lack of freedom. What Moses taught his people was this: you must live *with* the past, but not *in* the past. Those who are held captive by anger against their former persecutors are captive still. Those who let their enemies define who they are have not yet achieved liberty.[2]

*

I learned this from Holocaust survivors. I came to know them when I became a rabbi, and they became one of the great inspirations of my life. At first it was difficult to understand how they survived at all, how they lived with their memories, knowing what they knew and having seen what they saw. Many of them had lost their entire families. The world in which they grew up was gone. They had to begin again as strangers in a strange land.

Yet they were, and are, some of the most life-affirming people I have ever met. What struck me most was that they lived without resentment. They did not seek revenge. They did not hate. They cared, more than anyone else I knew, when other people were being massacred in Bosnia, Rwanda, Kosovo and Sudan. They let their pain sensitise them to the pain of others. In later life they began to tell their stories, especially to young people. They used to visit schools. Sometimes I went with them. They spoke about what had happened, and how they survived. But their fundamental message was not about the past at all. What they wanted young people to know was how precious freedom is, and how fragile; what a miracle it is that there is food to eat, windows you can open, gates you can walk out of, a future to look forward to. They spoke about tolerance and how important it is to care for the people who are different from you. Never take freedom for granted – that was their message. Work for it, fight for it, stand up especially for minorities, and never give way to hate even when others do.

How, I wondered, had they exorcised the pain that must have haunted them nightly, and led many, including Primo Levi, to commit suicide, sometimes many years later? Eventually I realised the answer. For decades they did not speak about the past, even to their spouses, even to their children. They focused single-mindedly on the future. They learned the language and culture of their new home. They worked and built careers. They married and had children. Only when they felt their future absolutely secure, forty or fifty years on, did they allow themselves to turn back and remember the past. That was what I learned from the survivors. *First you have to build the future. Only then can you revisit the past without being held captive by the past.*

That is what the biblical story of Lot's wife is about (Gen. 19:17–26). Messengers – angels – come to tell Lot and his family that they have to leave. The city is about to be destroyed. Lot hesitates, prevaricates, but eventually they depart. 'Don't look back,' say the angels, but Lot's wife does, and she is turned into a pillar of salt. As a child I thought this was a silly story, but as an adult I felt its power. Look back on a painful past, and you will not be able to move on. You will be immobilised by your tears. You will become a pillar of salt.

The people Moses was addressing were not survivors, but they were children of survivors. Their parents had lived through the first collective tragedy of the Jewish people. It was essential that he teach them to focus on the future, not to look back in anger or pain but to use the past constructively, creatively. The Mosaic books refer time and again to the Exodus and the imperative of memory: 'You shall remember that you were slaves in Egypt.' Yet never is this invoked as a reason for hatred, retaliation or revenge. Always it appears as part of the logic of the just and compassionate society the Israelites are commanded to create: the alternative order, the antithesis of Egypt. Don't enslave others, says Moses, or – because that was too much to ask at that stage of history – treat slaves honourably. Don't subject them to hard labour. Give them rest and freedom every seventh day. Release them every seventh year. Recognise them as *like you*, not ontologically inferior. No one is born to be a slave.

Give generously to the poor. Let them eat from the leftovers of the harvest. Leave them a corner of the field. Share your blessings with others. Don't deprive people of their livelihood. The entire structure of biblical law is rooted in the experience of slavery in Egypt, as if to say: you know in your heart what it feels like to be the victim of persecution, therefore do not persecute others. Biblical ethics is based on repeated acts of role reversal: the principle we saw in the Joseph story in chapter 8. You cannot stay moral in hard times and towards strangers without something stronger than Kantian logic or Humean sympathy. That 'something stronger' is memory.[3] In Exodus and Deuteronomy, memory becomes a moral force: not a way of preserving hate, but, to the contrary, a way of conquering hate by recalling what it feels like to be its victim. 'Remember' – not to *live* in the past but to *prevent a repetition* of the past.

*

The Sermon on the Mount tells us to love our enemies. That is a supremely beautiful idea, but it is not easy. Moses offers a more liveable solution. Help your enemy. You don't have to love him but you do have to assist him. That is the basis of the simple command in Exodus:

> If you see your enemy's donkey sagging under its burden, you shall not pass by. You shall surely release it with him. (Exod. 23:5)

Behind this law is a simple idea: your enemy is also a human being. He has a problem. Besides which, his donkey is suffering. Hostility may divide you, but something deeper connects you: the covenant of solidarity. Pain, distress, difficulty – these transcend the language of difference. A decent society will be one in which enemies do not allow their rancour or animosity to prevent them from coming to one another's aid when they need help. If someone is in trouble, act. Do not stop to ask whether they are friend or foe. Do as Moses did when he saw shepherds roughly handling the daughters of Jethro, or as Abraham did when he prayed for the people of the cities of the plain.

The rabbis noted that in Deuteronomy (22:4) a similar law appears, but this time in relation to friend, not foe: it speaks of 'your brother's donkey'. The Talmud rules that in a case of conflict, where your brother and your enemy both need your help 'you should first help your enemy – in order to suppress the evil inclination'.[4] Both may be equally in distress, but in the case of an enemy, there is more at stake: the challenge of overcoming estrangement, distance and ill-will. Therefore, it takes precedence. The ancient Aramaic translations (*Targum Onkelos*, and more explicitly *Targum Yonatan*) say something fascinating at this point. They take the phrase 'You shall surely release' to mean not just the physical burden weighing on the donkey, but also the psychological burden weighing on you. They translate the verse as: 'You shall surely *let go of the hate you have in your heart* towards him.'

What is powerful about this provision is that it is not utopian. It does not envisage a world without animosities. Your enemy may still be your enemy. Until the end of days, people will still fight over land, wealth and power. But strangers can still come to one another's assistance. During 9/11, in the World Trade Center, a Hassidic Jew rescued a Muslim at prayer. During the attack on the Jewish supermarket in Paris in January 2015, a Muslim worker at the shop rescued twenty Jewish customers by hiding them in a cold storage room. No one in real crisis stops to ask whether the person they are about to rescue is 'one of us'. That is when crisis brings out the best in us, not the worst.

*

Above all: never seek revenge. Do not believe you can rectify the past by avenging it. That way you merely succeed in perpetuating the past instead of healing it.

There is an element of the Hebrew Bible that is often misunderstood. It speaks about God's revenge. The Psalms sometimes pray for it. Why so in a religion dedicated to love, forgiveness and the future? One of the people who decoded the mystery is Yale theologian Miroslav Volf, a native Croatian who saw at first hand the bitter ethnic wars in the former Yugoslavia. Those experiences shaped his courageous book on reconciliation, *Exclusion and Embrace*.[5]

Having written for some three hundred pages on the need to open ourselves to the Other, he ends on an utterly unexpected note. He speaks of 'the close association between human non-violence and the affirmation of God's vengeance'. His thesis, shared by the Jewish scholar Henri Atlan,[6] is that *the belief that God will avenge wrongs spares human beings from having to do so*. Not all injustice, let alone perceived injustice, can be remedied by human beings. The attempt to do so creates more violence and more perceived injustice. 'Preserving the fundamental difference between God and non-God, the biblical tradition insists that there are things which only God may do.'

That is the meaning of 'Vengeance is mine, says the Lord' (Deut. 32:35; Rom. 12:19). We can never undo the past, nor can we fully remedy it. Killing your enemy does not bring your friend back to life. Yes, we must right past wrongs, apologise, atone, acknowledge people's sense of suffering and grievance. But there is no perfect justice in history, only a rough approximation, and that must do. The rest we must leave to God.

Jewish law *forbids* human beings from bearing a grudge or taking vengeance:

> You shall blot [any offences against you] out of your mind and not bear a grudge. For as long as one nurses a grievance and keeps it in mind, one may come to take vengeance. The Torah therefore emphatically warns us not to bear a grudge, so that the impression of the wrong should be completely obliterated and no longer remembered. This is the right principle. It alone makes civilized life and social interaction possible.[7]

This is the corollary of belief in divine justice. If vengeance belongs to God, it does not belong to us.

*

There is a connection between monotheism and letting go of hate. Here I want to clarify an idea alluded to briefly in the chapter about dualism. Different civilisations generate different character types. That is not because character is a matter of ethnicity: that is racism, and it is also untrue. Humans are culture-producing animals, and the way we act, even the way we feel, depends in no small measure on structures of the mind that we have internalised from our environment and habits of the heart we learned as children. Religions are culture-shaping institutions, and they include not just a theology, but also an anthropology. What we believe about God affects what we believe about ourselves.[8]

Monotheism *internalises* conflict, whereas myth *externalises* it. The Jesuit scholar Jack Miles, commenting on the difference between Oedipus and Hamlet, points out that the forces Oedipus confronts – fate, the Delphic oracle, the pre-scripted ending – have nothing to do with his thoughts, intentions or choices. They are 'out there'. Hamlet's battle, by contrast, is within, his 'native hue of resolution sicklied o'er by the pale cast of thought'.[9] Just as the clashing deities of myth become, in monotheism, inner conflicts within the mind of the one God, so the human drama takes place not on the battlefield but in the mind, the soul. As soon as Jacob can wrestle with the angel, he need no longer wrestle with Esau. The Hebrew Bible, indeed Judaism as a whole, is the story of an inner struggle. That rules out, in advance and on principle, the psychological alternative: *it was someone else's fault.*

That is the real difference between monotheism and dualism. When bad things happen to an individual or group, one can either ask, 'Who did this to me?' or, 'Given that this has happened, what then shall I do?' The first is the question a dualist asks, the second is the response of a consistent monotheist. So different are these questions that they generate two modes of being: respectively a *blame* culture and a *penitential* culture. The first focuses on external cause, the second on internal response. Blame looks to the past, penitence to the future. Blame is passive, penitence active. A penitential culture is constructed on the logic of responsibility. If bad things happen to us, it is up to us to put them right. When that is a culture's response to tragedy, a profound dignity is born.

That, essentially, is the prophetic voice. When mishaps befall the Israelites, they say, it is because *we the people* have sinned. We dishonoured the covenant, we betrayed God's trust. Never is *someone else* blamed for Israel's troubles. This is what makes Judaism a religion of guilt, repentance and atonement, made bearable by divine forgiveness. A penitential culture says, 'God, I blame no one but myself. Forgive me. Accept my broken heart. Then give me the strength to change.' Its peculiar power is that *penitence defies entropy*, the law that all systems lose energy over time. Penitence conserves energy by turning all suffering into an impetus to do better in the future. It spares its adherents 'the expense of spirit in a waste of shame'.[10]

It produces people of astonishing strength and resilience, like the late Viktor Frankl who found that even in Auschwitz he could retain a sense of freedom and dignity.[11] Atonement is the ultimate expression of freedom because it brings together the two mental acts – repentance and forgiveness – that have the power to break the iron grip of the past. Repentance testifies to our ability to change. Forgiveness expresses our refusal to be held captive by ill-will. Atonement is where divine and human freedom meet and create a new beginning. It is the act that defeats tragedy in the name of hope.

Dualism creates blame cultures. It says, 'It wasn't us, and it wasn't God, so it must be them.' The plague, the Black Death, the loss of a child, defeat in war, the failure of an economy, the disorienting effects of change itself – all these are the intentional act of a malevolent will, an evil presence, a satanic conspiracy whose very invisibility proves its cunning secrecy.

You don't have to be an evil person to think in such ways, but the result of such thinking is altruistic evil, and it begins when you see yourself, your nation or your people as the victim of someone else's crime. They can then be killed without compunction. Murder becomes a moral act. You are defending your people, avenging their humiliation, ridding the world of a pestilence, and helping to establish the victory of God, truth and right. Since not everyone understands this, you have constantly to educate the people to hate, through radio, television, the press, the Internet, social media, schools and families, so that even a three-and-a-half-year-old girl will know who are her enemies, whom she has to learn to mistrust and fear, so that one day she may blow herself up and thus earn her share in heaven, or encourage her children to do so when the time comes. Dualism is always potentially genocidal, and to avoid ever having to admit this, you must ceaselessly accuse your enemies of genocide.

This is troubling. It is also self-defeating. Defining yourself as a victim is ultimately a diminution of what makes us human. It teaches us to see ourselves as objects, not subjects. We become done-to, not doers; passive, not active. Blame bars the path to responsibility. The victim, ascribing his condition to others, locates the cause of his situation outside himself, thus rendering himself incapable of breaking free from his self-created trap. Because he attributes a real phenomenon (pain, poverty, illiteracy, disease) to a fictitious cause, he discovers that murdering the cause does not remove the symptom. Hence efforts must be redoubled. Blame cultures perpetuate every condition against which they are a protest.

This would be true even if people arrived at dualism through their own personal journey to understand the world. But usually they do not. Dualism is a cultural phenomenon devised by tyrants to manipulate people into becoming means, not ends. If you can teach a population to hate, you can get them to do whatever you want, and they will not turn against you because all their anger is turned outwards. This, as we have seen, is the classic function of the scapegoat.

That is why the secular-nationalist regimes against which the Arab Spring was a series of uprisings were able to survive so long under conditions of oppression, corruption, economic stagnation and educational underachievement. They did so by the manipulative use of antisemitism, often focused on the State of Israel but based on passages in the Qur'an and Hadith written more than a thousand years before the State existed. Astonishingly, the Islamist movements formed in opposition to the secular-nationalist regimes use the same antisemitism with even greater virulence, and will thus perpetuate the stagnation, corruption, brutality and underachievement against which they protest.

Some years ago I sat at the bedside of a young man in intensive care who had narrowly survived death. A twenty-year-old student at a rabbinic academy in the north of England, he had been sitting on a bus in London studying a volume of the Talmud, when he was stabbed twenty-two times. His assailant told the police when he was arrested: 'Israel are the murderers . . . So I stabbed him.'[12] An unprovoked attack on an innocent student – who, as it happened, was neither an Israeli nor a Zionist, just a Jew – became a form of self-defence.

Hate and the blame culture go hand in hand, for they are both strategies of denial: 'It wasn't me, it was them, I acted in self-defence, I am the victim not the perpetrator.' The murder of the innocent then becomes a holy deed. Victims *do* need our support. But they need our support to recover the power of agency. Taking responsibility for your own fate is not a luxury of the moral life, but a necessity. First build the future: that is how you redeem the past.

Freedom involves letting go of hate, because hate is the abdication of freedom. That is what Moses taught those who were about to enter the Promised Land. Don't hate the people who persecuted you. Instead, learn from that experience how to build a society without persecution. It is what the Holocaust survivors taught me: look forward, not back. Build a life, a family, a future, a hope. Hate makes us slaves; therefore let it go. Do not wage war on the children of darkness. Make sure instead that you and your children are sources of light.

15

The Will to Power or the Will to Life

Here in this transport
I am Eve
with Abel my son
If you see my older son
Cain son of Man
tell him that I

Dan Pagis, 'Written
with a Pencil in the Sealed Wagon'

It began with Cain and Abel and it is happening still. Much of this book has been about sibling rivalry, so it makes sense to conclude with the story of how it started: the first human children, the first religious act, and the first fratricide. Cain brings an offering to God. So does Abel. God accepts the second but not the first. Cain becomes angry. God urges him to control himself. Cain ignores the warning and murders his brother. God then says, 'The voice of your brother's blood is crying to me from the ground' (Gen. 4:10). So it was and so it is. The entire tragedy of religious history is foreshadowed in this drama.

Yet the story is undeniably odd. Why does God reject Cain's offering? Why does Cain respond by murdering his brother? What is the rivalry between the brothers about? Modern interpreters tend to read it as a story about the tension between shepherds (Abel) and farmers (Cain). Alternatively, suggesting non-Hebraic sources of the brothers' names, they argue that Abel means 'herdsman' and Cain 'metalsmith'. These readings miss the clue the Bible itself gives, namely the *Hebrew* meaning of the brothers' names.

Abel, in Hebrew *Hevel*, is among other things the keyword of

252

the book known in English as Ecclesiastes. Its second sentence includes the word *hevel* no less than five times. This is how the King James Version translates it: 'Vanity of vanities, saith the Preacher, vanity of vanities; all is vanity.' *Hevel* has also been translated as 'meaningless, pointless, futile, useless'. These translations miss the point.

Hevel is a word for 'breath'. Jews, like the Greeks, spoke of the soul, or the spiritual dimension of humankind, in language drawn from the act of breathing. In Hebrew, words for soul – such as *nefesh, ruach, neshamah* – are all types of breath. *Hevel* means a shallow, fleeting, ephemeral breath.

Ecclesiastes is a sustained meditation on mortality. Life is no more than a breath, and all the wealth and glory even the greatest accumulate means nothing because all that separates us from non-existence is a mere breath. Its mood is like the scene in which King Lear, at the end of the play that bears his name, holds the dead body of his daughter Cordelia – the one who loved him and whose love he failed to recognise until the end – and cries, 'Why should a dog, a horse, a rat have life, / And thou no breath at all?'

Abel represents human mortality – a mortality that comes less from sin than from the fact that we are embodied souls in a physical world subject to deterioration and decay. All that separates us from the grave is the breath God breathed into us: 'Then the Lord God formed man from the dust of the ground and breathed into his nostrils the breath of life, and the man became a living being' (Gen. 2:7). That is all we are: *hevel*, mere breath. But it is God's breath. Life is holy. That is common ground in Judaism, Christianity and Islam.

What eventually will kill Abel is Cain. Cain in Hebrew means 'to acquire, to possess, to own'. The Bible says so explicitly. 'Now Adam knew Eve his wife, and she conceived and bore Cain, saying, I have acquired [*kaniti*] a man with the help of the Lord.' The significance of this is lost on most translators, who read it as 'made', 'gotten', 'produced', 'created', 'given life to', and so on. These too miss the point.

Kaniti, 'I have acquired', is one of those verbs that, like the narratives analysed in this book, yield their meaning only in retrospect, when we have gone through the entire Hebrew Bible and then returned to read the text in the light of all that follows. It was Jean-Jacques Rousseau who unintentionally provided the deepest commentary. In his *Discourse on the Origin of Inequality*, he writes:

> The first man who, having fenced in a piece of land, said 'This is mine,' and found people naïve enough to believe him, that man was the true founder of civil society. From how many crimes, wars, and murders, from how many horrors and misfortunes might not any one have saved mankind, by pulling up the stakes, or filling up the ditch, and crying to his fellows: 'Beware of listening to this impostor; you are undone if you once forget that the fruits of the earth belong to us all, and the earth itself to nobody.'

The only word with which a reader of the Bible would disagree would be the last. 'The earth is the Lord's and the fullness thereof' (Ps. 24:1). It does not belong to nobody, it belongs to God.

The entire ethical-legal principle on which the Hebrew Bible is based is that we own nothing. Everything – the land, its produce, power, sovereignty, children and life itself – belongs to God. We are mere trustees, guardians, on his behalf. We possess but we do not own. That is the basis of the infrastructure of social justice that made the Bible unique in its time and still transformative today.

Cain represents the opposite: power as ownership, owner-ship as power. The Hebrew word *Baal*, the name of the chief Canaanite god, has the same range of meanings. The root means 'to own, to possess, to exercise power over someone or something'. That for the Bible is the ultimate idolatry. Rousseau was right. Violence begins in competition for scarce goods, of which the first is land.

Eve unwittingly gave her eldest son a name that would eventually lead him to murder. *Cain* represents the idea that what I own gives me power. When I give some of what I own to God in the form of a sacrifice, I am doing so in order to receive in return some of his power. That is pagan sacrifice: a way of propitiating, cajoling or bribing the gods. That kind of sacrifice God does not accept. The sacrifice he accepts, that of Abel/*hevel*, is one that comes from the humility of mortality. 'God, I am mere breath. But it is your breath I breathe, not mine.'

This, as the Bible understands it, is the fundamental conflict within the human condition: the struggle between the *will to power* and the *will to life*. Life, down here on earth, is holy. It is also exceptionally fragile. It is *hevel*, a mere breath. Almost in his last words, Moses tells his people, 'I call heaven and earth to witness against you today that I have set life and death, blessing and curse, before you. Therefore choose life so that you and your descendants may live!' (Deut. 30:19). Murder in pursuit of power while invoking the name of God is sacrilege, whoever does it, whoever the victim, whatever the faith.

That drama is still being enacted today in Syria, Iraq, Afghanistan, Nigeria, Somalia, Libya, and in acts of terror around the world. What drives ISIS and its kindred organisations is the restoration of the Caliphate and the return to its rule of all the lands it once controlled, from Israel to Spain.[1] These are political objectives. They have nothing to do with the God of Abraham. God does not accept human sacrifice. God does not sanctify the will to power. That is the way of Cain, not that of God. When religion turns men into murderers, God replies: 'The voice of your brother's blood is crying to me from the ground.'

*

What then will happen if we do nothing directly to confront the ideology that has led in our time to barbarism and bloodshed? First, the world will be more religious a generation from now, not less. This will be so even if religion fails to convert a single soul. It has to do with demography. The more religious people are, the more children they have. The more secular they are, the fewer children they have. The indigenous populations of Europe, the most secular continent on earth, are committing long, slow suicide. Their below-replacement birth rates mean that they will get older and fewer. Demographically, as Eric Kaufmann has shown, the religious will inherit the earth.

Within religion, the most extreme, anti-modern or anti-Western movements will prevail. This is happening in Judaism, Christianity and Islam. The old marriage of religion and culture has ended in divorce. Today the secular West has largely lost the values that used to be called the Judeo-Christian heritage. Instead it has chosen to worship the idols of the self – the market, consumerism, individualism, autonomy, rights and 'whatever works for you' – while relinquishing the codes of loyalty, reverence and respect that once preserved marriages, communities and the subtle bonds that tie us to one another, moving us to work for the common good.

Losing its religious faith, the West is beginning to lose the ideals that once made it inspiring to the altruistic: reverence, loyalty, human dignity, the relief of poverty, public service, collective responsibility, national identity and respect for religious values while at the same time making space for liberty of conscience and the peaceable co-existence of more than one faith. Today Western politics often seem bereft of vision beyond the mantra of 'freedom and democracy' and cost-benefit calculations of maximum services for the minimum of tax. Faced with a culture of individualism and hedonism, it is not surprising that young radicals, eager to change the world, turn elsewhere to express their altruism, even if it involves acts that are brutal and barbaric. 'The act of self-denial seems to confer on us the right to be harsh and merciless toward others,' said Eric Hoffer in *The True Believer*.[2] Altruism misdirected can lead to evil: that has been the thesis of this book. That is why the West must recover its ideals.

The moral relativism that prevails today in the secular West is no defence of freedom. To see this, all you have to do is to watch any interview between a Western journalist and an Islamist. The journalist will make a comment like, 'Surely killing people for blasphemy is wrong.' The Islamist will say, 'I can understand how you see it that way, but people have different moral views, and you surely understand that some people see it differently.' End of conversation. The journalist has no reply. He or she probably believes that morality is subjective, the only basic human values are autonomy and the right to choose, the supreme virtue is tolerance even towards the intolerant, and imposing your views on others is intellectual imperialism. The journalist has, in effect, signalled his defeat before he has even opened his mouth, and the Islamist knows this.

In a world of relativism, what talks is power. In that sense, the Islamist is a faithful child of the twenty-first century. He or she knows that what makes the West sit up and take notice is the brute assertion of force. The West has often had no serious response to religiously motivated violence beyond ridicule and crude assaults on religion as such.

It was a great sage of Islam, ibn Khaldun (1332–1406), who saw that as a society becomes affluent it becomes more individualistic. It loses what he called its *asabiyah*, its social cohesion. It then becomes prey to the 'desert dwellers', those who shun the luxuries of the city and are prepared for self-sacrifice in war. Bertrand Russell came to the identical conclusion from a diametrically opposed starting point. Creative civilisations like ancient Greece and Renaissance Italy, he said, found that 'the liberation from fetters made individuals energetic and creative, producing a rare florescence of genius', but 'the decay of morals' made them 'collectively impotent', and they fell to 'nations less civilised than themselves but not so destitute of social cohesion'.[3]

So there will be more terror, more bloodshed, and more civil war in the Middle East and Africa. Other countries, like Jordan and Lebanon, may be drawn into the abyss. There will be further barbaric new crimes against humanity, broadcast courtesy of the Internet. There will be rising tension in every European country. People will feel that their liberties are being threatened, but will have no clear idea of how to respond. Every time a movement like al-Qaeda is defeated, another will arise to take its place. Young people, in search of meaning, identity and community, will continue to be recruited to the cause.

The West, indeed the world, has never faced a challenge quite like this. Against it stands a movement more like a series of flash-mobs than a nation or a coalition, groups that can form, dissolve and reform almost at will. None of the normal conventions of war apply: uniforms distinguishing combatants from non-combatants, or the rules like those of the Geneva Conventions that constrain the cruelties that may be practised in the name of humanity. Indeed, the radicals pride themselves on their inhumanity. They have no qualms against butchering and beheading those with whom they disagree, using civilians as human shields, turning people into slaves and ten-year-old girls into suicide bombers.

Nor are they amenable to the kind of rational considerations that have governed international conflict in the past. They pride themselves on their willingness to die and they are utterly disinclined to compromise. According to Graeme Wood, ISIS 'rejects peace as a matter of principle' and 'hungers for genocide'.[4] It believes that time and God are on their side. Radical Islam has proved its ability to recruit anywhere via the Internet, by playing endless video scenes of suffering and humiliation, enlisting people to take revenge, sacrificing their own and other people's lives to win their place in heaven.

If we fail to address the issue seriously now, this will be our future. It is not one any of us should wish to bequeath to our grandchildren.

*

In chapters 3 and 4 I devoted what might seem to be a dispro-
portionate amount of space to antisemitism. This is not because
Jewish suffering is different from Christian or Muslim suffering. It is not. All human suffering matters, and matters equally.
Nor is it because Jews are suffering more than others today. They
are not. Everyone is a potential victim. Humanity as a whole is
suffering.

My point is that we still have not understood what antisemitism is and the role it plays in the legitimation of evil. It is the
first warning sign of a culture in a state of cognitive collapse. It
gives rise to that complex of psychological regressions that lead
to evil on a monumental scale: splitting, projection, pathological
dualism, dehumanisation, demonisation, a sense of victimhood,
and the use of a scapegoat to evade moral responsibility. It allows
a culture to blame others for its condition without ever coming to
terms with it themselves. The antisemitism flooding through the
Arab and Islamic world today is as widespread and virulent as it
was in Europe between 1880 and 1945, and it is being dissemi-
nated worldwide through the Internet.

Antisemitism is only contingently related to Jews. The real
targets of Christians in the age of the Crusades were the Muslims,
not the Jews. The targets of Nazi Germany were the European
nations that had defeated it in the First World War and humiliated
it thereafter. The real targets of the Islamists are secular Islamic
regimes and the West, especially those who defeated the Ottoman
Empire in 1922 and divided up its spoils.

Jews, however, played an essential function in the group psychology of these movements. By fulfilling the role of the scapegoat, they could be blamed for everything bad that happened to
the group. As the mysterious, omnipotent, all-embracing enemy,
they united the group, silenced dissent, distracted the mind from
painful truths and enabled otherwise utterly incompatible groups
to become allies. Today, for example, Islamist groups find it
hard to win Western support for the imposition of Sharia law,
the beheading of captives, the forced conversion of Christians or

the sentencing to death of blasphemers. But when they criticise Israel, they find they no longer stand alone. This brings within the fold such strange fellow travellers as the far right, the anti-globalisation left, and some notoriously politicised human rights organisations, surely the oddest coalition ever assembled in support of people practising terror to bring about theocracy.

Note that antisemitism, to succeed, must always disguise its motives. It did so in the Middle Ages by accusing Jews of killing Christian children and spreading the plague. It did so in Nazi Germany in terms drawn from medicine. Jews were the cancer in the midst of the Aryan nation. Today it does so by blaming Israel or Jews, in classic Blood Libel/*Protocols of the Elders of Zion* style, for controlling America, dominating Europe, manipulating the economy, owning the media, perpetrating 9/11 and all subsequent terrorist attacks, creating AIDS, Ebola, the 2004 tsunami and global warming.

In the Middle Ages Jews were hated for their religion, in the nineteenth and twentieth centuries for their race, and today for their nation state, Israel. In the West, antisemitism is now usually disguised as anti-Zionism. In Arabic, the rhetoric is usually more honest: it speaks openly of Jews. But the targets of Islamist terror in the West – the synagogue guard in Copenhagen, Jewish shoppers in a kosher supermarket in Paris, visitors to the Jewish Museum in Brussels, and so on – were Jewish, not Israeli. The reason is simple. *A scapegoat must be someone you can kill without risk of reprisal.* Israel can respond. Jews outside Israel cannot. Indeed, that is one compelling reason why Israel exists. It is the only thing protecting Jews from being the scapegoat-victims of the world for another thousand years.

No one I know confuses antisemitism with legitimate criticism of Israel. Jews believe that no human, certainly no nation, is above criticism. Judaism is one of the world's most self-critical cultures. The Hebrew Bible is an extended essay in self-criticism. Antisemitism is not criticism. It is the denial of Jews' collective right to exist. It changes form over time. In the 1930s, antisemites chanted 'Jews to Palestine'. Today they chant 'Jews out of Palestine'. As Israeli novelist Amos Oz put it: They don't want us to be here. They don't want us to be there. They don't want us to be.

The significance of antisemitism, though, is its effect not on Jews but on antisemites. It allows them to see themselves as victims. It enables them to abdicate moral responsibility. Whatever is wrong in the world, 'It isn't our fault, it's theirs. They did it to us. After all, they control the world.' The result is that hate paralyses the mind and perpetuates the very failures that caused defeat or underachievement in the first place. Antisemitism did not help Christians win the Crusades, or the Nazis win the Second World War. It will not help Muslims in the Middle East, Africa and Asia build societies that will honour God and his image in humankind. Those who hate Jews, hate freedom. Those who seek to eliminate Jews, seek to eliminate freedom. Antisemitism is a sickness that destroys all who harbour it. Hate harms the hated but it destroys the hater. There is no exception.

*

Can the world be changed? The answer is yes, and the proof is one of the most uplifting stories in the religious history of humankind: the changed relationship between Jews and Christians after the Holocaust. Here there are many heroes, Christians of moral courage, deep faith and surpassing humanity who realised that, after that terrible denouement, something must change. Among these, special praise must go to a series of popes: John XXIII who began the process leading to Vatican II and *Nostra Aetate*, Paul VI who completed it, and John Paul II and Benedict XVI, both of whom continued it in their own way.

Greater even than these, however, is the current Pope, Francis I. On 12 September 2013, in an open letter to the editor of an Italian newspaper, *La Repubblica*, he wrote, 'God's fidelity to the close covenant with Israel never failed, and . . . through the terrible trials of these centuries, the Jews have kept their faith in God. And for this we shall never be sufficiently grateful to them as Church but also as humanity.' This may be the first time that a pope has publicly recognised that in staying true to their faith, Jews were being loyal to God, not faithless to him. That is a statement capable of changing the world. The Church, in the West, has begun to overcome its sibling rivalry with Judaism. If it can happen between Christians and Jews, it can happen between them and Islam also.

Today Jews, Christians and Muslims must stand together, in defence of humanity, the sanctity of life, religious freedom and the honour of God himself. The real clash of the twenty-first century will not be *between* civilisations or religions, but *within* them. It will be between those who accept and those who reject the separation of religion and power. Those who believe that political problems have religious solutions are deluding themselves as well as failing to understand who Abraham was and what he represented. The confusion of religion and politics was what Abraham and his heirs opposed, not what they endorsed.

What then must we do? We must put the same long-term planning into strengthening religious freedom as was put into the spread of religious extremism. Radical Islam was a movement fuelled by Western petrodollars, used by oil-producing countries to fund networks of schools, madrassahs, university professorships and departments, dedicated to Wahhabi or Salafist interpretations of Islam, thus marginalising the more open, gracious, intellectual and mystical tendencies in Islam that were in the past the source of its greatness. It was a strategy remarkable in its long time-horizons, its precision, patience, detail and dedication. If moderation and religious freedom are to prevail, they will require no less. We must train a generation of religious leaders and educators who embrace the world in its diversity, and sacred texts in their maximal generosity.

There must be an international campaign against the teaching and preaching of hate. Most Western countries have anti-racist legislation that has proved virtually powerless against the vitriol spread through the social media. Education in many countries continues to be a disgrace. If children continue to be taught that non-believers are destined for hell and that Christians and Jews are the greater and lesser Satan, if radio, television, websites and social media pour out a non-stop stream of paranoia and incitement, then Article 18 of the Universal Declaration of Human Rights, with its commitment to religious freedom, will mean nothing. All the military interventions in the world will not stop the violence.

We need to recover the absolute values that make Abrahamic monotheism the humanising force it has been at its best: the sanctity of life, the dignity of the individual, the twin imperatives of justice and compassion, the moral responsibility of the rich for the poor, the commands to love the neighbour and stranger, the insistence on peaceful modes of conflict resolution and respectful listening to the other side of a case, forgiving the injuries of the past and focusing instead on building a future in which the children of the world, of all colours, faith and races, can live together in grace and peace. These are the ideals on which Jews, Christians and Muslims can converge, widening their embrace to include those of other faiths and none. This does not mean that human nature will change, or that politics will cease to be an arena of conflict. All it means is that politics will remain politics, and not become religion.

We need also to insist on the simplest moral principle of all, the first (as we saw in chapter 2) to be confirmed by computer simulation: the principle of reciprocal altruism, otherwise known as Tit-for-Tat. This says: as you behave to others, so will others behave to you. *If you seek respect, you must give respect. If you ask for tolerance, you must demonstrate tolerance. If you wish not to be offended, then you must make sure you do not offend.* As John Locke said, 'It is unreasonable that any should have a free liberty of their religion who do not acknowledge it as a principle of theirs that nobody ought to persecute or molest another because he dissents from him in religion.'⁵ This principle alone, properly applied, would have banned at the outset the preachers-of-hate who radicalised so many impressionable minds in the West, turning them into murderers in God's name.

Wars are won by weapons, but it takes ideas to win a peace. This book has been about one such idea: an alternative to the sibling rivalry that has been a source of fratricide and religious violence throughout history. Sibling rivalry as a contest for divine love is a bad idea and wrongly diminishes Abraham's God. The truth that shines through the Genesis texts is that we are each blessed by God, each precious in his sight, each with our role in his story, each with our own song in the music of humankind. To be a child of Abraham is to learn to respect the other children of Abraham even if their way is not ours, their covenant not ours, their understanding of God different from ours. We know that we are loved. That must be enough. To insist that being loved entails that others be unloved is to fail to understand love itself.⁶

It has also been about the dual covenant in Genesis, first with Noah, then with Abraham. This is the best solution I know to the potential violence implicit in the fact that we derive our identities from groups. Groups conflict, so that the altruism we show to the people like us goes hand in hand with the aggression we show to the people not like us, and both are deeply embedded in human nature. That is why the great attempts to escape from identity – into either universalism or individualism – have always failed, whether they were religious or secular. Sooner or later the tribes return, fully armed and breathing fire. The only adequate alternative, proposed by Genesis precisely as God's protest against violence, is to say that he has made two covenants with us, one in our common humanity, the other in our specific identity. The first is about the universality of justice, the second about the particularity of love, and in that order. *Our common humanity precedes our religious differences.* That must be the basis of any Abrahamic theology capable of defeating the false god of violence and the idolatry of the pursuit of power.

And yes, there are hard texts. There are passages in the sacred scriptures of each of the Abrahamic monotheisms which, interpreted literally, can lead to hatred, cruelty and war. But Judaism, Christianity and Islam all contain interpretive traditions that in the past have read them in the larger context of co-existence, respect for difference and the pursuit of peace, and can do so today. Fundamentalism – text without context, and application without interpretation – is not faith but an aberration of faith.

*

No soul was ever saved by hate. No truth was ever proved by violence. No redemption was ever brought by holy war. No religion won the admiration of the world by its capacity to inflict suffering on its enemies. Despite the fact that these things have been endorsed in their time by sincere religious believers, they are a travesty of faith, and until we learn this, religion will remain one of the great threats to the peace of the world.

The crimes of religion have one thing in common. They involve making God in our image instead of letting him remake us in his. The highest truth does not cast its mantle over our lowest instincts – the search for power, the urge for conquest, the use of religious language to spread the aura of sanctity over ignoble crimes. These are forms of imperialism, not faith.

Terror is the epitome of idolatry. Its language is force, its principle to kill those with whom you disagree. That is the oldest and most primitive form of conflict resolution. It is the way of Cain. If anything is evil, terror is. In suicide bombings and other terrorist attacks, the victims are chosen at random, arbitrarily and indiscriminately. Terrorists, writes Michael Walzer, 'are like killers on a rampage, except that their rampage is not just expressive of rage or madness; the rage is purposeful and programmatic. It aims at a general vulnerability: Kill these people in order to terrify those.'[7]

The victims of terror are not only the dead and injured, but the very values on which a free society is built: trust, security, civil liberty, tolerance, the willingness of countries to open their doors to asylum seekers, the gracious safety of public places. Religiously motivated terror desecrates and defames religion itself. It is sacrilege against God and the life he endowed with his image. Islam, like Judaism, counts a single life as a universe. Suicide and murder are forbidden in the Abrahamic faiths. Judaism, Christianity and Islam all know the phenomenon of martyrdom – but martyrdom means being willing to die for your faith. It does not mean being willing to kill for your faith.[8]

Terror is not a justifiable means to an acceptable end, because it does not end. Terrorists eventually turn against their own people. Walzer again: 'The terrorists aim to rule, and murder is their method. They have their own internal police, death squads, disappearances. They begin by killing or intimidating those comrades who stand in their way, and they proceed to do the same, if they can, among the people they claim to represent. If terrorists are successful, they rule tyrannically, and their people bear, without consent, the costs of the terrorists' rule.'[9] There is no route from terror to a free society.

Nor is it the cry of despair of the weak. The weak have different weapons. They know that justice is on their side. That is why the prophets used not weapons but words. It is why Gandhi and Martin Luther King preferred non-violent civil disobedience, knowing that it spoke to the world's conscience, not its fears. True need never needs terror to make its voice heard.

The deliberate targeting of the innocent is an evil means to an evil end, to achieve a solution that does violence to the humanity and integrity of those we oppose. To give religious justification to it is to commit sacrilege against the God of Abraham, who is the God of life. Altruistic evil is still evil, and not all the piety in the world can purify it. Abraham's God is the power that rescues the powerless, the God of glory who turns the radiance of his face to those without worldly glory: the poor, the destitute, the lonely, the marginal, the outsiders of the world. God hears the cry of the unheard, and so, if we follow him, do we.

Now is the time for Jews, Christians and Muslims to say what they failed to say in the past: We are all children of Abraham. And whether we are Isaac or Ishmael, Jacob or Esau, Leah or Rachel, Joseph or his brothers, we are precious in the sight of God. We are blessed. And to be blessed, no one has to be cursed. God's love does not work that way.

Today God is calling us, Jew, Christian and Muslim, to let go of hate and the preaching of hate, and live at last as brothers and sisters, true to our faith and a blessing to others regardless of their faith, honouring God's name by honouring his image, humankind.

Notes

Chapter 1

1. Joint report by the BBC World Service and the International Centre for the Study of Radicalisation (ICSR), King's College London, December 2014.
2. 'Islamic State Crucifying, Burying Children Alive in Iraq', Reuters, Geneva, 5 February 2015.
3. Lord Alton, speech, House of Lords, 24 July 2014. I am indebted to Lord Alton for many of the examples cited here.
4. Angela Shanahan, 'No Going Back for Egypt's Converted Copts', *The Australian*, 21 May 2011.
5. http://www.bbc.com/news/magazine-30883058.
6. Aid to the Church in Need, *Religious Freedom in the World Report 2014*.
7. *Sunday Times*, 16 November 2014.
8. Thomas Hobbes (1588–1679), *Of Man, Being the First Part of Leviathan*, Part 1, ch. 11, 'On the Difference of Manners', Harvard Classics, 1909–14.
9. C. Phillips and A. Axelrod, *Encyclopedia of Wars*, New York, Facts on File, 2004.
10. G. Austin, T. Kranock and T. Oommen, *God and War: An Audit and an Exploration*, BBC, 2003.
11. See H. Tajfel and J.C. Turner, 'The Social Identity Theory of Intergroup Behaviour', in S. Worchel and W.G. Austin (eds.), *Psychology of Intergroup Relations*, Chicago, Nelson-Hall, 1986, pp. 7–24. See also Donald M. Taylor and Janet R. Doria, 'Self-serving and Group-serving Bias in Attribution', *Journal of Social Psychology*, 113.2, April 1981, pp. 201–11.
12. Moisés Naím, *The End of Power*, New York, Basic Books, 2013, p. 5.

Chapter 2

1. Charles Darwin, *The Descent of Man*, vol. 1, London, John Murray, 1871, p. 163.
2. Richard Sosis, 'Religion and Intragroup Cooperation: Preliminary Results of a Comparative Analysis of Utopian Communities,' *Cross-Cultural Research*, 34.1, 2000, pp. 70–87; Richard Sosis and Candace Alcorta, 'Signaling, Solidarity, and the Sacred: The Evolution of Religious Behavior', *Evolutionary Anthropology: Issues, News, and Reviews*, 12.6, 2003, pp. 264–74; Richard Sosis and Eric R. Bressler, 'Cooperation and Commune Longevity: A Test of the Costly Signaling Theory of Religion,' *Cross-Cultural Research*, 37.2, 2003, pp. 211–39.
3. Nicholas K. Rauh, *The Sacred Bonds of Commerce: Religion, Economy, and Trade Society at Hellenistic Roman Delos, 166–87 BC*, Amsterdam, J.C. Gieben, 1993, p. 129.
4. Cited in Ara Norenzayan, *Big Gods: How Religion Transformed Cooperation and Conflict*, Princeton, NJ, Princeton University Press, 2013, pp. 66–7.
5. Ronald Inglehart and Wayne E. Baker, 'Modernization, Cultural Change, and the Persistence of Traditional Values,' *American Sociological Review*, 65.1, 2000, pp. 19–51.
6. John Locke, *Letter Concerning Toleration*, Indianapolis, Hackett, 1983, p. 51. Note that Locke would also have denied granting civil rights to Catholics, on the ground that their loyalty lay elsewhere (to the Pope), a charge similar to that raised by some antisemites today against Jews, in relation to the State of Israel.
7. Jonathan Haidt, *The Righteous Mind: Why Good People Are Divided by Politics and Religion*, New York, Pantheon Books, 2012, p. 151.
8. Norenzayan, *Big Gods*, p. 153.
9. Eric Hoffer, *The True Believer: Thoughts on the Nature of Mass Movements*, New York, Harper and Row, 1951; Scott Atran, *Talking to the Enemy: Violent Extremism, Sacred Values, and What It Means to Be Human*, London, Allen Lane, 2010.
10. Michael Ignatieff, *The Warrior's Honor: Ethnic War and the Modern Conscience*, New York, Metropolitan Books, 1997, p. 188.

Chapter 3

1. Sam Keen, *Faces of the Enemy: Reflections of the Hostile Imagination*, New York, HarperSanFrancisco, 1992.
2. Jeffrey B. Russell, *The Prince of Darkness*, Ithaca, NY, Cornell University Press, 1989, p. 20.
3. Ibid., p. 19.
4. Richard Dawkins, *The God Delusion*, London, Bantam Press, 2006, p. 31.
5. Richard Beck and Sara Taylor, 'The Emotional Burden of Monotheism: Satan, Theodicy, and Relationship with God', *Journal of Psychology and Theology*, 36.3, 2008, pp. 151–60.
6. On this, see e.g., Claudia Koonz, *The Nazi Conscience*, Cambridge, MA, Belknap Press of Harvard University Press, 2003, pp. 46–68.
7. Ingo Müller, *Hitler's Justice: The Courts of the Third Reich*, trans. Deborah Lucas Schneider, Cambridge, MA, Harvard University Press, 1991, pp. 92–6.
8. See Robert Jay Lifton, *The Nazi Doctors*, New York, Basic Books, 1986, p. 18.
9. John Weiss, *Ideology of Death: Why the Holocaust Happened in Germany*, Chicago, Ivan R. Dee, 1996, p. 296.
10. Mark Roseman, The *Villa, the Lake, the Meeting: Wannsee and the Final Solution*, London, Allen Lane, 2002, p. 67.
11. George Browder, *Hitler's Enforcers*, New York, Oxford University Press, 1996, pp. 136–8.
12. Julian Benda, *The Treason of the Intellectuals (Le Trahison des Clercs)*, trans. Richard Aldington, New York, Norton, 1928, p. 27.
13. Jeffrey Herf, *The Jewish Enemy*, Cambridge, MA, Belknap Press of Harvard University Press, 2008, p. 38.
14. Ibid., p. 121.
15. Koonz, *The Nazi Conscience*, p. 20.
16. Ibid., p. 24.
17. Ibid., p. 25.
18. Ibid., p. 130. Note that the mass killing began with the murder of the handicapped – people suffering from what were literally mental or physical defects, and who were therefore regarded as 'useless eaters' and *lebensunwertes Leben*. This idea was not invented by the Nazis but taken up by them after its invention by 'progressive' figures such as Karl Binding and Alfred Hoche in their 1920 book, *The Permission of*

Destroying Lives Unworthy of Life. (I am grateful to Robert P. George for this note.)

19. Lifton, *The Nazi Doctors*, p. 16.
20. Primo Levy, *If This is a Man*, London, Abacus, 1987, pp. 111–12.
21. Koonz, *The Nazi Conscience*, p. 137.
22. Cited in Weiss, *Ideology of Death*, p. 325.
23. Herf, *The Jewish Enemy*, p. 5.
24. Vamik Volkan, *Blind Trust*, Charlottesville, VA, Pitchstone Publishing, 2004, p. 136.
25. Ibid., p. 49.
26. Herf, *The Jewish Enemy*, p. 152.
27. Ibid., p. 87.
28. Ibid., p. 131.
29. Wolff Heinrichsdorff, *Die Judenfrage*, 18 September 1939.
30. Herf, *The Jewish Enemy*, p. 69.
31. Ibid., p. 77.
32. Ibid., p. 121.
33. Ibid., p. 98.
34. Max Domarus (ed.), *Hitler: Reden und Proklamationen*, vol. 2, Neustadt, Schmidt, 1962, p. 1055.
35. Joseph Goebbels, 'Wer will den Krieg', *Die Zeit ohne Beispiel, Reden und Aufsatze aus den Jahren 1939/40/41*, pp. 93–5.
36. Herf, *The Jewish Enemy*, p. 64.
37. Ibid., pp. 255–6.
38. *Mein Kampf*, ch. 2, quoted in Koonz, *The Nazi Conscience*, p. 17.
39. Cited in, e.g., Lucy Dawidowicz, *A Holocaust Reader*, New York, Behrman, 1976, pp. 120ff.
40. Dov Shilansky, *Musulman*, Tel Aviv, Menora, 1962. I am indebted for this reference to Emil Fackenheim, *To Mend the World*, New York, Schocken, 1982, p. 186.
41. Herf, *The Jewish Enemy*, pp. 261–2.
42. E.H. Gombrich, *Myth and Reality in German War-Time Broadcasts*, London, Athlone, 1970, p. 23.

Chapter 4

1. http://www.memri.org/clip_transcript/en/4641.htm.
2. http://www.memri.org/clip/en/0/0/0/0/0/0/4666.htm.
3. http://www.memritv.org/clip_transcript/en/4498.htm.

4. *Jakarta Globe*, 21 January 2010.

5. Tarek Fatah, *The Jew Is Not My Enemy*, Toronto, McClelland and Stewart, 2010, p. xxi.

6. Reported in Turkish daily paper *Aksam*, 12 September 2004.

7. Quoted in Gabriel Schoenfeld, *The Return of Anti-Semitism*, San Francisco, Encounter Books, 2004, p. 13.

8. Bernard Lewis, 'The Roots of Muslim Rage', *The Atlantic*, 1 September 1990.

9. Voltaire, *Oeuvres Complètes*, 1756, vol. 7, ch. 1; text in Paul R. Mendes-Flohr and Jehuda Reinharz (eds.), *The Jew in the Modern World: A Documentary History*, New York, Oxford University Press, 1980, pp. 252–3.

10. Immanuel Kant, *Streit*, in *Werke*, 11:321, cited in Paul Lawrence Rose, *Revolutionary Antisemitism in Germany from Kant to Wagner*, Princeton, NJ, Princeton University Press, 1990.

11. Georg Wilhelm Friedrich Hegel, *Early Theological Writings*, p. 201, cited in Rose, *Revolutionary Antisemitism*, p. 111.

12. Johann Gottlieb Fichte, 'On the French Revolution', in Mendes-Flohr and Reinharz (eds.), *The Jew in the Modern World*, p. 257; Poliakov, *The History of Antisemitism*, p. 180.

13. Accounts can be found in R. Po-chia Hsia, *The Myth of Ritual Murder: Jews and Magic in Reformation Germany*, New Haven, CT, Yale University Press, 1988; Hermann Strack, *The Jew and Human Sacrifice; Human Blood and Jewish Ritual, an Historical and Sociological Inquiry*, trans. Henry Blanchamp, New York, Blom, 1971; Joshua Trachtenberg, *The Devil and the Jews: The Medieval Conception of the Jew and its Relation to Modern Antisemitism*, Philadelphia, Jewish Publication Society, 1993; Alan Dundes (ed.), *The Blood Libel Legend: A Casebook in Anti-Semitic Folklore*, Madison, University of Wisconsin Press, 1991; Ronald Florence, *Blood Libel: The Damascus Affair of 1840*, Madison, University of Wisconsin Press, 2004.

14. They include a work by a French cleric, Abbé Barruel, blaming the French Revolution on the Order of Templars; a second written by a German, E.E. Eckert, about Freemasons; and the third, a fictional dialogue between Montesquieu and Machiavelli, written by Maurice Joly in 1864.

15. The classic historical account is Norman Cohn, *Warrant for Genocide*, London, Eyre and Spottiswoode, 1967. See also Hadassa Ben-Itto, *The Lie that Wouldn't Die: The Protocols of the Elders of Zion*, London, Vallentine Mitchell, 2005.

16. Goebbels, entry for 13 May 1943, *Die Tagebucher von Joseph Goebbels*, 11/8, pp. 287–91.
17. Robert Wistrich, *A Lethal Obsession*, New York, Random House, 2010, p. 792.
18. Judith Apter Klinghoffer, 'Blood Libel', *History News Network*, 19 December 2006.
19. A survey of reactions can be found in MEMRI *Inquiry and Analysis Series, No. 114*, 'Arab Press Debates Antisemitic Egyptian Series "Knight Without a Horse" – Part III', 10 December 2002.
20. MEMRI *Inquiry and Analysis Series, No. 610*, 18 November 2003.
21. http://www.centerforsecuritypolicy.org/wp-content/uploads/2014/05/Explanatory_Memoradum.pdf. The document is cited in Andrew C. McCarthy, *The Grand Jihad*, New York, Encounter, 2010; Lorenzo Vidino, *The New Muslim Brotherhood in the West*, New York, Columbia University Press, 2010; Jan McDaniel, *Irredentist Islam and Multicultural America*, 2008; Thomas M. Pick, *Home-grown Terrorism*, Amsterdam, IOS Press, 2009; and Zeyno Baran, *Citizen Islam*, New York, Bloomsbury Academic, 2011.
22. Bernard Lewis, *Semites and Anti-Semites: An Inquiry into Conflict and Prejudice*, New York, Norton, 1986, p. 259.

Chapter 5

1. Horace, *Epodes* 7, 17–20.
2. Sigmund Freud, James Strachey, Anna Freud, Carrie Lee Rothgeb and Angela Richards, *The Standard Edition of the Complete Psychological Works of Sigmund Freud*, London, Hogarth Press, 1953, p. 250.
3. *The Letters of Sigmund Freud 1873–1939*, London, Hogarth Press, 1970, p. 428.
4. Sigmund Freud, *Femininity* (1933), in *Complete Psychological Works*, vol. 22, p. 123.
5. See Ernest Jones, *The Life and Work of Sigmund Freud*, New York, Basic Books, 1953, p. 9.
6. Douglas W. Mock, *More than Kin and Less than Kind: The Evolution of Family Conflict*, Cambridge, MA, Belknap Press of Harvard University Press, 2004.
7. Geoffrey Wigoder, *Jewish–Christian Relations since the Second World War*, Manchester, Manchester University Press, 1988.
8. Rosemary Radford Ruether, *Faith and Fratricide: The Theological Roots*

of Anti-Semitism, New York, Seabury Press, 1974; Gregory Baum, *The Jews and the Gospel: A Re-Examination of the New Testament*, Westminster, MD, Newman Press, 1961; Edward H. Flannery, *The Anguish of the Jews: Twenty-Three Centuries of Anti-Semitism*, New York, Macmillan, 1965; Paul M. van Buren, *A Theology of the Jewish-Christian Reality*, Lanham, MD, University Press of America, 1995; R. Kendall Soulen, *The God of Israel and Christian Theology*, Minneapolis, Fortress Press, 1996; Mary C. Boys, *Has God Only One Blessing? Judaism as a Source of Christian Self-Understanding*, New York, Paulist Press, 2000; James Carroll, *Constantine's Sword: The Church and the Jews: A History*, Boston, Houghton Mifflin, 2001.

9. Yosef Hayim Yerushalmi, 'Response to Rosemary Ruether', in Eva Fleischner (ed.), *Auschwitz, Beginning of a New Era? Reflections on the Holocaust: Papers Given at the International Symposium on the Holocaust, Held at the Cathedral of Saint John the Divine, New York City, June 3 to 6, 1974*, New York, KTAV Pub. Co., 1977, pp. 97–108.

10. Alan Edelstein, *An Unacknowledged Harmony: Philo-Semitism and the Survival of European Jewry*, Westport, CT, Greenwood Press, 1982.

11. Robert Satloff, *Among the Righteous: Lost Stories from the Holocaust's Long Reach into Arab Lands*, New York, PublicAffairs, 2006.

12. To be sure, there are other passages in Paul – especially Romans 11 – that suggest a more benign view of Jews and Judaism. See John Gager, *Origins of Anti-Semitism*, New York, Oxford University Press, 1983.

13. Cyprian, *Three Books of Testimonies against the Jews*, 20; quoted in Ruether, *Faith and Fratricide*, p. 135.

14. Ruether, *Faith and Fratricide*, p. 135.

15. Prudentius, *Apotheosis*, 541–50; Ruether, *Faith and Fratricide*, p. 134. For more on this subject, see Galit Hasan-Rokem and Alan Dundes (eds.), *The Wandering Jew: Essays in the Interpretation of a Christian Legend*, Bloomington, Indiana University Press, 1986.

Chapter 6

1. Gen. 16:9–12; 17:20; 21:13, 18.

2. A Midrash portrays the episode in terms of a conflict between God and the angels: When Ishmael was dying of thirst, the angels said to the Holy One, 'Will you create a well of water for one whose descendants will one day refuse to give water to your children the Israelites when they are dying with thirst?' God asked the angels: 'What is Ishmael at

this moment: righteous or wicked?' 'Righteous,' replied the angels. 'I only judge a person,' said God, 'by how he is now.' See below for the rabbinic re-reading of the entire narrative.

3. Gen. 17:17; 18:12, 13, 15; 21:6 (twice) and 21:9. The name *Yitzchak* ('he will laugh') also appears seven times during this section of the narrative: Gen. 17:19, 21; 21:3, 4, 5, 8, 10. The same verb, *z-ch-k*, occurs at two other critical junctures. The first is when the two angels visit Lot in Sodom and tell him to leave. He reports their warning to his sons-in-law, 'but his sons-in-law *thought he was joking*' (19:14). The second occurs when Isaac – by now married – is forced by famine to go to the land of the Philistines. Afraid that the people will kill him in order to take Rebekah, he says that she is his sister. One day, Abimelech looks out of the window and sees Isaac 'being familiar with her' (26:8) and immediately understands that they are not brother and sister but husband and wife. The range of senses of this single word is thus very wide indeed, but its thematic centrality is unmistakable.

4. See Umberto Cassuto, *A Commentary on the Book of Genesis*, trans. from Hebrew by Israel Abrahams, Jerusalem, Magnes Press, 1964.

5. Nahmanides, Commentary to Gen. 16:6. An English translation is available in *Ramban: Commentary on the Torah*, trans. and annotated by Rabbi Dr Charles Chavel, New York, Shilo, 1971, vol. 1, p. 213.

6. In most of the literary treatments – poems and novels – about Sarah and Hagar, Isaac and Ishmael, the sympathies of the writer are with Hagar and Ishmael. As Sol Liptzin puts it: 'modern poets and novelists have been almost unanimous in their sympathy for her [Hagar] and in their condemnation of her master and mistress . . . In the Hagar story, our sympathy is not with Abraham but rather with the princess who became a bondwoman, the concubine who was misused by her master and mistress and then abandoned. She is at the centre of our interest, and not the patriarch . . .' (Sol Liptzin, *Biblical Themes in World Literature*, Hoboken, NJ, KTAV, 1985, pp. 39, 52–3).

Shakespeare, in *The Merchant of Venice*, sees Shylock – and by implication Jews in general – as fated to undergo an ironic role reversal. Now it is the children of Isaac and Jacob who have become outcasts in a world of 'Hagar's offspring' (Act 2, sc. 5, l. 44).

In 'The Seed Growing Secretly', Henry Vaughan casts Ishmael as a symbol of the Gentiles, apparently cast off, but nonetheless the eventual recipients of God's saving grace: 'If pious griefs Heavens joys awake / O fill his bottle! Thy childe weeps!'

Ishmael's most noted literary appearance is as the narrator of Herman Melville's *Moby Dick*, with its famous opening line, 'Call me Ishmael.' In his *Ishmael: A Study of the Symbolic Mode in Primitivism* (Baltimore, Johns Hopkins University Press, 1956), James Baird argues that 'Ishmael is the overseer of every major work in [Melville's] literary record': Tom in *Typee*, Paul in *Omoo*, Taji in *Mardi*, the young sailor-heroes in *Redburn* and *White-Jacket*, the tragic hero of *Pierre* in his early life, the handsome sailor of *Billy Budd*, and so on: 'He is Ishmael, the outcast, condemned to wander' (pp. 92–3). For these references, see Antony Westenbroek, 'Ishmael', in *Genesis: The Book of Beginnings*, Oxford, Lion Classic Bible Series, 1997, pp. 91–3.

These writers – as did post-biblical Jewish tradition – sensed the lonely dignity of Hagar and her son. The story of Isaac and Ishmael is not a tragedy, but neither is it a simple moral tale of black and white, good and evil, chosen and rejected.

7. Jack Miles, *God: A Biography*, New York, Alfred A. Knopf, 1995, p. 406.
8. John Milton, 'Sonnet: On His Blindness' (1650s).
9. On Midrash, the classic work is Isaac Heineman, *Darkhei ha-Aggadah* [Hebrew], Jerusalem, Magnes Press, 1970. For English introductions, see Michael Fishbane (ed.), *The Midrashic Imagination: Jewish Exegesis, Thought, and History*, Albany, State University of New York Press, 1993; *The Exegetical Imagination: On Jewish Thought and Theology*, Cambridge, MA, Harvard University Press, 1998; Moshe Halbertal, *People of the Book: Canon, Meaning, and Authority*, Cambridge, MA, Harvard University Press, 1997; Geoffrey H. Hartman and Sanford Budick (eds.), *Midrash and Literature*, New Haven, CT, Yale University Press, 1986; Jacob Neusner, *Judaism and the Interpretation of Scripture: Introduction to the Rabbinic Midrash*, New York, Hendrickson Publishers, 2004; *Midrash in Context: Exegesis in Formative Judaism*, Philadelphia, Fortress Press, 1983. On the continuity between Midrash and the Hebrew Bible itself, see Michael Fishbane's path-breaking work, *Biblical Interpretation in Ancient Israel*, Oxford, Clarendon Press, 1985.
10. Midrash Hagadol, Gen. 24:62; see also Genesis Rabbah 60:14.
11. One example is the two anonymous Israelites who object when the young Moses intervenes in their dispute. The Midrash identifies them with Dathan and Aviram, the two men who subsequently objected to Moses' leadership during the Korah rebellion many years later. On the midrashic principle, see Heineman, *Darkhei ha-Aggadah*, pp. 27–34.

12. Midrash Tanhuma, Hayyei Sarah, 8; Pirkei deRabbi Eliezer, 29.

13. In a perceptive comment, Moshe Lichtenstein suggests that Midrash operates not on a *correspondence* theory of truth (does it match the facts?) but on a *coherence* theory (does it provide an internally consistent narrative?). M. Lichtenstein, *Tsir va-tson* [Hebrew], Alon Shvut, Israel, Yeshivat Har Etzion, 2002, p. 219.

14. Pirkei deRabbi Eliezer, 30. The work is generally dated as belonging to the eighth century, and contains references to the Umayyad dynasty of Islam.

15. Targum Jonathan to Gen. 25:11.

Chapter 7

1. See, in this context, Roland Barthes' fine essay, 'The Struggle with the Angel', in Roland Barthes, *Image, Music, Text*, London, Fontana, 1977, pp. 125–410. Barthes shows in detail how the narrative subverts the conventions of the folktale – as, I argue, is the case with all the counter-narratives in Genesis.

2. Rashi, quoting Midrash, gives a fine interpretation: '*He was exceedingly afraid* – lest he be killed; *he was distressed* – lest he be forced to kill.' Even killing in self-defence should occasion moral qualms, despite the fact that it is morally warranted. See the fine analysis in Everett Gendler, 'War in the Jewish Tradition', in Menachem Kellner (ed.), *Contemporary Jewish Ethics*, New York, Sanhedrin Press, 1978, pp. 189–210.

3. Genesis Rabbah 77:3; 78:3.

4. English translations tend to miss this point, which is essential to the counter-narrative. Thus, the New International Version has, 'Please accept the present that was brought to you'; the New English Translation: 'Please take my present that was brought to you'; the Revised Standard Version, 'Accept, I pray you, my gift that is brought to you.' The King James Version, however, reads, 'Take, I pray thee, my blessing that is brought to thee.'

5. Again the translations tend to miss the point. Thus the King James Version has, 'because I have enough'; The New International Version, 'I have all I need'; the New American Bible, 'I have an abundance.' The Hebrew original, however, makes a pointed distinction between Esau's 'I have much' (*yesh li rav*) and Jacob's 'I have everything' (*yesh li khol*).

6. 'Face' is, of course, a fundamental element of Emmanuel Levinas's philosophy of 'the Other'. See, among his many writings, *Alterity*

and *Transcendence*, trans. Michael B. Smith, New York, Columbia University Press, 1999; *Humanism of the Other*, trans. Nidra Poller, Urbana, Chicago, University of Illinois Press, 2003; *Of God Who Comes to Mind*, trans. Bettina Bergo, Stanford, Stanford University Press, 1998; *Otherwise than Being: Or, Beyond Essence*, trans. Alphonso Lingis, The Hague, M. Nijhoff, 1981; *Proper Names*, trans. Michael B. Smith, Stanford, Stanford University Press, 1996; *Totality and Infinity: An Essay on Exteriority*, trans. Alphonso Lingis, The Hague, M. Nijhoff, 1979. A useful introduction is Seán Hand (ed.), *The Levinas Reader*, Oxford, Blackwell, 1989. Alain Finkielkraut's *The Wisdom of Love*, trans. Kevin O'Neill and David Suchoff, Lincoln, University of Nebraska Press, 1997, is an accessible work based on Levinas's philosophy of 'the face'. For a discussion of Levinas's views on otherness, see Jeffrey Bloechl (ed.), *The Face of the Other and the Trace of God: Essays on the Philosophy of Emmanuel Levinas*, New York, Fordham University Press, 2000; and Simon Critchley and Robert Bernasconi (eds.), *The Cambridge Companion to Levinas*, Cambridge, Cambridge University Press, 2002.

7. Thus, for example, Abraham is promised the land five times – Gen. 12:7; 13:14–18; 15:7, 18–21; 17:1–8 – and children five times – 12:2; 13:16; 15:5; 17:2, 5–6. See also David J.A. Clines, *The Theme of the Pentateuch*, Sheffield, Dept. of Biblical Studies, University of Sheffield, 1978.

8. Zohar 146b; see also Deuteronomy Rabbah 1:15.

9. See Rashi, Commentary to Gen. 25:25.

10. R. Zvi Hirsch Chajes explains that Midrash, using the Bible as an ethics textbook, is forced to turn its characters into clearly demarcated heroes and villains. Biblical narrative is full of nuance. There are no villains without virtues, no heroes without shortcomings. This very subtlety, however, makes it hard to use as a teaching text. See Maharatz Chajes, *Mavo ha-Aggadot*, printed at the beginning of standard editions of *Ein Yaakov*. The problem Chajes addresses is well illustrated in John Barton, *Ethics and the Old Testament*, Harrisburg, PA, Trinity Press International, 1998.

11. As I mention in the text, René Girard calls this 'mimetic' desire – the desire to be like, and hence in place of, the other: 'In the temporal plan of the system there is not a moment when those involved in the action do not see themselves separated from their rivals by formidable differences. When one of the "brothers" assumes the role of father and king, the other cannot but feel himself to be the disinherited son. That

explains why the antagonists only rarely perceive the reciprocal nature of their involvement' (*Violence and the Sacred*, trans. Patrick Gregory, Baltimore, Johns Hopkins University Press, 1977, pp. 143–68).

12. A midrash, *Pesikta Rabbati* 13, makes the same point. See Menahem Kasher, Torah Shelemah to Gen. 33:11.

13. R. David Kimche (Radak) and R. Yosef ibn Kaspi, Commentaries to Gen. 25:23.

14. See, for example, Gen. 29:26; 43:33; 48:14.

15. See Rashi, Rashbam, Ibn Ezra, Chizkuni to Gen. 25:22; Nahmanides, Commentary to Gen. 27:4.

16. Nahmanides, Commentary to Gen. 25:22.

17. The readings given in this and the following chapters are not necessarily to be found in the classic Jewish exegetical literature, but that is the point: there is, I argue, a meaning below the surface that is different from the one on the surface. This approach is similar to the phrase used by Rabbi Samuel ben Meir (Rashbam, c. 1085–1158) in his phrase 'the deep plain sense of Scripture' (*omek peshuto shel mikra*); see his Commentary to Gen. 37:2.

18. Girard, *Violence and the Sacred*, p. 169.

19. Maimonides holds that the wrestling match took place in a vision (*The Guide for the Perplexed*, II:42). Nahmanides strongly objects: if the encounter was a vision, why did Jacob limp subsequently? (Nahmanides, Commentary to Gen. 18:1). Gersonides and Abrabanel defend Maimonides' interpretation: it is possible for an intense psychological experience to have psychosomatic effects.

20. There is, of course, a famous verse (Mal. 1:2–3) that seems to contradict this: '"Was not Esau Jacob's brother?" the Lord says. "Yet I have loved Jacob, but Esau I have hated."' This, however, refers to specific circumstances in Israel's later history, during a period of conflict between the Israelites and the Edomites. In any case, Nahmanides and R. David Kimche (Commentaries to Gen. 29:31) point out that the word *senuah*, when contrasted with *ahuvah* ('loved'), does not mean 'hated', but rather 'loved, but loved less intensely'. That is also its meaning in Deut. 21:15.

   R. Elijah of Vilna (the Vilna Gaon), in his notes at the end of *Sa'arat Eliyahu*, translates the phrase in Malachi as 'I hate *the subsidiary part* of Esau, but the main part – his head – is hidden next to our Father in Heaven, and that is why Jacob says, "I have seen your face and it is like seeing the face of God."' This passage is developed at length by R. Abraham Isaac Kook (*Iggerot Rayah*, vol. 1, letter 112), to prove that eventually there will be a reconciliation between Jacob and Esau, i.e. between Jews and Christians, as also between Jews and Muslims ('the brotherly love of Esau and Jacob, of Isaac and Ishmael, will assert itself above all the confusion that the evil brought on by our bodily nature has engendered'). For an English translation, see Ben Zion Bokser, *Abraham Isaac Kook: The Lights of Penitence, The Moral Principles, Lights of Holiness, Essays, Letters, and Poems*, New York, Paulist Press, 1978, pp. 338–9.

Chapter 8

1. Mishnah, Avot 2:5.
2. For literary analyses of the Joseph narrative, see Eric I. Lowenthal, *The Joseph Narrative in Genesis*, New York, KTAV, 1973; Uriel Simon, *Joseph and his Brothers: A Story of Change*, trans. David Louvish, Ramat Gan, Israel, Lookstein Center, 2002; James L. Kugel, *In Potiphar's House: The Interpretive Life of Biblical Texts*, Cambridge, MA, Harvard University Press, 1994.
3. Gen. 24:67.
4. Gen. 29:18, 20, 30.
5. Gen. 37:3, 4; 44:20.
6. Rashi, Commentary to Gen. 37:2, on the basis of Genesis Rabbah 84:3.
7. R. Hayyim of Kossov, Torat Hayyim to Gen. 37:18.
8. See previous chapter, note 6.
9. See Rashi, Commentary ad loc., who attributes this phrase to 'the holy spirit'. The classic Jewish commentators are unused to the concept of irony. On the use of irony in the Bible, see Edwin M. Good, *Irony in the Old Testament*, Philadelphia, Westminster Press, 1965.
10. See Ephraim E. Urbach, *The Sages, their Concepts and Beliefs*, trans. Israel Abrahams, Cambridge, MA, Harvard University Press, 1987, pp. 462–71.
11. See especially Rom. 7:7–24.
12. See Urbach, *The Sages*, pp. 471–83; Solomon Schechter, *Aspects of Rabbinic Theology: Major Concepts of the Talmud*, New York, Schocken, 1961, pp. 219–343.
13. Maimonides, Mishneh Torah, Teshuvah, 2:2.
14. Ibid., 2:1.
15. Esau had earlier said, 'The days of mourning for my father are near;

then I will kill my brother Jacob' (Gen. 27:41). Apparently, fraternal revenge was not permitted during a father's lifetime.

16. I am indebted for these examples to Bill Bryson, *Mother Tongue*, London, Penguin, 1991, p. 63.

Chapter 9

1. See David Diringer, *Writing*, New York, Praeger, 1962; *The Alphabet: A Key to the History of Mankind*, New York, Funk & Wagnalls, 1968; *The Story of the Aleph Beth*, New York, Yoseloff, 1958; Robert K. Logan, *The Alphabet Effect: A Media Ecology Understanding of the Making of Western Civilization*, Cresskill, NJ, Hampton Press, 2004; John Man, *Alpha Beta: How our Alphabet Changed the Western World*, London, Headline, 2000; David Sacks, *The Alphabet: Unravelling the Mystery of the Alphabet from A to Z*, London, Hutchinson, 2003. On early semitic scripts, see Joseph Naveh, *Early History of the Alphabet: An Introduction to West Semitic Epigraphy and Palaeography*, Jerusalem, Magnes Press, 1982. On Hebrew letters, see Marc-Alain Ouaknin's delightful *Mysteries of the Alphabet: The Origins of Writing*, trans. Josephine Bacon, New York, Abbeville Press, 1999. On the impact of literacy on consciousness, see Walter J. Ong's masterly and suggestive works, *The Presence of the Word: Some Prolegomena for Cultural and Religious History*, New Haven, CT, Yale University Press, 1967; and *Orality and Literacy: The Technologizing of the Word*, London, Routledge, 1991. See also Jack Goody, *The Domestication of the Savage Mind*, Cambridge, Cambridge University Press, 1977; *The Logic of Writing and the Organization of Society*, Cambridge, Cambridge University Press, 1986; *The Interface between the Written and the Oral*, Cambridge, Cambridge University Press, 1987.

2. There are many biblical examples. Every seven years the king was commanded to assemble the nation and 'read aloud this Torah before them in their hearing' (Deut. 31: 10–13). When 'the book of the law' was rediscovered in the reign of King Josiah, 'He went up to the temple of the Lord with the men of Judah, the priests and the prophets – all the people from the least to the greatest – and read in their hearing all the words of the book of the covenant which had been found in the Temple of the Lord' (2 Kgs 23:2). In the historic gathering of those who had returned from Babylon, Ezra 'read [the Torah] aloud from daybreak till noon, in the presence of the men, women and others who

could understand, and all the people listened attentively to the book of the Torah' (Neh. 8:3).

3. Nahmanides and R. David Kimche, Commentaries ad loc.
4. Targum Onkelos and Rashbam, Commentary ad loc.
5. Ibn Ezra, Commentary ad loc.
6. R. Naftali Berlin, Ha'amek Davar ad loc., suggests that Leah was unable to go out with the flocks because the bright sunlight hurt her eyes.
7. Genesis Rabbah 70:16; Midrash Sekhel Tov (Buber), 29:17; 30:7.
8. There is a rabbinic tradition that the patriarchs kept the commands of the Mosaic covenant before it was given to the nation at Mount Sinai. Nahmanides explains, however, that they did so only in the land of Israel. Jacob's deathbed blessings were uttered in Egypt. See Nahmanides, Commentary to Gen. 26:5.
9. Rashi to Gen. 22:1.

Chapter 10

1. Jonathan Haidt, *The Righteous Mind: Why Good People Are Divided by Politics and Religion*, New York, Pantheon Books, 2012.
2. One of the most powerful of all stories of role reversal is, however, a religious one. After King David has fallen in love with Bathsheba, wife of Uriah the Hittite, he sends her husband into battle knowing that he will be killed. He then marries her. Nathan the prophet approaches the king, ostensibly to seek his advice. He tells him the following story. There are two men in a certain town, one rich, the other poor. The rich man has large flocks and herds, the poor one only a single lamb which he cherishes as if it were his child. A traveller arrives, and the rich man, preparing a feast for the visitor, is reluctant to kill one of his own animals, so he takes the poor man's sheep instead. As the story proceeds, David gets more and more angry, until he bursts out, saying, 'The man who did this deserves to die.' Then Nathan said to David, 'You are the man.' The story is told in 2 Samuel 11–12. It is the most effective example of role reversal I know.
3. See Yosef Hayim Yerushalmi, *Zakhor: Jewish History and Jewish Memory*, Seattle, University of Washington Press, 1982.
4. See Julia Kristeva, *Desire in Language: A Semiotic Approach to Literature and Art*, New York, Columbia University Press, 1980; Michael Fishbane, *Biblical Interpretation in Ancient Israel*, Oxford, Clarendon Press, 1985.
5. Talmud Yerushalmi, Rosh Hashanah 3:5.

Chapter 11

1. Samuel Huntington, *The Clash of Civilizations and the Remaking of World Order*, New York, Simon & Schuster, 1996, p. 310.
2. The Talmud Yerushalmi, Megillah 1:11, 71b, records a dispute between R. Eliezer and R. Johanan, on just this question. One holds that Gen. 10 describes the situation after Gen. 11. The other maintains that the two chapters are in correct chronological sequence.
3. J. Richard Middleton, *The Liberating Image: The Imago Dei in Genesis 1*, Grand Rapids, MI, Brazos, 2005, p. 224.
4. Maimonides, Mishneh Torah, Melakhim 9:1. See David Novak, *The Image of the Non-Jew in Judaism: An Historical and Constructive Study of the Noahide Laws*, New York, E. Mellen Press, 1983; *Natural Law in Judaism*, Cambridge, Cambridge University Press, 1998.
5. I say this mindful of centuries of criticism of the idea. See, for a recent example, Clifford Longley, *Chosen People: The Big Idea that Shaped England and America*, London, Hodder & Stoughton, 2002.
6. Mishnah, Sanhedrin 4:5.
7. Rabbinic tradition speaks of Abraham making disciples, but that is oral tradition, not written, explicit text.
8. R. Abraham Isaac Kook, *Orot haKodesh*, vol. 3, 15.
9. Tosefta, Sanhedrin 13:2.
10. Mishnah, Avot 3:14.
11. The title of an article by B.S. Lewis puts it bluntly: 'I'm right, you're wrong, go to hell', *The Atlantic Monthly*, May 2003.

Chapter 12

1. William Blake, 'The Everlasting Gospel' (c. 1818).
2. Sanhedrin 71a.
3. Babylonian Talmud, Kiddushin 49a.
4. Shakespeare, *The Merchant of Venice*, Act 1, scene 3.
5. Babylonian Talmud, Berakhot 28a.
6. Maimonides, Mishneh Torah, Melakhim 5:4.
7. Maimonides, Mishneh Torah, Melakhim 6:5.
8. See Rabbi N.L. Rabinovitch, *Responsa Melomdei Milchamah*, Maaleh Adumim, Maaliyot, 1993, pp. 22–5.
9. Levi Yitzhak of Berditchev, *Kedushat Levi*, Jerusalem, 2001, section on Purim; Gerald Cromer, 'Amalek as Other, Other as Amalek:

Interpreting a Violent Narrative', *Qualitative Sociology*, 24.2, 2001, pp. 191–202.

10. See David Cook, *Understanding Jihad*, Berkeley, University of California Press, 2005.
11. Mishnah, Shabbat 6:4.
12. Babylonian Talmud, Shabbat 63a.
13. Babylonian Talmud, Kiddushin 30b.
14. Babylonian Talmud, Megillah 10b.
15. Bamidbar Rabbah 13:15.
16. Maharsha, Chiddushei Aggadot to Berakhot 58a.

Chapter 13

1. Babylonian Talmud, Yoma 86b.
2. See the interesting essay on Josephus as survivor in Elias Canetti, *Crowds and Power*, Harmondsworth, Penguin, 1973, pp. 274–82.
3. Josephus, *The Jewish War*, trans. G.A. Williamson, Harmondsworth, Penguin, 1959, chs. 9–23.
4. Tosefta, Chagigah 2:9.
5. *The Jewish War*, p. 264.
6. Ibid., p. 135.
7. For a balanced survey of the subject, see David Biale, *Power and Powerlessness in Jewish History*, New York, Schocken Books, 1986.
8. Abraham Lincoln, 'Second Inaugural Address', in Andrew Delbanco (ed.), *The Portable Abraham Lincoln*, New York, Viking, 1992, p. 321.
9. Stephen Toulmin, *Cosmopolis: The Hidden Agenda of Modernity*, Chicago, University of Chicago Press, 1992, p. 55.
10. Alexis de Tocqueville, *Democracy in America*, abridged with an introduction by Thomas Bender, New York, Modern Library, 1981, p. 185.
11. Ibid., pp. 187–88.
12. R. Naftali Zvi Yehudah Berlin (Netziv), Ha-amek Davar to Gen. 11:4.
13. Karl Popper, *The Open Society and Its Enemies*, vol. 1, new edn., London, Routledge Classics, 2002.
14. Aristotle, *The Politics*, ed. Stephen Everson, Cambridge, Cambridge University Press, 1988, 1261a16-23, p. 21.
15. For a good summary, see Harry Redner, *Ethical Life: The Past and Present of Ethical Cultures*, Lanham, MD, Rowman & Littlefield, 2001, pp. 68–85.
16. 1 Sam. 8:7.

17. Thomas Paine, *Political Writings*, ed. Bruce Kuklick, Cambridge, Cambridge University Press, 2000, p. 3.
18. Oliver Goldsmith, *The Traveller* (1764), l. 427.
19. Michael Novak, *The Spirit of Democratic Capitalism*, London, Institute of Economic Affairs, 1991, p. 53.
20. Rousseau called his secular substitute 'civil religion'. J.-J. Rousseau, *The Social Contract and Other Later Political Writings*, ed. and trans. Victor Gourevitch, Cambridge, Cambridge University Press, 1997.
21. Babylonian Talmud, Shabbat 88a; Avodah Zarah 2b.
22. Eric Voegelin, *Order and History*, vol. 1, *Israel and Revelation*, Baton Rouge, Louisiana State University Press, 1956, p. 37.
23. Graeme Wood, 'What ISIS Really Wants', *The Atlantic*, March 2015.
24. The classic work on the subject is Norman Cohn, *The Pursuit of the Millennium*, London, Paladin, 1972.
25. Matthew Arnold, 'Stanzas from the Grande Chartreuse' (c. 1850).
26. J.L. Talmon, *The Origins of Totalitarian Democracy*, Harmondsworth, Peregrine, 1986.
27. Michael Walzer, *Exodus and Revolution*, New York, Basic Books, 1985, p. 145.
28. Talmon, *The Origins of Totalitarian Democracy*, p. 253.
29. Maharal, *Be'er haGolah*, Jerusalem, 1972, pp. 150–51.
30. John Stuart Mill, 'Utilitarianism', *On Liberty, Considerations on Representative Government*, ed. H.B. Acton, London, Dent, Everyman's Library, 1972, p. 85.
31. Kierkegaard actually said, 'The tyrant dies and his rule is over; the martyr dies and his rule begins.'

Chapter 14

1. Martin Luther King, *Strength to Love*, New York, Harper & Row, 1963.
2. That is what is so offensive about Jean-Paul Sartre's book, *Sur le Question Juif*, published in 1946. Written immediately after the Holocaust, it is ostensibly a book *against* antisemitism. Sartre's central thesis is that Jews do not create antisemitism; antisemitism creates Jews. Jews, he says, have nothing in common except that they are the objects of hatred. Therefore to be Jewish is to defy that hatred. By Sartre's own standards, this is 'inauthentic' existence. Authenticity, he believed, meant living in a certain way because you have chosen to, not because someone else has

forced you to. Yet this is the only form of existence he accords to Jews: Jews exist because other people hate them. Such is the power of antisemitism that Sartre, seeking to reject it, reinvents it.

3. On memory, see Yosef Hayim Yerushalmi, *Zakhor, Jewish History and Jewish Memory*, Seattle, University of Washington Press, 1982; Maurice Halbwachs, *On Collective Memory*, ed., trans., and with an introduction by Lewis A. Coser, Chicago, University of Chicago Press, 1992; Eviatar Zerubavel, *Time Maps: Collective Memory and the Social Shape of the Past*, Chicago, University of Chicago Press, 2003. On the misuse of memory in modern ethnic conflict, see Stuart J. Kaufman, *Modern Hatreds: The Symbolic Politics of Ethnic War*, Ithaca, NY, Cornell University Press, 2001.

4. Babylonian Talmud, Baba Metzia 32b.

5. Miroslav Volf, *Exclusion and Embrace: A Theological Exploration of Identity, Otherness, and Reconciliation*, Nashville, Abingdon Press, 1996.

6. Henri Atlan, 'Founding Violence and Divine Referent', in Paul Dumouchel (ed.), *Violence and Truth: On the Work of René Girard*, Stanford, Stanford University Press, 1988, pp. 198–208.

7. Maimonides, Mishneh Torah, Deot 7:8.

8. See Jonathan Sacks, *To Heal a Fractured World*, London, Continuum, 2005, pp. 175–84.

9. Jack Miles, *God: A Biography*, New York, Alfred A. Knopf, 1995, pp. 397–408.

10. William Shakespeare, *Sonnets*, 129.

11. Viktor E. Frankl, *Man's Search for Meaning: An Introduction to Logotherapy*, trans. Ilse Lasch, Boston, Beacon Press, 1992.

12. Phyllis Chesler, *The New Anti-Semitism: The Current Crisis and What We Must Do About It*, San Francisco, Jossey-Bass, 2003, p. 105.

Chapter 15

1. See Graeme Wood, 'What ISIS Really Wants', *The Atlantic*, March 2015.

2. Eric Hoffer, *The True Believer: Thoughts on the Nature of Mass Movements*, London, Secker and Warburg, 1952, p. 103.

3. Bertrand Russell, *History of Western Philosophy*, London, Allen and Unwin, 1961, Introduction.

4. Wood, 'What ISIS Really Wants'.

5. John Locke, *Political Essays*, Cambridge, Cambridge University Press, 1997, p. 152.

6. Spinoza – in some ways a very un-Jewish thinker, in others a very Jewish one – writes: 'Every man's true happiness and blessedness consists solely in the enjoyment of what is good, not in the pride that he alone is enjoying it, to the exclusion of others. He who thinks himself the more blessed because he is enjoying benefits which others are not, or because he is more blessed or more fortunate than his fellows, is ignorant of true happiness and blessedness, and the joy which he feels is either childish or envious or malicious. For instance, a man's true happiness consists only in wisdom, and knowledge of the truth, not at all in the fact that he is wiser than others, or that others lack such knowledge: such considerations do not increase his wisdom or true happiness. Whoever, therefore, rejoices for such reasons, rejoices in another's misfortune, and is, so far, malicious and bad, knowing neither true happiness nor the peace of the true life.' Or, in the language of contemporary economics, blessedness is not a positional good. Benedict Spinoza, *A Theologico-Political Treatise*, trans. R.H.M. Elwes, Mineola, NY, Dover Publications, 2004, p. 43.

7. Michael Walzer, *Arguing about War*, New Haven, CT, Yale University Press, 2004, p. 51.

8. 'Does our religion agree with the idea of suicide? Is the Muslim permitted to blow himself up among others because they are enemies? The sacred [Islamic] sources referred to this as one of the greatest sins. Throughout 14 centuries, all the [jurisprudent] literature regarding Jihad has not permitted harming innocent women and children. Moreover, even if the enemy has violated all things sacred and killed [Muslim] women and children, [Islam] forbids responding in kind' (Dr Abd Al-Hamid Al-Ansari, *Al-Raya*, Qatar, 25 July 2005).

9. Walzer, *Arguing about War*, p. 65.

Bibliography

Chapter 1

Armstrong, Karen, *The Battle for God*, New York, Alfred A. Knopf, 2000.

Armstrong, Karen, *Fields of Blood: Religion and the History of Violence*, New York, Alfred A. Knopf, 2014.

Berger, Peter L., *The Desecularization of the World*, Washington, DC, Ethics and Public Policy Center, 1999.

Brafman, Ori, and Rod A. Beckstrom, *The Starfish and the Spider: The Unstoppable Power of Leaderless Organizations*, New York, Portfolio, 2006.

Carlson, John D., and Jonathan H. Ebel, *From Jeremiad to Jihad: Religion, Violence, and America*, Berkeley, University of California, 2012.

Gopin, Marc, *Holy War, Holy Peace: How Religion Can Bring Peace to the Middle East*, New York, Oxford University Press, 2002.

Hill, Christopher, *The English Bible and the Seventeenth-Century Revolution*, London, Allen Lane, 1993.

Hill, Christopher, *The World Turned Upside Down: Radical Ideas during the English Revolution*, New York, Viking, 1972.

Ignatieff, Michael, *Blood and Belonging: Journeys into the New Nationalism*, New York, Farrar, Straus, and Giroux, 1994.

Ignatieff, Michael, *The Lesser Evil: Political Ethics in an Age of Terror*, Princeton, NJ, Princeton University Press, 2004.

Ignatieff, Michael, *The Warrior's Honor: Ethnic War and the Modern Conscience*, New York, Metropolitan Books, 1998.

Juergensmeyer, Mark, *Terror in the Mind of God: The Global Rise of Religious Violence*, Berkeley, University of California Press, 2000.

Juergensmeyer, Mark, and Margo Kitts, *Princeton Readings in Religion and Violence*, Princeton, NJ, Princeton University Press, 2011.

Kaufman, Stuart J., *Modern Hatreds: The Symbolic Politics of Ethnic War*, Ithaca, NY, Cornell University Press, 2001.

Kaufmann, Eric P., *Shall the Religious Inherit the Earth? Demography and Politics in the Twenty-First Century*, London, Profile, 2010.

Naím, Moisés, *The End of Power: From Boardrooms to Battlefields and Churches to States, Why Being in Charge Isn't What It Used to Be*, New York, Basic Books, 2013.

New, David S., *Holy War: The Rise of Militant Christian, Jewish, and Islamic Fundamentalism*, Jefferson, NC, McFarland & Co., 2002.

Phillips, Charles, and Alan Axelrod, *Encyclopedia of Wars*, New York, Facts on File, 2004.

Renard, John, *Fighting Words: Religion, Violence, and the Interpretation of Sacred Texts*, Berkeley, University of California Press, 2012.

Schwartz, Regina M., *The Curse of Cain: The Violent Legacy of Monotheism*, Chicago, University of Chicago Press, 1997.

Walzer, Michael, *The Revolution of the Saints: A Study in the Origins of Radical Politics*, Cambridge, MA, Harvard University Press, 1965.

Chapter 2

Atran, Scott, *In Gods We Trust: The Evolutionary Landscape of Religion*, Oxford, Oxford University Press, 2002.

Atran, Scott, *Talking to the Enemy: Violent Extremism, Sacred Values, and What It Means to Be Human*, London, Allen Lane, 2010.

Axelrod, Robert, *The Evolution of Cooperation*, New York, Basic Books, 1984.

Bloom, Paul, *Just Babies: The Origins of Good and Evil*, London, The Bodley Head, 2013.

Boniolo, G., and G. De Anna, *Evolutionary Ethics and Contemporary Biology*, Cambridge, Cambridge University Press, 2006.

Buller, D., *Evolutionary Psychology and the Persistent Quest for Human Nature*, Cambridge, MA, MIT Press, 2005.

Churchland, Patricia Smith, *Braintrust: What Neuroscience Tells Us about Morality*, Princeton, NJ, Princeton University Press, 2011.

Darwin, Charles, *The Descent of Man, and Selection in Relation to Sex*, London, John Murray, 1871.

Darwin, Charles, *On the Origin of Species*, London, John Murray, 1859.

Diamond, Jared, *The Third Chimpanzee: The Evolution and Future of the Human Animal*, New York, HarperCollins, 1992.

Durkheim, Émile, *Suicide, a Study in Sociology*, Glencoe, IL, Free Press, 1951.

Foot, Philippa, *Natural Goodness*, Oxford, Oxford University Press, 2001.

Glover, Jonathan, *Humanity: A Moral History of the 20th Century*, New Haven, CT, Yale University Press, 2000.

Greene, Joshua David, *Moral Tribes: Emotion, Reason, and the Gap between Us and Them*, New York, Penguin, 2013.

Haidt, Jonathan, *The Righteous Mind: Why Good People Are Divided by Politics and Religion*, New York, Pantheon, 2012.

Hamilton, W.D., 'The Genetical Evolution of Social Behavior', I and II, *Journal of Theoretical Biology*, 1964, 7:1–52.

Hoffer, Eric, *The True Believer: Thoughts on the Nature of Mass Movements*, New York, Harper and Row, 1951.

Hrdy, Sarah Blaffer, *Mothers and Others: The Evolutionary Origins of Mutual Understanding*, Cambridge, MA, Belknap Press of Harvard University Press, 2009.

Kitcher, P., *The Ethical Project*, Cambridge, MA, Harvard University Press, 2011.

Maynard Smith, John, *Evolution and the Theory of Games*, Cambridge, Cambridge University Press, 1982.

Norenzayan, Ara, *Big Gods: How Religion Transformed Cooperation and Conflict*, Princeton, NJ, Princeton University Press, 2013.

Pinker, Steven, *The Better Angels of Our Nature: Why Violence Has Declined*, New York, Viking, 2011.

Pinker, Steven, *The Blank Slate: The Modern Denial of Human Nature*, New York, Viking, 2002.

Putnam, Robert D., and David E. Campbell, *American Grace: How Religion Divides and Unites Us*, New York, Simon & Schuster, 2010.

Ridley, Matt, *The Origins of Virtue: Human Instincts and the Evolution of Cooperation*, New York, Viking, 1997.

Sober, E., and D.S. Wilson, *Unto Others: The Evolution and Psychology of Unselfish Behavior*, Cambridge, MA, Harvard University Press, 1998.

Trivers, R., 'The Evolution of Reciprocal Altruism', *Quarterly Review of Biology*, 1971, 46:35–57.

Waal, F.B.M. de, *The Bonobo and the Atheist: In Search of Humanism among the Primates*, New York, W.W. Norton & Company, 2014.

Waal, F.B.M. de, *Good Natured: The Origins of Right and Wrong in Humans and Other Animals*, Cambridge, MA, Harvard University Press, 1996.

Waal, F.B.M. de, *Primates and Philosophers*, Princeton, NJ, Princeton University Press, 2006.

Wilson, David Sloan, *Darwin's Cathedral: Evolution, Religion, and the Nature of Society*, Chicago, University of Chicago Press, 2002.

Wilson, E.O., *On Human Nature*, Cambridge, MA, Harvard University Press, 1978.

Wilson, J.Q., *The Moral Sense*, New York, Free Press, 1993.

Wright, R., *The Moral Animal: The New Science of Evolutionary Psychology*, New York, Pantheon, 1994.

Chapter 3

Barnstone, Willis, *The Other Bible: Gnostic Scriptures, Jewish Pseudepigrapha, Christian Apocrypha, Kabbalah, Dead Sea Scrolls*, San Francisco, Harper & Row, 1984.

Baumeister, Roy F., *Evil: Inside Human Cruelty and Violence*, New York, W.H. Freeman, 1997.

Beck, Aaron T., *Prisoners of Hate: The Cognitive Basis of Anger, Hostility and Violence*, New York, HarperCollins, 1999.

Herf, Jeffrey, *The Jewish Enemy*, Cambridge, MA, Belknap Press of Harvard University Press, 2008.

Jonas, Hans, *The Gnostic Religion*, Boston, Beacon Press, 1963.

King, Karen L., *What is Gnosticism?*, Cambridge, MA, Belknap Press of Harvard University Press, 2003.

Koonz, Claudia, *The Nazi Conscience*, Cambridge, MA, Belknap Press of Harvard University Press, 2003.

Lifton, Robert Jay, *The Nazi Doctors*, New York, Basic Books, 1986.

Müller, Ingo, *Hitler's Justice*, Cambridge, MA, Harvard University Press, 1991.

Pagels, Elaine H., *Adam, Eve, and the Serpent*, New York, Random House, 1988.

Pagels, Elaine H., *Beyond Belief*, New York, Random House, 2003.

Pagels, Elaine H., *The Gnostic Gospels*, New York, Random House, 1979.

Pagels, Elaine H., *The Gnostic Paul*, Philadelphia, Trinity Press International, 1992.

Pagels, Elaine H., *The Johannine Gospel in Gnostic Exegesis: Heracleon's Commentary on John*, Nashville, Abingdon Press, 1973.

Pagels, Elaine H., *The Origin of Satan*, New York, Random House, 1995.

Pagels, Elaine H., *Revelations*, New York, Viking, 2012.

Robinson, James, *The Nag Hammadi Library in English*, San Francisco, Harper & Row, 1978.

Roseman, Mark, *The Villa, the Lake, the Meeting*, London, Allen Lane/Penguin, 2002.

Russell, Jeffrey Burton, *The Devil*, Ithaca, NY, Cornell University Press, 1977.

Russell, Jeffrey Burton, *Lucifer: The Devil in the Middle Ages*, Ithaca, NY, Cornell University Press, 1984.

Russell, Jeffrey Burton, *The Prince of Darkness*, Ithaca, NY, Cornell University Press, 1988.

Russell, Jeffrey Burton, *Satan*, Ithaca, NY, Cornell University Press, 1981.

Volkan, Vamik D., *Blind Trust: Large Groups and their Leaders in Times of Crisis and Terror*, Charlottesville, VA, Pitchstone Publishing, 2004.

Volkan, Vamik D., *Bloodlines*, New York, Farrar, Straus, and Giroux, 1997.

Volkan, Vamik D., *Killing in the Name of Identity: A Study of Bloody Conflicts*, Charlottesville, VA, Pitchstone Publishing, 2006.

Volkan, Vamik D., *The Need to Have Enemies and Allies*, Northvale, NJ, Jason Aronson, Inc., 1988.

Chapter 4

Armstrong, Karen, *Holy War: The Crusades and their Impact on Today's World*, New York, Anchor Books, 2001.

Baumeister, Roy F., *Evil: Inside Human Cruelty and Violence*, New York, W.H. Freeman, 1997.

Beck, Aaron T., *Prisoners of Hate: The Cognitive Basis of Anger, Hostility and Violence*, New York, HarperCollins, 1999.

Carmichael, Joel, *The Satanizing of the Jews: Origin and Development of Mystical Anti-Semitism*, New York, Fromm, 1992.

Carroll, James, *Constantine's Sword: The Church and the Jews: A History*, Boston, Houghton Mifflin, 2001.

Chazan, Robert (ed.), *Church, State, and Jew in the Middle Ages*, New York, Behrman House, 1980.

Chazan, Robert, *European Jewry and the First Crusade*, Berkeley, University of California Press, 1987.

Chazan, Robert, *God, Humanity, and History: The Hebrew First Crusade Narratives*, Berkeley, University of California Press, 2000.

Chazan, Robert, *In the Year 1096: The First Crusade and the Jews*, Philadelphia, Jewish Publication Society, 1996.

Chazan, Robert, *Medieval Stereotypes and Modern Anti-Semitism*, Berkeley, University of California Press, 1997.

Chesler, Phyllis, *The New Anti-Semitism: The Current Crisis and What We Must Do About It*, San Francisco, Jossey-Bass, 2003.

Eidelberg, Shlomo (ed. and trans.), *The Jews and the Crusaders: The Hebrew Chronicles of the First and Second Crusades*, Hoboken, NJ, KTAV Publishing House, 1996.

Flannery, Edward H., *The Anguish of the Jews: Twenty-Three Centuries of Anti-Semitism*, New York, Paulist Press, 1985.

Foxman, Abraham H., *Never Again? The Threat of the New Anti-Semitism*, San Francisco, HarperSanFrancisco, 2003.

Freud, Sigmund, *Totem and Taboo: Some Points of Agreement between the Mental Lives of Savages and Neurotics*, trans. James Strachey, London, Routledge and Kegan Paul, n.d.

Gager, John G., *The Origins of Anti-Semitism: Attitudes toward Judaism in Pagan and Christian Antiquity*, New York, Oxford University Press, 1983.

Girard, René, *The Scapegoat*, trans. Yvonne Freccero, Baltimore, Johns Hopkins University Press, 1986.

Girard, René, *Things Hidden since the Foundation of the World*, research undertaken in collaboration with Jean-Michel Oughourlian and Guy Lefort, trans. Stephen Bann (Books II and III) and Michael Metteer (Book I), Stanford, Stanford University Press, 1987.

Girard, René, *Violence and the Sacred*, trans. Patrick Gregory, Baltimore, Johns Hopkins University Press, 1977.

Glick, Leonard B., *Abraham's Heirs: Jews and Christians in Medieval Europe*, Syracuse, NY, Syracuse University Press, 1999.

Glover, Jonathan, *Humanity: A Moral History of the Twentieth Century*, London, Jonathan Cape, 1999.

Iganski, Paul, and Barry Kosmin (eds.), *The New Antisemitism? Debating Judeophobia in 21st-Century Britain*, London, Profile, 2003.

Isaac, Jules, *Has Anti-Semitism Roots in Christianity?*, trans. Dorothy and James Parkes, New York, National Conference of Christians and Jews, 1961.

Isaac, Jules, *Jesus and Israel*, ed. with a foreword by Claire Huchet Bishop, trans. Sally Gran, New York, Holt, Rinehart and Winston, 1971.

Isaac, Jules, *The Teaching of Contempt: Christian Roots of Anti-Semitism*, trans. Helen Weaver, New York, Holt, Rinehart and Winston, 1964.

Kearney, Richard, *Strangers, Gods, and Monsters: Ideas of Otherness*, London, Routledge, 2002.

Lang, Berel, *Heidegger's Silence*, Ithaca, NY, Cornell University Press, 1996.

Mack, Michael, *German Idealism and the Jew: The Inner Anti-Semitism of Philosophy and German Jewish Responses*, Chicago, University of Chicago Press, 2003.

Netanyahu, B., *The Origins of the Inquisition in Fifteenth Century Spain*, New York, Random House, 1995.

New, David S., *Holy War: The Rise of Militant Christian, Jewish, and Islamic Fundamentalism*, Jefferson, NC, McFarland & Co., 2002.

Nicholls, William, *Christian Anti-Semitism: A History of Hate*, Northvale, NJ, Jason Aronson Inc., 1993.

Poliakov, León, *The History of Anti-Semitism*, 4 vols., Philadelphia, University of Pennsylvania Press, 2003.

Rose, Paul Lawrence, *Revolutionary Antisemitism in Germany from Kant to Wagner*, Princeton, NJ, Princeton University Press, 1990.

Rosenbaum, Ron (ed.), *Those Who Forget the Past: The Question of Anti-Semitism*, New York, Random House, 2004.

Rotenstreich, Nathan, *Jews and German Philosophy: The Polemics of Emancipation*, New York, Schocken Books, 1984.

Rotenstreich, Nathan, *The Recurring Pattern: Studies in Anti-Judaism in Modern Thought*, New York, Horizon Press, 1964.

Ruether, Rosemary Radford, *Faith and Fratricide: The Theological Roots of Anti-Semitism*, New York, Seabury Press, 1974.

Schoenfeld, Gabriel, *The Return of Anti-Semitism*, San Francisco, Encounter Books, 2004.

Schwartz, Regina M., *The Curse of Cain: The Violent Legacy of Monotheism*, Chicago, University of Chicago Press, 1997.

Signer, Michael A., and John Van Engen (eds.), *Jews and Christians in Twelfth-Century Europe*, Notre Dame, IN, University of Notre Dame Press, 2001.

Simon, Marcel, *Verus Israel: A Study of the Relations between Christians and Jews in the Roman Empire*, London, Littman Library of Jewish Civilization, 1986.

Timmerman, Kenneth R., *Preachers of Hate: Islam and the War on America*, New York, Crown Forum, 2003.

Wistrich, Robert S., *Antisemitism: The Longest Hatred*, New York, Schocken Books, 1994.

Wistrich, Robert S., *A Lethal Obsession*, New York, Random House, 2010.

Chapter 5

Baum, Gregory, *The Jews and the Gospel, A Re-Examination of the New Testament*, Westminster, MD, Newman Press, 1961.

Boys, Mary C., *Has God Only One Blessing? Judaism as a Source of Christian Self-understanding*, New York, Paulist Press, 2000.

Buren, Paul M. van, *A Theology of the Jewish-Christian Reality*, Lanham, MD, University Press of America, 1995.

Carroll, James, *Constantine's Sword: The Church and the Jews: A History*, Boston, Houghton Mifflin, 2001.

Edelstein, Alan, *An Unacknowledged Harmony: Philo-Semitism and the Survival of European Jewry*, Westport, CT, Greenwood Press, 1982.

Flannery, Edward H., *The Anguish of the Jews: Twenty-Three Centuries of Anti-Semitism*, New York, Macmillan, 1965.

Freud, Sigmund, *Femininity* (1933), *The Standard Edition of the Complete Psychological Works of Sigmund Freud*, London, Hogarth, vol. XXII, 1933.

Freud, Sigmund, *The Letters of Sigmund Freud 1873–1939*, Hogarth Press, London, 1970.

Freud, Sigmund, James Strachey, Anna Freud, Carrie Lee Rothgeb and Angela Richards, *The Standard Edition of the Complete Psychological Works of Sigmund Freud*, London, Hogarth, 1953.

Gager, John, *Origins of Anti-Semitism*, New York, Oxford University Press, 1983.

Girard, René, *Violence and the Sacred*, Baltimore, Johns Hopkins University Press, 1977.

Hasan-Rokem, Galit, and Alan Dundes (eds.), *The Wandering Jew*, Bloomington, Indiana University Press, 1986.

Jones, Ernest, *The Life and Work of Sigmund Freud*, New York, Basic Books, 1953.

Mock, Douglas W., *More than Kin and Less than Kind: The Evolution of Family Conflict*, Cambridge, MA, Belknap Press of Harvard University Press, 2004.

Nirenberg, David, *Anti-Judaism*, New York, W.W. Norton & Co., 2013.

Ruether, Rosemary Radford, *Faith and Fratricide: The Theological Roots of Anti-Semitism*, New York, Seabury Press, 1974.

Satloff, Robert, *Among the Righteous: Lost Stories from the Holocaust's Long Reach into Arab Lands*, New York, Public-Affairs, 2006.

Shepardson, Christine C., *Anti-Judaism and Christian Orthodoxy*, Washington, DC, Catholic University of America Press, 2008.

Soulen, R. Kendall, *The God of Israel and Christian Theology*, Minneapolis, Fortress Press, 1996.

Wigoder, Geoffrey, *Jewish–Christian Relations since the Second World War*, Manchester, Manchester University Press, 1988.

Chapters 6–9

Alter, Robert, *The Art of Biblical Narrative*, New York, Basic Books, 1981.

Alter, Robert, *The Art of Biblical Poetry*, New York, Basic Books, 1985.

Alter, Robert, *On Biblical Narrative*, Eugene, University of Oregon Books, 2000.

Alter, Robert, *The World of Biblical Literature*, New York, Basic Books, 1992.

Alter, Robert, and Frank Kermode (eds.), *The Literary Guide to the Bible*, Cambridge, MA, Belknap Press of Harvard University Press, 1987.

Berlin, Adele, *The Jewish Study Bible*, New York, Oxford University Press, 2004.

Berlin, Adele, *Poetics and Interpretation of Biblical Narrative*, Winona Lake, IN, Eisenbrauns, 1994.

Clines, David J.A., *The Theme of the Pentateuch*, Sheffield, Dept. of Biblical Studies, University of Sheffield, 1978.

Fisch, Harold, *A Remembered Future: A Study in Literary Mythology*, Bloomington, Indiana University Press, 1984.

Fishbane, Michael, *Biblical Interpretation in Ancient Israel*, Oxford, Clarendon Press, 1985.

Fishbane, Michael, *The Exegetical Imagination: On Jewish Thought and Theology*, Cambridge, MA, Harvard University Press, 1998.

Fishbane, Michael, *The Garments of Torah: Essays in Biblical Hermeneutics*, Bloomington, Indiana University Press, 1989.

Fishbane, Michael (ed.), *The Midrashic Imagination: Jewish Exegesis, Thought, and History*, Albany, State University of New York Press, 1993.

Fishbane, Michael, *Text and Texture: Close Readings of Selected Biblical Texts*, New York, Schocken Books, 1979.

Fokkelman, J.P., *Narrative Art in Genesis: Specimens of Stylistic and Structural Analysis*, Assen, Van Gorcum, 1975.

Fokkelman, J.P., *Reading Biblical Narrative*, Louisville, KY, Westminster John Knox Press, 1999.

Kugel, James L., *The Bible As It Was*, Cambridge, MA, Belknap Press of Harvard University Press, 1997.

Kugel, James L., *In Potiphar's House: The Interpretive Life of Biblical Texts*, Cambridge, MA, Harvard University Press, 1994.

Kugel, James L., *On Being a Jew*, Baltimore, Johns Hopkins University Press, 1998.

Levenson, Jon D., *Creation and the Persistence of Evil: The Jewish Drama of Divine Omnipotence*, Princeton, NJ, Princeton University Press, 1994.

Levenson, Jon D., *The Hebrew Bible, the Old Testament, and Historical Criticism: Jews and Christians in Biblical Studies*, Louisville, KY, Westminster John Knox Press, 1993.

Levenson, Jon D., *Sinai and Zion: An Entry into the Jewish Bible*, Minneapolis, Winston Press, 1985.

Levenson, Jon D., *The Universal Horizon of Biblical Particularism*, New York, American Jewish Committee, Institute of Human Relations, 1985.

Sacks, Jonathan, *Exodus: The Book of Redemption*, New Milford, CT, Maggid Books & The Orthodox Union, 2010.

Sacks, Jonathan, *Genesis: The Book of Beginnings*, New Milford, CT, Maggid Books & The Orthodox Union, 2009.

Sacks, Jonathan, *Leviticus: The Book of Holiness*, New Milford, CT, Maggid Books & The Orthodox Union, 2015.

Sternberg, Meir, *The Poetics of Biblical Narrative: Ideological Literature and the Drama of Reading*, Bloomington, Indiana University Press, 1985.

Chapters 10–15

Ahmed, Akbar S., *Discovering Islam: Making Sense of Muslim History and Society*, London, Routledge, 2002.

Ahmed, Akbar S., *Islam under Siege: Living Dangerously in a Post-Honor World*, Cambridge, Polity, 2003.

Ahmed, Akbar S., *Postmodernism and Islam: Predicament and Promise*, New York, Routledge, 2004.

Aristotle, *The Politics*, ed. Stephen Everson, Cambridge, Cambridge University Press, 1996.

Berlin, Isaiah, and Henry Hardy, *The Crooked Timber of Humanity*, New York, Knopf, 1991.

Biale, David, *Power and Powerlessness in Jewish History*, New York, Schocken Books, 1986.

Canetti, Elias, *Crowds and Power*, Harmondsworth, Penguin, 1973.

Chesler, Phyllis, *The New Anti-Semitism: The Current Crisis and What We Must Do About It*, San Francisco, Jossey-Bass, 2003.

Cohn, Norman, *The Pursuit of the Millennium*, London, Paladin, 1972.

Cook, David, *Understanding Jihad*, Berkeley, University of California Press, 2005.

Dumouchel, Paul (ed.), *Violence and Truth: On the Work of René Girard*, Stanford, Stanford University Press, 1988.

Esposito, John L., *Islam and Politics*, Syracuse, NY, Syracuse University Press, 1998.

Esposito, John L., *Islam: The Straight Path*, 3rd edn., updated with new epilogue, New York, Oxford University Press, 2005.

Esposito, John L., *The Islamic Threat: Myth or Reality?*, 3rd edn., New York, Oxford University Press, 1999.

Esposito, John L. (ed.), *The Oxford History of Islam*, New York, Oxford University Press, 1999.

Esposito, John L. (ed.), *Political Islam: Revolution, Radicalism, or Reform?*, Boulder, CO, Lynne Rienner, 1997.

Esposito, John L., *Unholy War: Terror in the Name of Islam*, New York, Oxford University Press, 2002.

Esposito, John L. (ed.), *Voices of Resurgent Islam*, New York, Oxford University Press, 1983.

Esposito, John L., *What Everyone Needs to Know about Islam*, Oxford, Oxford University Press, 2002.

Fishbane, Michael A., *Biblical Interpretation in Ancient Israel*, Oxford, Clarendon Press, 1985.

Frankl, Viktor E., *Man's Search for Meaning: An Introduction to Logotherapy*, trans. Ilse Lasch, Boston, Beacon Press, 1992.

Gopin, Marc, *Between Eden and Armageddon: The Future of World Religions, Violence, and Peacemaking*, Oxford and New York, Oxford University Press, 2000.

Gopin, Marc, *Holy War, Holy Peace: How Religion Can Bring Peace to the Middle East*, New York, Oxford University Press, 2002.

Haidt, Jonathan, *The Righteous Mind*, New York, Pantheon Books, 2012.

Halbwachs, Maurice, *On Collective Memory*, ed., trans., and with an introduction by Lewis A. Coser, Chicago, University of Chicago Press, 1992.

Hiro, Dilip, *Holy Wars: The Rise of Islamic Fundamentalism*, New York, Routledge, 1989.

Huntington, Samuel, *The Clash of Civilizations and the Remaking of World Order*, New York, Simon & Schuster, 1996.

Josephus, Flavius, *The Jewish War*, trans. G.A. Williamson, Harmondsworth, Penguin, 1959.

Kaufman, Stuart J., *Modern Hatreds: The Symbolic Politics of Ethnic War*, Ithaca, NY, Cornell University Press, 2001.

Kepel, Gilles, *Jihad: The Trail of Political Islam*, trans. Anthony F. Roberts, Cambridge, MA, Harvard University Press, 2002.

Kepel, Gilles, *The Revenge of God: The Resurgence of Islam, Christianity, and Judaism in the Modern World*, trans. Alan Braley, University Park, Pennsylvania State University Press, 1994.

Kepel, Gilles, *The War for Muslim Minds: Islam and the West*, trans. Pascale Ghazaleh, Cambridge, MA, Belknap Press of Harvard University Press, 2004.

King, Martin Luther, *Strength to Love*, New York, Harper & Row, 1963.

Kristeva, Julia, *Desire in Language*, New York, Columbia University Press, 1980.

Lewis, Bernard, *The Assassins: A Radical Sect in Islam*, New York, Basic Books, 2003.

Lewis, Bernard, *The Crisis of Islam: Holy War and Unholy Terror*, New York, Modern Library, 2003.

Lewis, Bernard, *Cultures in Conflict: Christians, Muslims, and Jews in the Age of Discovery*, New York, Oxford University Press, 1995.

Lewis, Bernard, *Islam and the Arab World: Faith, People, Culture*, New York, Knopf, 1976.

Lewis, Bernard, *Islam and the West*, New York, Oxford University Press, 1993.

Lewis, Bernard, *Islam in History: Ideas, People, and Events in the Middle East*, Chicago, Open Court, 1993.

Lewis, Bernard, *The Jews of Islam*, Princeton, NJ, Princeton University Press, 1984.

Lewis, Bernard, *The Middle East: 2,000 Years of History from the Rise of Christianity to the Present Day*, London, Weidenfeld & Nicolson, 1995.

Lewis, Bernard, *The Muslim Discovery of Europe*, New York, W.W. Norton, 2001.

Lewis, Bernard, *The Political Language of Islam*, Karachi, Oxford University Press, 2002.

Lewis, Bernard, *Semites and Anti-Semites: An Inquiry into Conflict and Prejudice*, New York, Norton, 1986.

Lewis, Bernard, *What Went Wrong? Western Impact and Middle Eastern Response*, Oxford, Oxford University Press, 2002.

Lewis, Bernard, and Benjamin Braude (eds.), *Christians and Jews in the Ottoman Empire: The Functioning of a Plural Society*, New York, Holmes & Meier Publishers, 1982.

Longley, Clifford, *Chosen People: The Big Idea that Shaped England and America*, London, Hodder & Stoughton, 2002.

Miles, Jack, *God: A Biography*, New York, Alfred A. Knopf, 1995.

Mill, John Stuart, *On Liberty, Considerations on Representative Government*, ed. H.B. Acton, London, Dent, Everyman's Library, 1972.

Nelson, Eric, *The Hebrew Republic*, Cambridge, MA, Harvard University Press, 2010.

Novak, David, *Natural Law in Judaism*, Cambridge, Cambridge University Press, 1998.

Novak, David, and Matthew Lagrone, *The Image of the Non-Jew in Judaism*, Oxford, Littman Library of Jewish Civilization, 2011.

Novak, Michael, *The Spirit of Democratic Capitalism*, London, Institute of Economic Affairs, 1991.

Paine, Thomas, *Political Writings*, ed. Bruce Kuklick, Cambridge, Cambridge University Press, 2000.

Popper, Karl, *The Open Society and Its Enemies*, vol. 1, new edn., London, Routledge Classics, 2002.

Price, Randall, *Unholy War*, Eugene, OR, Harvest House Publishers, 2002.

Rabinovitch, N.L., *Responsa Melomdei Milchamah*, Maaleh Adumim, Maaliyot, 1993.

Redner, Harry, *Ethical Life: The Past and Present of Ethical Cultures*, Lanham, MD, Rowman & Littlefield, 2001.

Rousseau, J.J., *The Social Contract and Other Later Political Writings*, ed. and trans. Victor Gourevitch, Cambridge, Cambridge University Press, 1997.

Sacks, Jonathan, *The Dignity of Difference*, London, Continuum, 2002.

Sacks, Jonathan, *The Home We Build Together*, London, Continuum, 2007.

Sacks, Jonathan, *To Heal a Fractured World*, London, Continuum, 2005.

Spinoza, Benedict, *A Theologico-Political Treatise*, trans. R.H.M. Elwes, Mineola, NY, Dover Publications, 2004.

Talmon, J.L., *The Origins of Totalitarian Democracy*, London, Secker & Warburg, 1952.

Tocqueville, Alexis de, *Democracy in America*, abridged with an introduction by Thomas Bender, New York, Modern Library, 1981.

Toulmin, Stephen, *Cosmopolis: The Hidden Agenda of Modernity*, Chicago, University of Chicago Press, 1992.

Voegelin, Eric, *Order and History*, vol. 1, *Israel and Revelation*, Baton Rouge, Louisiana State University Press, 1956.

Volf, Miroslav, *Exclusion and Embrace: A Theological Exploration of Identity, Otherness, and Reconciliation*, Nashville, Abingdon Press, 1996.

Walzer, Michael, *Arguing about War*, New Haven, CT, Yale University Press, 2004.

Walzer, Michael, *Exodus and Revolution*, New York, Basic Books, 1985.

Walzer, Michael, *In God's Shadow*, New Haven, CT, Yale University Press, 2012.

Walzer, Michael, *Law, Politics, and Morality in Judaism*, Princeton, NJ, Princeton University Press, 2006.

Walzer, Michael, *On Toleration*, New Haven, CT, Yale University Press, 1997.

Walzer, Michael, *Politics and Passion*, New Haven, CT, Yale University Press, 2004.

Yerushalmi, Yosef Hayim, *Zakhor, Jewish History and Jewish Memory*, Seattle, University of Washington Press, 1982.

Zerubavel, Eviatar, *Time Maps: Collective Memory and the Social Shape of the Past*, Chicago, University of Chicago Press, 2003.